ROAD RACER

RACER

IT'S IN MY BLOOD

MICHAEL DUNLOP

ROAD RACER

IT'S IN MY BLOOD

Michael O'Mara Books Limited

This paperback edition first published in 2018

First published in Great Britain in 2017 by
Michael O'Mara Books Limited
9 Lion Yard
Tremadoc Road
London SW4 7NQ

Copyright © Michael Dunlop 2017, 2018
Text written by Jeff Hudson 2017
Text copyright © Michael O'Mara Books Limited 2017, 2018

A CIP catalogue record for this book is available from the
British Library.

Papers used by Michael O'Mara Books Limited are natural,
recyclable products made from wood grown in sustainable
forests. The manufacturing processes conform to the
environmental regulations of the country of origin.

ISBN: 978-1-78243-779-6 in hardback print format
ISBN: 978-1-78243-792-5 in trade paperback format
ISBN: 978-1-78243-909-7 in mass market paperback format
ISBN: 978-1-78243-801-4 in ebook format

3 5 7 9 10 8 6 4 2

Follow us on Twitter @OMaraBooks

www.mombooks.com

Designed and typeset by Mark Bracey

Printed and bound by CPI Group (UK) Ltd, Croydon, CR0 4YY

For my dad. My hero. My inspiration.

CONTENTS

PROLOGUE

Road Racer

WHEEL-TO-WHEEL RACING. There's nothing like it.

I'm doing 160 miles an hour, inches from Christian Elkin, the British Champion, and John McGuinness, winner of everything. We're that close you can smell each other's cologne. One false move from any of us will take the pack down like dominoes. That's not going to happen. I'm not going to fall. I'm not going to fail. I can't afford not to win this race.

It's 17 May 2008, the North West 200, the most popular sporting event in Northern Ireland and one of the fastest road races in the world. There are more than 30,000 spectators lining the streets of the nine-mile 'Triangle' course, and to them we're a neck-ache-inducing blur. But from where I'm sitting, I see everything.

I see the people. They're everywhere. Along the pavements. Waving out of houses. They're on roundabouts, in shops, sitting on post boxes and walls. At 100 miles an hour or 200 miles an hour, I see them all.

I see the lamp posts. I see the kerbs. I see the flowerpots, the jagged country walls, the signposts, the shops, the hotels, the pubs, the trees. And the hedges. I go so close to them my overalls will be green by the end. It's not advised. It's not sensible. In fact it's bloody dangerous. But it's me. It's how I ride.

I'm nineteen. I've got a lot on my mind. I don't actually remember much about the race until this moment, until this, the start of the very last lap. Everything from here is as clear as if it happened yesterday.

Elkin and McGuinness have both just passed me. More fool them. It's the wakeup call I need.

I'm not having this.

It's like a switch goes on in my head. Elkin, he's hungry for this race, he really wants the North West on his CV. And the wee bugger can ride. McGuinness is McGuinness. Great driver, always there or thereabouts, a legendary figure. He was impressive in qualifying but now it's different. He's not racing the clock any more. He's racing me. And that boy's going to know about it. By the time we start the last lap, I've got my place back from him.

We're going across the start and finish line, three peas in a pod, synchronized swimmers on two wheels. We're bombing along Millbank Avenue, up Primrose Hill. I get past Elkin. But at what cost? The hairpin at York Corner is coming up quicker than I can deal with.

I'm not going to make it. I'm not going to make it. I'm not going to make it ...

I smack the brakes on, I throw that Honda down left and, for a moment, I think she's put me off. I think it's all over.

But I'm not in the mood to quit. I wrestle her back just as Elkin goes past again. It's okay, I've got time. The two of us are at it the whole way round the anti-clockwise course. I'm having a go at him and he's having a go at me. There is no love given, no love lost. I'm thinking, *He has no choice, I am going past or through him.* I don't mind which.

Then *boom*, it's done.

We're going round the Metropol, I am in the lead and I'm pushing and pushing. It's the last leg. I'm on the edge and I'm drifting. I know the chicane at Juniper Hill is coming. I know it's the last place where a normal racer can pass you. I know that Elkin will be having a go if he gets half a chance. I don't care what it takes.

I have to be first through here.

I'm going flat out, so fast I don't know if I can stop. Somehow the brakes bite, the tyres grip and I find the strength to force her round right, then left.

We're bombing up the hill again now. As we come to the top, I can see people out of the corner of my eye going bananas. The chequered flag is within touching distance. I soar across the line and lift my visor. I have to hear the crowds. They're cheering, they're jumping, they're having a party – all in my name.

I've never heard anything like it. I'm not one who really likes the crowds or the fuss, but this must be what it's like for Mick Jagger or Paul McCartney or one of those boys when they go on stage. Thousands and thousands of people screaming for you, showing their love. It never happens to me. It never happens to any racer. But then, what I've just done has never happened before.

The second the race finishes I'm done. I'm not seeing anything. My visor's open but it's steamed up. My head's full of tears. I'm numb. I'm spent. I pull up before I get to the pits and am vaguely aware of Christian slapping me on one side and John patting me on the other. I'm really not in control of anything. I've won the race but I can't find any happiness in it. There's no celebration to be had today, for one simple reason.

Tomorrow I bury my father.

Death is a familiar foe to road racers. She's always there, just out of the corner of your eye. Watching, waiting. Since the Isle of Man Touring Trophy began in 1907 there have been 252 fatalities on that famous Snaefell Mountain Course, not including the losses to spectators and officials. My uncle, Joey Dunlop, the legendary 'King of the Mountain', died during a race in Estonia. There've been fifteen deaths at the Ulster Grand Prix, five at the Killinchy 150, five at Tandragee, and nineteen here at the North West. My dad, Robert Dunlop, was number fifteen.

Death is responsible for the man I am today – my dad going, my winning that race the day before his funeral, continuing the Dunlop 'dynasty' – those events shaped me in ways I could never have imagined if they hadn't happened. I know that. All my achievements, everything, it started then. I'm the fastest man in history around the TT track. I hold the lap records virtually everywhere I've ever ridden. I've got thirteen TT trophies so far. I've achieved everything there is to achieve in my sport – and I'm only twenty-eight. What burns me is that my dad never saw any of it.

I'd give it all up tomorrow to have him back just for a day. But then this would be a much shorter book. And anyway, that's not the way of things. You don't get to write your own script. Life moves on. Life will wait for nobody. Not me, not the prime minister, not the Queen. Not even my dad.

Like it or not, this is my life. This is the script I've been given. This is who I am.

I'm Michael Dunlop: Road Racer.

ONE

That's Dunlop Country

LEEDS, ENGLAND. A BIT OF YORKSHIRE. I'm over to take a look at a bike with a mechanic I've known for a while. I trust his judgement. Before we can leave, he has a car in his yard that needs fixing. While he's finishing, the owner walks in.

'All right?' the fella says to me. I'm standing in the doorway. My boy is under the bonnet, just dotting the I's, crossing the T's. 'Won't keep you a minute, Davey,' he calls out.

So Davey chats to me. He asks me what I'm up to and I say I'm in the market for a motorbike.

'Ah,' he says. My accent, the word 'motorbike', and he's off, telling me about the Isle of Man TT he's seen on the TV, and the fact he thinks the competitors are all 'lunatics', the way they ride. 'Two hundred miles per hour past a pub and a post office? They need their heads testing, the lot of them.'

My boy under the bonnet shuts the lid, wipes his hands and walks over.

'You ever heard of the Dunlops?' he asks.

'Those boys from Ireland?'

'They're the ones.'

'Of course I've heard of them. They're mad. Mad and dead, most of them. Joey and Robert? Great riders, great men. Sorely missed.'

'Have you ever heard of Michael?'

Davey laughs. 'That crazy wanker? I watched him on TV only the other day. I'll tell you this: that boy is not right in the head.'

I'm standing there, loving it. Seriously, really loving it. This guy, who I've never met before – he's an expert. He'd recognize me in my helmet, no bother. But my fat face is like any other poor sod's. I'm anonymous off my bike, I know that. But apparently my notoriety, if you want to call it that, goes before me. I think there's a bit more fun to be had with the guy, but my friend puts him out of his misery.

'Davey,' he says, 'this is Michael. Michael Dunlop.'

The guy's mouth just falls open. He's trying to play over in his head exactly what he's just said. Looking me up and down, wondering whether or not I'm the sort of boy who's going to lamp him for speaking out of turn. But he's heard of me. He knows exactly what I'm like. What was it he called me? A wanker? He wouldn't be the first. And he wouldn't necessarily be that wrong either.

Honestly, I don't care what he thinks. I don't care what anyone thinks. Most riders my age still have the stabilizers on.

I'm twenty-eight and I hold the lap record for the hardest road race in the world.

You say 'wanker', I say 'winner'. Who's to say who's right? Maybe you decide ...

You never forget your first set of wheels.

I was three years old and was that excited my head dropped clean off. I went bananas, actually hyperventilated. They had to slap me two or three times to get me round. I had never seen anything more beautiful in my life. But there she was. Just for me.

My own little ... *tractor*.

It was only this wee pedal thing, but to me that green John Deere was a Rolls-Royce and a red Ferrari rolled into one. It had a yellow bucket on the front and I'd bomb around the garden, pretending to cut the grass, pulling up weeds and loading her up. I was happy as a pig in shite. I drove it for years. I swear that if it still fitted me now I'd be out on it. Best set of wheels I ever owned.

Motorbikes? My dad thought they were the bee's knees. Me? I thought they were okay.

But can they pick up grass?

I was born on 10 April 1989 to Robert and Louise Dunlop. According to the birth certificate, I arrived at a hospital in a place called Ballymoney, a wee town at the top end of Northern Ireland. The maps will tell you that it's part of County Antrim, but ask any motorbike fan the world over if they've heard of it and they'll say the same thing.

'That's Dunlop country.'

No word of a lie – and it had nothing to do with me. Not yet.

In 1952, my grandparents, Willy and May Dunlop, had the first of their seven children. Joey was his name, and despite being the eldest of quite a rabble, he was quiet, shy even, and kept himself to himself. The fella wouldn't say boo to a goose. But there was one place he made himself heard, and that was on a motorbike.

Road racing in Northern Ireland is a pastime going back generations. There are a dozen or so towns that, for a few days every year, block off their streets and invite motorcyclists to hurtle down high roads at 200 mph and take roundabouts at barely half that speed. Locals and enthusiasts from all over the globe line the streets, waving, drinking and in all honesty, risking their lives, being within touching distance of these two-wheeled missiles. The biggest of them all, the North West 200, regularly gets 150,000 visitors, making it the most popular regular sporting event in the country. Even the smaller events quadruple their hosts' populations for the extent of the meets.

Joey Dunlop, the boy from Ballymoney, was untouchable at every circuit he raced. But the one where he was the undisputed master isn't in Ireland at all.

The Isle of Man Touring Trophy is the pinnacle of the sport. Even little old dears who've never heard of road racing have heard of the TT. It's got legendary status, up there with the World Cup, Wimbledon and the Monte Carlo Grand Prix. It's a big-bollocks affair, no question. And for twenty-three years nobody's bollocks were bigger than Uncle Joey's.

Between 1977 and 2000 he won twenty-six races around the mountain circuit – a record that stands today. And for every single one of those victories, Ballymoney got a bit more famous. When he won his last, the town put on an open-top-bus parade and the whole region turned out to give him a wave. If you knew Joey, you'll know how much he would have hated that. But people need to show their affection.

Uncle Joey was a trailblazer, no mistake, but he wasn't the only one dragging the town into the headlines. When Joey brought home another winged lady trophy, there wasn't a prouder person in all of Ballymoney than his wee brother. Eight years younger, Robert idolized his big brother, like everyone did. Scratching around for something to do with his own life, Robert decided he'd follow in Joey's footsteps, but by anyone's standards those are some boots to fill. The weight of the Dunlop name, people said, would be too great for him. The media, even my grandad, they all said he needed to find his own way in life or forever be compared to big brother Joe. And maybe they would have been right, assuming that all Robert wanted to do was win.

To a degree I think my dad chose to ride because the craic – the good time – was there. The boys are away every weekend, having a laugh, drinking beer, chasing women, and he wanted a slice of that. So he took up the bike as a way to get in on the fun. That's my honest opinion. Then a thing happened: my dad realized he was actually good at it. Bloody good. Joey Dunlop fans are not going to like this, but a lot of experts said that my dad was a rare talent. On plenty of tracks he was every bit as good as Joey and maybe on some days even better.

I'm not saying that to disrespect Joey in any way, because he was the undisputed king of the roads. He was The Man. Our entire family owes everything to that boy, as does our town. But I think if my dad had come to racing earlier in his life he might have made more of a name for himself. By the time he became the British 125 champion, he was maybe a little bit old. When you're thirty-one and you have people in their teens doing Grand Prix, you get passed over by the big factory teams. He was fast enough, though, and more than that, he was happy. Give that boy a motorbike and a road ahead and you never saw him complain.

While Joey had a reputation for being withdrawn and quiet, my dad was happy to live up to his title as the 'George Best of racing'. But that was a bit of a con, to tell the truth. When my dad was trying to make his way out of Joey's shadow, it was actually my mum who suggested he try to come out of his shell a bit and grab a few headlines. 'Let people know you're there, Robert.' So, to an extent, that party-boy image (which he genuinely enjoyed) was cultivated as a way of differentiating himself from his brother. Away from the media he was a different fella.

Joey loved Robert being there on race weekends. Racing is a very private sport; you need your own people and your own space around you. But if Joey had a problem on his bike, he knew there was one man on the grid who'd give up his own engine if it meant his hero getting over the finish line first. And afterwards they'd both go for a glass of red wine with the boys, both get a bit lairy, and when the journalists came sniffing for a quote, Robert would be the man leading the singing and dancing. Joey loved that. The fewer the people wanting a word with him, the happier he was.

They were peas in a pod, Joey and Robert. They'd walk over hot coals for a sniff of a race and I think that's what people respected. I've been into pubs in the middle of nowhere and there's a photo of one or both of them on the wall. I've been in Hong Kong and had people who don't speak English shake my hand because of those boys.

I've even experienced a couple of scenarios where I've had strangers go down on their knees and bow to me, in Ballymoney and beyond. So, yeah, Dunlop country is a thing.

No pressure on the rest of us then.

Mum was a horse rider and trainer from Norfolk. In 1982 she was in Northern Ireland racing and met Dad at an evening out with friends. I don't believe it was love at first sight. Not for Mum, anyway. Dad could be a cocky so-and-so, the cheeky chappy of the group, always out for the craic – the laugh – and I'm not sure Mum was up for that. On their first date he took her to the rope bridge at Carrick-a-Rede, the old National Trust place over near Ballintoy on the Antrim coast. Dad being Dad, he waited till she was halfway across, then bounced the hell out of the bridge. One hundred feet up in the air, just the sea and a ton of rocks below, I can tell you she was not a happy lady. But somehow Mum managed not to be sick and Dad managed to get her to agree to see him again, so it was win-win. Two years later they were wed and that was it: Mum's life in England was over. But she never stopped working the horses.

All my life, animals were around us. One of my earliest memories is of this couple of Great Danes we had. Massive bastards, they towered over me. They were like horses. Mum could have trained them to jump, I swear. I love my animals but I've gone the other way. I've got two dogs, little Yorkshire terriers, plus John, my dad's old mutt. He's what we call an 'outdoors' dog: he has his kennel in the yard, loves the big walks. Getting washed ... not so much. The other two are the type you'd see in a woman's handbag. I don't think people realize they're mine. Nothing gives me greater pleasure than walking the dogs in the fields near my house. I can be gone for hours. Most days I don't need any company other than the four-legged kind. I now part-own a veterinary practice down in Dublin with a couple of friends. I'll go down there once a week, put in a few hours when I can. It helps to keep me sane.

My parents had three kids. First was William, in 1985. Two years later came Daniel. Then, after another two years, out shot yours truly, all chubby, all kicking, all screaming. Some say I've not changed much.

I was the runt of the family, the baby, and the bane of my brothers' lives. Sometimes my mum and dad's, too. If there was a way to get into trouble, I'd find it. It was my gift.

The first house I remember was this massive old country pile called Ballynacree out on Glenstall Road. It was a proper serious piece of real estate, with a sweeping drive, large pillars at the front door and in the hallway, and a courtyard and stables at the rear. But it was run-down – pretty decrepit. That's the only reason Mum and Dad had been able to afford to buy it, so people said.

But I think there was another reason.

Ballynacree was massive. You could start hide 'n' seek at breakfast and not find a living soul by dinner. There was one room you'd never hide in, though. Not that there was a choice. If you look at the house from the front, there are five windows downstairs and six across the top. One for each room. But when you go inside, there are five doors downstairs, and upstairs only five again. That's freaky, right? How is there no door to the last room? I admit, that used to creep me out. I couldn't be upstairs on my own.

Not once I realized. The Great Danes were no bloody use. Most dogs you can't stop from tearing upstairs. These brave beasts, oh-so-noble and fierce when they feel like it, they wouldn't go up those stairs if you carried them. If you asked me as a five-year-old, I'd have said the place was haunted. Twenty-three years later you'll still get the same response.

Mum never engaged with any of that shit. She's not one for spooks, ghouls and superstitions. But looking back, no one would stay there. If Mum and Dad went away somewhere, there was no way they could persuade babysitters to stay in the house for love or money. Someone knew something, then. At least, though, it explained how Dad was able to afford it in the first place.

Ghosts or not, Dad had plans for Ballynacree. He wanted to do it up and run it as a B&B. The potential was huge. There were a load of trees and outbuildings, and I could play for hours climbing or hiding in both. But however much space there was, it was never enough. That's the way of kids, isn't it? We were playing football one day, and we were too near the house, and of course I sent the ball smashing through a window.

My dad was not best pleased.

I remember the three of us boys standing there, all examining our shoes, and Dad shouting, 'Who's done this?'

Head down: not me. *I'm not suffering a slap this day.*

'No one, eh?' Dad says. 'Okay, here's the thing. Unless one of you owns up, you're all getting a whack.'

Shit.

I just carried on staring at my dirty shoes, listening to Dad getting more and more furious. It seemed to go on forever and eventually the guilt got too much.

William stepped forward.

'It was me, Dad,' he says. 'I'm sorry.'

To protect the innocent Daniel, he'd rather take the clog himself. That's the kind of boy William was and still is. Whereas me, I'd just as likely drop everyone in the shit.

Sometimes literally.

Money was tight when I was very young, so Mum would put us all in the bath together to save water. Now, if you want to know what sort of kid I was, my favourite game was something we called 'Dodgeball'. Except there was no ball. Just a big turd. Nothing made me laugh more than taking a crap in the bath so that I'd see William and Daniel scrambling over each other to get out the way. They'd drown each other rather than let it touch them.

No word of a lie, I could be a nightmare for those boys. I was a brat. But they had their moments. Any stupid idea they came up with, I'd go along with it. I never realized they were usually setting me up as the fall guy.

One time we were up on the road, and the boys had come up with this scam. Only problem is it requires someone to lie down in the road. Now, this is an area where drivers and speed limits don't really mix. It's all blind turns and high hedges. But I'm a five-year-old idiot; I'm not thinking of safety. My brothers say, 'Will you do it?' and I say, 'Aye, why not.'

So down I go in the road, for all the world a dead body, and I hear this engine coming in the distance. I know it's travelling, I can hear the gears. Where I'm lying is a bit of straight section but if the person behind the wheel is fiddling with his radio or looking in his mirrors he's going too fast to avoid me.

The engine gets louder and louder as the car gets nearer, and for the first time I'm thinking, 'Why's it me lying down here and not Daniel or William?' But then it's too late. The car pelts round the bend and I've got about five seconds before I know whether the driver has seen me or not.

Five, four, three, two ... Suddenly there's a squeal of brakes and the car stops. It's so close I can feel the heat from the bonnet. I hear the driver fling open the door and he's shouting, 'Oh, what have I done,' when suddenly there's a splat and he starts swearing. The second he's out of the car my brothers are leaping up and bombing the poor bastard with eggs. He doesn't know what day of the week it is, his emotions are all wrapped round his sphincter, but what he does realize quick enough is that the chubby kid on the road is not dead. I have about ten seconds to get myself resurrected, up and off over into the farmer's field before he can lay his hands on me.

I thought it was a great craic and I never worked out it was always me taking all the risk. I mean, not only could I have actually got run over, the dumb pricks had picked the slowest runner out of the three of us.

There used to be a sweetie shop up in the town. We'd be allowed there every so often for a treat but as kids obviously we wanted more. It was fifteen minutes there and fifteen minutes back. We worked out that we could go at a certain time between Mum thinking we were in our rooms and Dad coming home from work. Except, of course, it was never all of us who'd go there, just little fat chops here. When I was a kid I was a chubby little sod. Running was not my forte, let's put it like that. I used to stagger most of the journey and get back just in time to chuck the sweets through the window as Dad's van swept up the drive. If I ever got caught with my fat arse hanging over the sill, no amount of William taking the blame would spare me the lash.

I got lucky more times than I didn't, but I was no stranger to a slap, from either Mum or Dad. To be fair, I never got a whack unless I deserved it. I can honestly say that. If we were really out of line, Dad would line us up and say, 'Right, go down to the garden and get yourselves a stick.' That would be the thing he whacked us with. Obviously I brought up a twig. That was my statement.

To a point, Daniel, William and I raised ourselves. Mum had her horses and the home to run, and Dad worked every hour under the sun in the steel construction game, erecting sheds and outbuildings, fences and the like, either by himself or with his brother Jim. When he wasn't working he'd be away racing or in his workshop stripping down one of his bikes. He'd be out there all hours, taking bits off, putting bits on. So us boys had a lot of time on our hands.

Growing up in this big property with its nine acres, it felt like the whole world was a playground to us. There was one particular tree I loved to climb and from up there the fields went on for as far as the eye could see. None of them belonged to us, mind, but that just made them all the more explorable.

There was a farmer next door who every year would harvest his hay, tie it into cylindrical bales and cover these in giant black plastic sheets to keep the rain out. Like huge cotton reels they looked. That was his year's income tied up in plastic right there. To three kids under ten years of age, it was a climbing frame. Hours we spent over there, shinning up to the top, sliding down, jumping up and down, whatever we felt like. A few weeks later, we got the knock at the door. It's the farmer.

'Are you all right there, Robert? I'm wondering if I could have a word with your lads.'

Dad called us into the room.

'Have you boys been playing on my hay bales?' the farmer asked.

'No,' we all said. Perfect harmony, like a boys' choir.

'Only the plastic that covers my bales has been ripped to shreds. It's ruined, the lot of it.'

I wasn't bothered by the farmer, but Dad was staring right at me. We held firm, though, and with no proof of anything, the farmer went on his way.

You'd think that'd be a lesson learned, but the next harvest, up went the bales – and so did we. Same fun, same disaster for the farmer, same denial, denial, denial from us.

Third year, we're over there, same story, except something goes wrong. Because of their shape, where four of the bales are pushed together you get big gaps in the middle. We were all scrambling over one of them and, of course, wee fat chops here falls down the hole. I'm trying to clamber up but I can't get a foothold. William's leaning down trying to grab me. He's holding Daniel by the legs and he can't reach. I'm getting a bit panicky; William, being the elder boy, he's shitting himself.

'I'm gonna have to get me dad,' he says.

'Don't, he'll kill us.'

'You're gonna suffocate down there.'

'That's nothing to what Dad's gonna do.'

I wasn't wrong. He couldn't care less about the bales but we'd made him look a liar in front of the farmer and there we were, banged to rights. I don't think any of us sat down for a week after that.

I think running Ballynacree cost a bit more than Dad was happy to admit. We always had a meal on the table but there were no real frills, not in my earliest years. Clothes were hand-me-downs, which isn't unusual in big families. I knew that whatever William was wearing I'd see Daniel in it soon enough, then it'd be my turn, if there was any life left in the thing. More often than not, by the time they got to me the jumpers had patches sewn in the sleeves and the trousers were darned around the kneecaps. It was no bother. Never troubled me one bit. I don't think I really noticed. Every so often a cousin would come to visit wearing a nice jumper; then, soon enough after, Mum would be dressing me in something identical. I used to think she just shopped at the same stores as my aunties.

It wasn't just clothes we got second dibs on. One of the doors we weren't allowed to open at Ballynacree led down to the cellar. Usually it was kept locked.

'You're not to go down, boys; it's too dangerous for children.'

So we didn't. Not until we did.

You know yourself, if you're told you're not allowed somewhere, where are you going to go? As a kid, you're going through that door. No other reason than to see why you're not allowed. That's child logic right there. So one day, when Daniel notices the door's unlocked, and Mum and Dad are out, we snatch our chance.

I'm five years old and I've never been more excited than about climbing down those stairs. It's a dark and freezing winter's morning and you could see your own breath, but down we go, all giggly and, hand on heart, scared to bits. What could it be that my dad says is so dangerous? Then William, being the tallest, finds a light switch.

'There's nothing here.'

Daniel's as disappointed as the rest of us. There're no

guns, no tools, no machinery to hurt ourselves with. Just over in one corner, there was a box of clothes, one or two books, a few little action men sort of things and, behind the box, an old bicycle that looked just like the one my cousin used to ride. What there wasn't was any kind of Big Secret.

'It's just a load of rubbish down here,' William says, angry as the rest of us. 'Let's go upstairs before we get caught.'

Up we trudge, despondent as you like. We close the door and pray Mum and Dad never discover what we've been up to.

A few weeks later, it's Christmas morning and we're all excited. We know there's no big pile of cash in the house so whatever gifts we get are gonna be pretty basic, and probably of the second-hand variety. Mum's fussing around getting some little treats to eat and drink, then Dad appears with our presents. We all tear the paper off and William and Daniel are dead chuffed with what they've got. I was not disappointed either. I'd asked for a bike, more in hope than expectation, but unless I was mistaken, the thing Dad was holding behind his back was exactly that.

'There you go, Micky lad,' he says. 'Happy Christmas.'

I'm happy as Larry – and it solves another mystery. 'Hey, look, it's the one we saw in the cellar.'

William and Daniel looked at me funny. Almost like they were trying to speak without moving their lips. Then I realized, too late, what they were trying to say.

Shut up, you fat idiot.

Dad was ahead of them. He knew exactly what they meant and he knew exactly what we'd done. He scooped the load of presents up, chucked them back through the cellar door and gave us something else to remember Christmas by instead.

Not one of my brighter days, I have to admit.

My dad was no bully. He wasn't a violent man, not by any means. He lived in a man's world where there were plenty of people quick to go from words to fists, and when they did he was always the pacifier, the referee cooling everyone down. But he hated liars. He believed you're only as good as your word and that went double for his boys. He never dished out more than we deserved, I believe that. I think I knew it even then.

Apart from my brothers, there was no person on the planet I wanted to spend more time with. I idolized that man. In summer I'd sit in my tree near the end of the drive and listen out for his van bombing up the road. Then, before he was out, I'd be climbing up him, hugging his leg while he's trying to walk. I gave him more trouble than the Great Danes, and they loved him too.

I don't have that many pictures of me with the old fella, but the majority have got me climbing all over him, glued to him while he's trying to sit down or eat or have an ale. I love my mum, don't get me wrong, but I always think that mums who have boys may as well have dogs. It's the same difference. You feed them, you look after them and as long as they get their walks you can cope with them. That's what the three of us were like, no question. Especially me. Mum just about kept me on the lead but I was Daddy's boy, through and through. We all were. That man could do no wrong in our eyes.

I hated him going off to race. Not because it was danger-ous – I had no idea about that side of things. As a three-, four- and five-year-old I only cared about myself. I just resented him not being around. I got, near enough, that he needed to work during the week. At the weekends, though, I thought he should be with me. What really pissed me off was not being allowed to go with him either, because Mum wasn't interested and Dad was too busy to look after a clingy kid.

The workshop I loved, though. I honestly had no idea what my dad was doing with those bikes, but I thought I was his right-hand man. He's up to his elbows in engine fluid and I'm handing him a spanner or a hammer like I have a clue what I'm doing. I liked watching my dad work. He wasn't a chatty man but he explained what was what if I asked. My questions were pretty basic.

'Will it make you go faster?'

'Aye, that's the hope.'

'Will it make you win?'

'What? Of course it will.'

'Can I come and watch?'

'Ask your mum.'

In other words, 'No.'

Sometimes Uncle Joey would come over and he'd help Dad out. Or Joey would bring his own bike and Dad would take a look at that. Occasionally, Dad's main man, 'LB' – Liam Beckett – would be there as well, just in case Dad needed a bit more help than I was able to give. I didn't mind. The more the merrier. Just watching your dad do his thing was sometimes all that a little kid needed to be happy.

Then, come race weekend, he'd load his van and I'd help him, mainly by keeping out of the way. Off he'd go, and I'd find my brothers and get up to mischief. On some of the bigger races there'd be radio commentary that Mum would let me listen to in the kitchen. For the really big ones, you'd even get the practices covered. I'd sit at the table, listening, literally screaming when I heard my dad's name.

I never knew my dad was famous. I never knew he was the bee's knees in Ballymoney. All I really knew for sure was that I wanted him to win and wanted him to come back home. Most weekends he did that.

And then, one day, he went off to race and he never came back.

TWO

You're Not the Same Brand

IT WASN'T QUITE 'NEVER' but, to a kid, it felt like it.

May 1994. I'd recently turned five years old and my superhero, my dad, was taking part in practice at the 1994 Isle of Man TT. Mum said I could listen as soon as the races started. There might even be a bit on the TV. With the meeting spread over a fortnight, I should be able to catch something.

The TT was such a big name in our house. Whenever I heard relatives or people in shops or visitors to the house talk about Uncle Joey or my dad, they all mentioned those two letters. *TT*. This wasn't Dad's first rodeo. Not by any means. He was a boy who'd competed thirty-one times over eleven years. That's maybe 120 laps of the 37-mile circuit, 4,440 miles or so at a conservative estimate, not including practice. No way, in my eyes, does this boy have an accident. Or, if he does, no way, no way does anything this boy has done cause it. This is Robert Dunlop we're talking about. He won his first of eight Cookstown 100 races in 1985. He took the chequered flag at the Macau Grand Prix in 1989; he took Supercup wins and a double at the prestigious North West 200; and by 1994 had racked up five victories on the TT circuit, including wins during the Manx GP. After several years in Uncle Joey's shadow, there was no doubt he was making a name for himself, and after a period of struggle, some money as well. He was a Dunlop. He was just doing what Dunlops did. And it was beginning to pay.

But this is what they said happened. Dad came into Ballaugh Bridge at the seventeen-mile mark on his Honda RC45, for some reason lost control during a long left turn and crashed into a wall. That's the story I heard then. That's the story the radio was reporting. And that's the story that turned my mum's face snow white and got her packing her bags the second she heard the news.

Dad's injuries were so severe, to his right hand and leg especially, he couldn't leave the Isle of Man. His mechanic and friend, Liam Beckett, was on the blower to Mum. He said there was a private plane waiting for her but the doctors needed Dad to be kept sedated and they were worried if she arrived too full-on he might wake up. Nothing's ever straightforward with this family. But my mum was over there in a shot – as soon as she managed to find a relative who'd look after us in the haunted house. Apparently it took a while before the doctors could stem the bleeding. When he was just about stable, Dad was sent to a surgeon in England. The best, apparently – at least that's what you tell yourself. Eventually they managed to get on top of the damage and my dad was redirected to the Royal Hospital in Belfast.

It'd been two months since the accident and I hadn't set eyes on him once.

I thought when he was moved to Belfast that would change. The truth is, Mum didn't want us to see him, not given the state he was in. Looking back, she didn't want us to be having nightmares. But I didn't know how Dad was looking; no one would tell me anything. Even when Mum went to see him, obviously she couldn't leave us at home. But she wouldn't take us inside. 'Not till your dad's ready.' The three of us just stayed in the car trying to kill each other. Or not kill each other, depending on which end of the punches you were on. It was the only way to pass the time.

After a couple more weeks Mum relented. Dad had been asking for us since he'd arrived in Belfast. We were allowed to go in on the condition that we were quiet as mice. I was two parts excited, two parts terrified. You build a picture in your mind of what he's going to look like. It was a bit of an anti-climax really. He was asleep when we got there and asleep when we left. But I remember he had more bandages covering him than an Egyptian mummy.

Two months, three months, four, five, six. To a dumb kid, such numbers become meaningless. What was meaningful to me was that Dad missed most of spring, all of summer as well as the most momentous – and tortuous – day of my life so far.

Starting school.

There was a place in Ballymoney where my brothers were already going. When I started going too, I didn't really understand why. Maybe I was just thinking about my dad. Maybe I simply wasn't interested. Whatever, every day after school I'd be raring to get home. Monday, Tuesday, Wednesday, Thursday or Friday – no matter what day it was, I was convinced that this was the day my dad would be coming home. There was no rhyme or reason for me to think this. Mum never said anything beyond, 'He'll be back soon enough.' But I translated that as 'tomorrow'. Day after day, week after week, I kept it up. Always disappointed, always ready to believe that the next day was the one.

May, June, July, August, September, October. Day after day, month after month, the same disappointment. Mum knew nothing. Or if she did, she never let on.

'You'll know when I do.'

I believed her. But it wasn't true. I came home from school one day and Mum said, 'Guess who's upstairs.'

I stared at her for a second, then I was out the door like lightning. Anything else she said was lost in the mad dash down the corridor and up the massive staircase. I remember running along the landing and opening the door, seeing Dad lying there with one leg hoisted up in the air, and flinging myself straight at him.

Not for one second did I think about his injuries.

I'll tell you now, I was not the lightest of children. He yelped and screamed and squealed, and then he screamed some more. There were tears in that brave man's eyes and it took me a second or two to work out why. Then Mum appeared in the door and dragged me off. I thought Dad was the tough one but she laced me good and proper. She was upset, obviously; a bit stressed that he was home. I was just so relieved to see my hero again, and Dad was in bits shouting, 'Leave him alone, Louise, leave him alone; he didn't know.'

Not exactly the big family reunion any of us had hoped for.

When things calmed down, Mum talked me through Dad's wounds. His right side was in bits. His right hand was mashed so much it had lost its ability to contact the brain, so they'd taken nerves out of his back and put them in his arm. One of his legs had been operated on so much it was two inches shorter than the other. Whichever way you looked at it, these were life-changing injuries, Mum said.

She needed us to know that Dad wouldn't be the Dad we remembered.

Really he should still have been in hospital but he'd threatened to sign himself out if they didn't let him out into my mum's care.

I still don't think it all sunk in. I never cried, I never thought any of it was that serious. In my eyes, Dad was superman. You see a bit of plaster on his hip, his arm or his leg – he looks like he's top to toe wrapped in toilet roll – but you don't think it's fatal. Five-year-olds aren't programmed to think like that.

In any case, it wasn't anything he hadn't been through before, right? I knew it wasn't my dad's first big stay in hospital – far from it. When he was young, about eighteen years old, Mum said, he crashed his van and went clean through the windscreen, breaking his neck and needing six months in traction, most of it in hospital. But he got through that and I think sheer pig-headedness played a part, same as it did with everything. When he rode his very first bike race, at Temple in 1979, he actually turned up still wearing his neck brace. If the clerk of the course had noticed he'd have been disqualified, no question about it. But he never let that injury stop him and I knew in my naïve young heart he wouldn't let this smash get the better of him either.

He's my dad. He's gonna live forever.

Those months with Dad in hospital were rough as dogs. Obviously he wasn't pulling in any money from his steel erection business but the big loss was his race winnings. You don't pick up that much for a win in the local events but with a bit of consistency in the bigger meetings you can pocket a tidy few grand. All of that was gone, so Mum was scrimping and scraping, working every hour to earn money herself as well as looking after us.

When my dad came home it didn't get any easier. She was still the only one pulling in an income of any description so our house was full of aunties and friends to look after us and Dad while she worked. My Auntie Margaret – Dad's twin – and their sisters, Helen, Linda and Virginia, virtually moved in, they were there that often. Luckily, Ballynacree was that big it never felt cramped. There were nurses as well, because obviously Dad needed to be washed in bed. And there was no shortage of jobs for us boys either: running up and down with water, food, fresh bedding, clothes, and a newspaper when he was feeling a bit better. There was always something to do.

Uncle Joey wasn't much of a nurse but he was a regular visitor, keeping an eye on his wee brother. After the accident, he'd gone with Robert to the hospital, then went back to the circuit to do the only thing he knew how: race. Come on, it's the TT. What do you expect? The first thing my dad said to him was, 'How'd you get on?'

He'd got a win, of course. For my dad.

Some people might find that odd, that he's racing like nothing's happened. That's the way of the sport. Unless they cancel the race, someone still has to win. Better it's a Dunlop. My dad knew it, my uncle knew it, we all knew it.

Several of the racing boys came along to the house to visit, quite a few of his friends. Believe it or not, Joey wasn't actually the biggest racing name who swung by.

Carl Fogarty, the World Superbike Champion at the time, was a good pal of my dad's because Dad had wanted to get into the WSB, given that's where all the money is, and they'd become tight. Carl stayed at the house a few times to rally the old boy's spirits. He believed Dad was on track to make a big name for himself in the sport. He said the accident had robbed the world of a great future rivalry.

Mum did a grand job of keeping the visitors to a minimum in the early days – to protect Dad's strength, she said. That suited me fine. When I got a moment to myself I liked just to sit with him. He didn't say much – no change there. Like I say, he and Joey were more peas in a pod than the public realized. Never saying a word if it wasn't needed. If you brought an audience or a TV camera upstairs, my dad was a different man. He'd put on a show. Which my mum knew, which is why she kept people at bay.

There is nothing that woman would not have done for my dad. All the visitors were cooing over the patient but she was the one run ragged. There was no heating in Ballynacree and even in summer some of the rooms could get very chilly. Being bedridden, Dad was always cold. First thing in the morning, Mum would get up and light the fire downstairs. The chimney ran up through the room where my dad was, so he'd get the heat by the time he woke up. Same pattern every day. Get up, light the fire, get on with the jobs, go and wake my dad up with some breakfast. The woman was a saint. She was run to the bone.

Maybe that's why she nearly killed him …

It's a warmish day, I'm already up and playing outside and I hear this shouting. *It's my dad.* Something must be hurting him. Thinking I'm the hero, I barrel indoors in time to see Mum flying up the staircase. Dad's still hollering. We get to his room, fling open the door and we can't see. It's black. The whole room is filled with smoke. Dad's on his bed, coughing and shouting, eyes watering. I'm still on the landing and I'm already choking, it's that bad. Mum darts in and throws open the window.

My dad says, 'What are you doing, woman? Are you trying to finish me off?'

It turned out a bird's nest had been built in the chimney, backing up the smoke. It would have been all right but there was a wee leak in the chimney wall in Dad's room. If Dad hadn't woken up he'd have choked to death. Luckily, he saw the funny side.

The way they spoke to each other cracked me up. No airs and graces with those two. From the day Dad had scared my mum half out of her life by making the rope bridge bounce, she'd had his card marked. She gave as good as she got, believe you me. But somehow my dad always had the final laugh. I remember once she was out in the fields, training this big bugger of a horse. It was miserable, slippery mud everywhere, and she got thrown into a ditch filled with water.

Then the horse lands right on top.

She's got a ton of panicked horse trapping her legs, water around her ears. Luckily she knows my dad has seen it all. He's running over. Coming to save the day. He gets there and his first words to his terrified wife are: 'Come on, girl, get yourself up. Are you going to lie in that ditch all day?'

'Robert Dunlop,' Mum says. 'My hero.'

The thing about being a kid is that adults forget you're there. If you're quiet enough, that is. People used to talk about Dad downstairs and I'd pick up snatches. The family would chat this way and that and the doctors would be bombarded with questions the second they came down from seeing him. I probably heard things I shouldn't have done. Things I wish I hadn't.

The medical opinion was that my dad was to all extent and purposes a disabled man. If he walked again unaided he'd have to take that as a win. He'd need to make radical adjustments to his life, probably find a new career. His right hand was bust, it would never be able to hold a mug let alone steel beams. And as for the bikes, the only Dunlop that would be riding now was his big brother.

The grown-ups all whispered and fretted and pondered how Robert was going to come through all this. He was such an active man. Racing was the only thing that got him out of bed in the morning. He was going to be a broken man, no question.

I heard all this and I didn't believe they were talking about my dad. I thought, *That man is no quitter. He's not going to let a wee accident stop him living his life.*

I was young; what the hell did I know? As it turned out, a lot more than those doctors.

In all the months I sat by his bed, I don't recall any change in my dad's personality, contrary to what they'd said would happen. The fire never went out. Yes, he could be a bit grumpy at times for the simple reason he was in a lot of pain. But he never let anything get on top of him. He never let things beat him, however bad they were. For a man having to eat and piss and crap in his own bed, that takes some doing.

I think Dad was smart enough to realize he had brought it on himself. He never blamed anybody else for what he'd done so he never felt sorry for himself. Some of his friends weren't of the same persuasion. They'd watched the accident on TV. There were tapes of it flying around. Dad's come round the corner and there's nothing he's done, the back wheel's just gone. Mechanical fault, everyone was saying. Family kept trying to persuade him to sue for compensation. The team he was riding for had to bear responsibility.

'Somebody has to pay for what you've gone through, Robert, plain as day.'

But Dad wouldn't hear of it.

'I chose to ride that bike. That's the end of the matter.'

Christmas came and it was bleak. The family scrambled around and we got a few gifts, but Dad was still bedridden. At least he hadn't been smoked out recently, so that was a positive. By the time I turned six, things weren't much improved. Maybe a month later, though, a full year after the accident, there were a few shoots of recovery. Knowing the old fella, he just wanted to be up for the TT. But he was happy enough with being able to swing his legs out of bed and begin to think about maybe one day leaving the house. Against the doctors' orders, by the way. He still needed his food cut up, though, on account of not being able to hold a knife in his right hand.

For the rest of us, life had to continue as best it could. To get us out from under her feet, Mum enrolled the three of us boys into Sunday school. There used to be a bus that went from up our road into town and back. Our lane was that creepy that if it was dark we'd just run as fast as we could before the monsters got us.

I'm not sure if Dad agreed with us going. One of the things Northern Ireland is known for is its religion. Or *religions*. You think of Northern Ireland in that period and obviously you think of 'The Troubles'. Crown versus republic, Protestants versus Catholics. You'll know things got very nasty indeed. Rightly or wrongly, my dad would not have religion in the house. Whatever your allegiance, you left your colours at the doorstep or you left. I don't know whether he had a particular dislike of the conflict, or whether it was for more practical reasons. My dad, you see, was raised a Protestant. My mum, on the other hand, arrived in Belfast a fully fledged Catholic. You can see why there might be a problem.

Growing up, you heard about the bad stuff all the time. Dad's generation had it worse. When you look down the road and you see the flags and the graffiti and you know the problems the Troubles have caused, and still cause, you have to wonder what it's all for. You can't do anything about what side of the fence you're born on, it's true, but if you want to go through life making your religion the only thing that defines you, the thing that's going to stop you getting on with another person, good luck to you. I think it's a stupid way to carry on.

I don't even know which side I'm on. My dad was one thing, my mum the other. What does that make me? A Jaffa cake, I reckon. But some people will make a decision for you, no bother.

I've walked into pubs and people will get into a

conversation with you and you think, *This is a friendly place.* But they're just having a listen to your voice. Even though they don't know your religion, if they know where you're from they'll make a judgement.

When I was twenty, I walked into a pub and sat down. I was on my way back from work with three lads. We're sitting at the bar, having a couple of pints on our way home. This boy turns round to me and says, 'What are you doing in here?'

'I'm having a pint.'

'Not in here you're not.'

I say, 'And why would that be?'

'Because you're not the same brand.'

I says, 'No harm to you, fella, but I bought these pints and I'll be drinking them. And after I've drunk them, if I feel I want another one, I'll have another one. If I don't want another one, I will leave then.'

I was more of an arrogant prick then than I am now. And I had my mates with me.

Anyway, the fella says, 'Young man, you'll be leaving. Either of your own accord or being carried out. That is my promise to you.'

Behind him I see a dozen others getting a bit restless. Even I can do the maths. That doesn't mean I'm going to go quietly, mind. That is not in my nature. I figure I've got probably thirty seconds to make my mind up, when the man behind the bar comes over. He steps right between us.

'Are you that young Dunlop?' he asks.

I says, 'Aye. I am indeed.'

'Then you stay where you are.'

Then he says to the other guy, 'This man's dad drank in here, his uncle drank in here, he is welcome in here any time.'

Don't get me wrong. That barman would have seen us

all carried out on stretchers if we'd been anyone else. He was no saint. But he was a fan of the Dunlops.

With everything else going on you'd think people would have better things to worry about. But that's the world we live in. To this day, though, I respect my dad's view of religion the only way I know how – and that is by walking through any door that takes my fancy. I'm not the sort for letting any colours or signs or flags get in my way. But the thing about doors is that they open both ways. I can assure you now that there have been a couple of occasions when I've been told to leave and, no bother, *I have left*.

Similar story. There were me and a couple of other boys in a pub once. It was busy, ten of the regulars to each one of us. We order our pints, we drink them, we have a craic. I get another round in, then head for the gents. I'm doing my business and this boy comes up and says, 'Look Dunlop, I think it's time you left.'

'You do, do you?'

Who do you think you are?

'Aye. I've nothing against you. But one of your boys at the bar said a couple of things he shouldn't have said. So we will need you to leave. And if you don't, the door will be locked and there *will* be problems.'

In life you need to know when to hold them and when to fold them. That was a time to fold them.

'You're all right, fella,' I says. 'We're just leaving.'

I think my dad's time was a lot worse. Dunlop or not, he was actually shot at. He once had a green and white bus that he used for his race lorry. There was a roadblock on the way home one evening. A couple of cars, not the police variety, were lined across the street, and some fellas flagged him down. Dad knew something was up. A quick look in the mirrors: there's another car behind and nowhere to turn.

The countryside at that time was filled with burned-out shells of cars and lorries. Some of them still had their drivers and passengers inside. Dad was not letting that happen.

'Boys,' he says to the lads in the back of the bus, 'hold on!'

He floors the pedal, shifts down and that old diesel engine squeals for its life as it picks up speed. When the men by the cars realize he's not stopping, they leap out of the way and start shooting. By then the bus has smacked the two cars, skittled them aside. It's through, the boys are alive – but there are bullet holes all up the side and back. Somehow, there's not even a scratch on Dad's bikes.

I'm not saying I'm not religious. Everyone's got their own reasons for doing something. I just feel there is no need to have it dominating everything all the time. There's too much evil in the world done in the name of religion. You need your head searching for any logic to it.

And at the end of the day, what's the point in picking out differences in each other? Catholics shit through their arseholes, same as Protestants.

A lot of my dad's more devoutly religious friends found his views on the local conflict pig-headed, to say the least. It's a funny expression. I hear it said about me a lot. Usually it's meant as an insult. Same for my dad. But when it came to his health, I swear to you now that that very pig-headedness was what got him through.

After the accident he was a year in bed. While there,

he listened to various doctors and experts tell him how crippled he was going to be, how he'd probably be on benefits for income, and how he'd have one working hand and be walking with sticks for the rest of his life. They all wanted to prepare him for the worst. My dad listened to them. They were the professionals. They'd saved his life more than once. But when they left and my mum came in to tell him to take it easy on doctors' orders, he said the same thing.

'With respect, they can fuck right off.'

My dad never saw himself as disabled, even when he needed help getting across the room. He never saw himself as permanently damaged, even while his right hand hung limp at the end of his arm. The doctors' opinion was that getting out of his bed was what Dad should have been aiming for. That was all he was ever going to achieve. Dad could not disagree more. He saw it as a step on a journey to getting better and he was by no means there yet. In my dad's mind he was on the TT, three laps in of six. Halfway.

Half to go.

And he had a plan how to finish the race. He got in contact with a physiotherapist called Fiona Gilligan. This woman worked miracles, but I don't think she knew what she was letting herself in for. Dad told her he wanted to get back to normal and was prepared to do whatever it took. Even if it meant leaving his beloved Ballynacree. And his family. Telling my mum was harder than telling his physio.

'I'll be moving out for a month or two,' he says. 'I need to work on my own to get better.'

'What are you talking about, man? This is your home. Stay here. Rest here. Get better here.'

'Ah, there's the thing,' he says. 'I don't want to just get better, Louise. I want to be normal again.'

You have to feel for my mum. She's the person who's always overlooked in my dad's story. The strain on her must have been immense. She'd put up with Dad's racing, knowing that each weekend could be his last. Then, when he does have an accident that by rights should have killed him, she puts her life on hold while she nurses him for more than a year. She keeps the family together and just about affords to hang on to the house. And what thanks does she get? She's told he'll never get better if she makes him too comfortable.

I'm none the happier. As a kid you're thinking, *What the hell? Why's he going away? Did I do something wrong?* It didn't make sense. Why wouldn't he want to stay at home? Was he scared the house was haunted as well?

But Dad was in no mood for budging. He took himself off to a wee cottage on the edge of town, just him, the dog and his bicycle. And started living like a monk. The way he saw it, he needed to change his way of life to get himself sorted. And he couldn't do that if people kept helping him. His right hand was useless, he knew that. So he needed to train himself to use his left. For everything. Eating, writing, picking his nose, wiping his backside. It was going to be difficult, he knew that, and he didn't want anyone watching.

He didn't want anyone to see him fail.

Fiona Gilligan went there every day to help him walk, to help him switch hands as best he could. Strength, mobility, muscle elasticity – they worked on everything. On his mind as well. There's no point having a fit body if your outlook is shot to pieces.

The things he put himself through. Dad didn't want any home comforts, and that included visitors, but eventually I persuaded my mum to drop me off for the day. It was in the middle of nowhere, and all he had was a bicycle he couldn't ride. That was the good news. My fridge is warmer than that house was. It had old stone walls, no heating, no electricity. Dad didn't want anything to distract him from his sole aim of recuperation, inside and out. Books, TV, his family, a bit of warmth, they were all on the 'banned' list. Rocky Balboa punching those beef carcasses in the deep freeze was a more preferable way to live than what my dad chose.

But he wanted to put himself through that. He wanted to fight: to be angry and uncomfortable enough to get back on his feet – both of them – and put right all the hardships his family had gone through, starting with improving Ballynacree. And the way he was going to do that was simple.

'I'm going to ride again,' he told my mum, 'and I'm going to make enough money to renovate Ballynacree to the standard you and the kids deserve.'

'Oh, Robert.'

'What, Louise?' he says. 'What's wrong?'

'You're too late, Robert.'

'What are you talking about?'

'It's Ballynacree,' Mum says. 'I've sold it. We move out next week.'

THREE

Bikers Welcome

YOU HAVE TO FEEL FOR THE WOMAN.

Maybe my mum knew Ballynacree was haunted after all. I don't know. What I can say is that she understood full well what that house meant to my dad. The man had a dream in life and that was to build a palace for his family. If he couldn't do that, buying one was the next best thing. You only have to look at what the recent owners have done to the place to see its potential. Dad saw it too, nearly thirty years ago. He saw him and my mum raising us, opening their B&B there and growing old together while the house paid its own way.

That wasn't going to happen now.

Dad tried to fight it. He said he'd give his support to his racing team in suing the wheel constructor accused of being responsible for his accident and, therefore, for his loss of earnings and house. But as he knew, that wouldn't be a quick fix, even if he won. In the meantime, the bank accounts were empty, Dad's income stream was nonexistent and my mum was working to feed five mouths and run two homes. And that's before the animals. Something had to give.

He wasn't a big man – I'm five foot seven, and he was a couple of inches shorter, depending on which leg he stood on – but my dad had a massive heart. I swear it was the idea of riding again that pulled him through. After three months locked away in that ice block of a cottage, he decided he was ready to come back out and take on the world. The last thing he wanted was to be a drain on the rest of us, Mum especially.

Dad coming out coincided with us having to move. I didn't have much to do with that; I didn't really understand what it meant. Even when we arrived at this little white rented bungalow at the junction of two country roads, about a mile away in Ballymoney, I still thought nothing of it. It was basically a kitchen, a lounge and one bedroom. Mum and Dad took that for themselves and hived off a bit of space there for us lads. We had one bed between us but I have to say in winter that was all that kept us alive.

That house was small but it was cold. You wouldn't give it to your wife's boyfriend to sleep in. It had no central heating and no insulation on the walls. You could see the breezeblocks inside and out. We'd stay around the stove as long as we could and at night the three of us boys would spoon up together in bed. There were some days we would be at each other's throats for this reason or that, but come night-time it's all forgotten and we're snuggling up. Shared bodily warmth, that's what they call it. Huddle up or freeze.

I don't think my dad noticed the temperature. It was no worse than where he'd chosen to spend the last few months. And the discomfort was certainly nothing like he'd gone through in the past year.

The cold is what it is. There was nothing I could do;

this was where my mum and dad had said I was living now. No problem to me, I just got on with it. What I mostly remember is the lack of land. There were no trees to climb, no big sweeping drives to run down in my John Deere tractor, and our windows looked straight on to the road. It wasn't busy, by any means, but when a car turned the corner it'd light up the whole room, throwing shadows everywhere. But at least it wasn't haunted.

My dad must have been pretty miserable going from owning a mansion to barely being able to afford the rent on a no-up two-down. But he never let it show. He forced himself to get back to work with his brother Jim. Uncle Jim had had a moment as a racer, too. There was a clan of them, led by Joey. Then Jim took a big smash down in the south of Ireland: he broke his pelvis and his back and he never got going after that. He was just about the only one of us who knew what my dad was going through. But even he couldn't understand why the old fella wouldn't let go of the crazy idea of getting back on a bike.

Dad said, 'The gain outweighs the pain, Jim. A man needs to ride.'

Jim knew that wasn't true. Not for him, anyway.

I don't know what my mum thought of it all. She listened to the doctors when they said Dad would be disabled all his life. And she listened to my dad when he said he was going to return to the TT and settle a few scores on that king of courses. Two people, two conflicting opinions. But there was only one person she was ever going to believe. My dad. He may have been small but they didn't call him the 'Mighty Micro' for nothing. The man was a force of nature. He had willpower enough to power the whole of Ballymoney. If he said he was doing something, only a fool or someone who'd never met him would disagree. So my mum never tried to stop him. She never said, 'You'll not be satisfied till you kill yourself.' Her outlook was, 'He'll do what makes him happy – and as long as he's genuinely healthy enough to take part, that's as much as I can hope.' Remember, this is a girl who goes toe to hoof with beasts double her size. If one of them takes against her, she's toast. Taking away my dad's bikes would be like taking away her horses. She understood.

Maybe in the back of her mind, my mum thought it would never happen. Dad had forced himself to be able to control his right hand but he still couldn't close it, not into a real grip, and definitely not tight enough to operate the front brake and the clutch on a bike. And if you're gonna be riding – and I mean *riding* – you really need those.

Once again, you reach a point in his story where a normal person usually gives up. Walks away and says, 'Okay, I tried but it's not to be.' I don't think my dad was ever normal that way. You might say, 'Show me a Dunlop who is.'

Dad looked at his bike and said, 'If I can't brake and change the clutch with my right hand I'll just have to do it with my left.' So that's what he did. He went into his workshop and rewired his bike so that the brake was on the left with the throttle, operated by his thumb. It's mad when you think about it. But to him it was logical. See problem: solve problem. Job done.

I watched him do all this. Of course I did. The house might be different, it might be smaller than our old kitchen, and the workshop was more crammed, but the same magic took place. And every minute that Dad was there, so was I, handing him spanners or wrenches; whatever he didn't need, usually. He put up with it, head down, quietly getting on with his work.

About the only concession Dad did make to his physical limitations was in the weight of bike. Superbikes – basically

the beasts of the sport – were just too much of a handful
with his restricted strength. Even 250s were hard work.
But that still left 125cc. So no bother. He'd won 125 races
all over. Including five at the famous Cookstown 100, the
traditional curtain-raiser to the road-racing season. That
weekend may as well have had a target pinned to its back
because my dad was gunning for it. In his mind, if he was
going to get back on the horse, that was where he wanted it
to be.

So: 20 April 1996, Orritor Road, County Tyrone. Almost
two years since Dad nearly died. A year since he was still
tucked up in bed. Six months after he was locked up alone
in the rehab cottage. If you'd seen him loading the van that
morning you'd never have guessed what had gone before. I
was so proud. We all were. I desperately wanted to climb in
with Dad and his boy LB but no way could they look after
me at a track.

'When you're old enough to look after yourself you can
come.'

Seems fair enough now, but I was genuinely pissed off.

We were glued to the radio. It wasn't blanket coverage
but there were plenty of mentions of Dad because of the
historic comeback. Loads of press interviews and the like.
Normally he would have loved it, played up to the cameras
and the microphones, but for once he just wanted to get his
visor down. He was nervous about coming back, even if he
never admitted it. He was as interested as the media and
the fans to see if he could still cut it.

But he could. Of course he could. I think he was pretty
happy with ninth place. My mum was just satisfied he came
home in one piece. I wanted to hear all about it. You could
tell he was hurting from the exertion, but I think he was
proud. Uncle Joey came first. Keep it in the family, that's
what they say.

I thought my dad was a superman. Not just for riding a bike with all the controls on one side. I'd see him get out of bed in the mornings. That was a man going through fifty shades of pain. Whatever he was telling the rest of us about being mended, the truth was written there on his face those first few minutes in the morning. Basic functions tore him to bits. But he got through it. He never moaned. If he knew someone was watching, he even smiled and pretended nothing was hurting. But he didn't always hear me coming. I saw the grimaces and the winces when he thought no one was around.

Seeing all this as a wee boy taught me a lot about the way a man should be. *Don't show weakness.* That message came over loud and clear. He didn't have to sit me down and spell it out.

But there was another rule.

If you put your mind to it, you can overcome any obstacle.

The craic was a big driver for my dad. One of the things he missed most in being laid up was not being with the boys. He could have them all visit every day, but that wasn't the same. I'm with him on that to a certain extent. You're not an equal if it's a pity visit.

If it wasn't to be on the track, there was no better place to get the noise going than in a little pub on Seymour Street in Ballymoney. 'Joey's Bar' was just about the flashiest thing my uncle ever spent a penny on. And it wasn't bought to be a show-off. He wanted a haven, if you like, for the boys to assemble. There were only two rules. Number one: leave your religion at the door. And number two: bikers welcome.

Dad loved it there. They all did. Joey would pull pints and run the place in his own quiet way, but he was happy to disappear into a corner with his brothers when they came by. It was paradise. My dad could go and have a red wine with Joey, Jim, his dad and their friends, and talk for hours if he felt in the mood. And even if Dad stepped inside and there was no one there he recognized, plenty of the fellas would know exactly who he was.

'Oh, you're that Robert Dunlop. What are you? Made of metal now? Let me buy you a drink.'

As a kid in the 1990s you got to go in more places than maybe you would today, with the rules and that. Nobody thought about the smoking or the late nights, or if they did, it wasn't something to get in the way of the good times. After one of the local races, Joey and my dad would head to Seymour Street and often my mum would drop us boys off there to catch up with the old fellas' news. That'd take about a minute, then they're knocking back the wine with their mates and I'm chasing my cousins around the pub. Joey had five kids and together we could make some noise. We're Dunlop kids in a Dunlop pub in Dunlop country. No bugger dared complain.

My favourite nights were the ones that got a bit messy. The lock-ins at Joey's Bar were legendary. Those were the nights I'd be allowed – no, I'd be *told* – to hop behind the bar and pour my uncle a beer. Next to me much of the time was one cousin or another. We were partners in crime, no mistake. I remember pulling a pint one day and thinking, *I'm running this place and I'm only nine!*

I thought I was class.

The thing about my dad and his brother was that they were both capable of sitting there in peace, comfortable in their own minds. But if there was a crowd and someone needed to bring the craic, the banter, my dad could, no problem. So could Joey. To the outside world he wouldn't say boo to a goose, but inside his own circle he could tear it up like no one's business.

I think I'm the same. I'll happily go a week or two without a jar or maybe only have a few tins at home. And I can go into a pub and sit there minding my own business. But if called upon, I kid you not, I can raise the roof. It's not something I need to do but it's something that's within me when the occasion arises.

These days, if I do fancy a swift half with the boys, I'll most likely ring a couple of lads I know in their forties rather than the fellas closer to my own age. Nothing against the younger lads because, trust me, there is a time and place for what those boys can bring, but you go through life at different speeds. What I've seen and done at twenty-seven, twenty-eight, is closer to what guys of my dad's generation have gone through, so most nights those are the kind of conversations I want to be having, not throwing back the shot glasses and hitting on the bar girls. Not always, anyway.

My dad was the same and so was my uncle. Joey loved his own company so much that he would drive to races all over Europe, totally on his own, as much to get away from the fuss back home as to win the races. And when there wasn't a race, he started driving charity donations out to Eastern Europe. He saw a news report one day saying kids were starving in Romania so he loaded up his race lorry with food and clothes and just drove off. He became a hero again twice over for that, and rightly so. The Queen even gave him an OBE.

Walking in your brother's shadow wasn't just something my dad had to put up with. From an early age I knew that money wasn't in abundant supply in our house. I also knew that whatever there was trickled down to me last. For example, all my school uniform had Daniel's name written on the tag. I didn't mind. It's not as though I liked school enough to care what anyone there thought of me. The only problem was that I was a different shape to my brother. He's more in William's mould, thin and gangly, whereas I regularly bust a button or two on my shirts on account of having a bit of a 'nelly'. Where it was more of a kicker was hearing William chatting to Dad about getting his own bike one day. Much as I loved my tractor, something with two wheels was the new dream.

For now, I was too young. I knew that. If anyone, it would be Daniel who got the chance before me. But here's the thing about my brother. Not only did he weigh less than me at two years older, he could not give less of a shit about bikes. I'm not saying he hated them, but he didn't care. He'd sit by our dad fettling away in the workshop if it was maybe raining outside, and he had a book but he'd not be bothered. He'd watch Dad go off to race and have no interest at all. Bikes and Daniel just weren't meant to be.

Daniel's idea of fun was being outdoors, alone in nature if possible. At ten years old he'd be walking out into the forest and we wouldn't see him for a day and a half. Bang, away he goes, not a care in the world, he'd lie like a bear in the wild, making a den, eating what he could scavenge, wiping his backside with leaves – I'm guessing there but I wouldn't be surprised. He's just one of them people. We have a word for weird behaviour like that: 'rare'. I thought his behaviour was rare. I thought *he* was rare. He thought the same about me.

I says to him, 'What the hell do you want to go lying in the forest for?'

'Why do you wanna be messing with motorbikes you're too young to drive?'

We couldn't agree on nothing.

While I was my dad's shadow every minute he was home, Daniel was more into Mum's side of things. He liked to ride a horse, and he did a wee bit of horse and cart riding to a decent standard, I'd say. Mum tried to get me up on one of the nags, but it would have been easier to get one of them to agree to ride me. I'm not a fan of the horses. They are very single-minded. And they're powerful. I don't like being on an animal bigger than me. You want to be the most powerful person in the room. You want to be the one making the decisions. On a motorbike, as formidable as it is, it's still the rider who calls the shots. Horses have a mind of their own. If my mum got me on one I'd put on full race helmet, proper protection. I'd sit on it and be led here and there. Sometimes I'd dig my heels in and tell it to turn left or right. That's about as much as I could get it to do. Honestly, they scare the hell out of me.

Daniel loved them. But then he loved anything I hated. He kept snakes and spiders and all I cared about was dogs. Literally, to this day I don't think we have anything in common apart from the fact he drinks beer and I drink beer.

We had our moments, though, when we were young. All three of us brothers played football together for about five minutes. I remember we had a spell playing in this little place called Balnamore, about a fifteen-minute walk from us. Not far, but you had to cross this busy road. My dad always told us, 'Be home before it's dark because there's no lights on the road.'

'Okay, Dad, that's grand. We'll be back before it's dark.'

Yeah, yeah, yeah.

But I always used to push it. One day we're there and Daniel says it's time to go.

'Just a few more minutes,' I say, but that turns into another ten, so Daniel, being smart, buggers off. By the time I'm set to go there's just me and William booting a ball around, and it's already dark.

Crap.

There was this shortcut through the fields, which avoided the roads, so because it's so late we thought we'd take that. A few minutes later, we're screwed. It's pitch black, I can't see the nose on my face and we're wandering around what feels like this maze. Who knows how many times we go back on ourselves. I'm getting scared, obviously. I don't know which way's up. Even Mr Placid, William, is beginning to sweat a bit. Finally, we hear a car so we push our way through the crops towards the sound and there, thank God, is the road.

With Dad's car crawling along it.

Obviously he's out looking for us, full beam on, yelling his head off trying to find us. It's ten o'clock and he is not happy. He thought we'd been hit by a car on the way home. After the slap he gave us when we got back, it felt like I had.

I remember thinking, *He's got his strength back anyway.*

Daniel joined the army later. He was serving in Afghanistan when the shit was hitting the fan. It makes sense when you look at how he grew up. But I still think he has a screw loose.

Road racing is all about the TT and 1997 was no different. Before the annual Isle of Man pilgrimage came the North West 200 where my dad just happened to be the possessor, at the time, of the most trophies in the race's history. He had big hopes for it that year but it wasn't to be. It was his first time back after the big smash and so people were looking at him with interest. The clerk of the course was more interested than most. When he noticed my dad eating a meal and having to cut his food with his left hand, the alarm bells in the fella's head started ringing.

'A man who can't hold a knife with his right hand can't possibly hold on to a bike at 200 mph,' he said. 'Robert, I'm sorry to tell you this, but I can't let you race. It's for your own good.'

In that situation I would blow a gasket. My dad was a bit more measured. He just packed up the lorry and said, 'I'll show them ...'

The TT was just around the corner. That was the real challenge. The place where his career – and his life – had nearly come to a premature end. I don't think Dad was scared of returning to the track. But the idea of thirty-seven miles, again and again and again, must have been a spectre that haunted him. It didn't matter how fit he said he was, the gruelling Snaeffel Mountain Course was going to hurt.

You get a number of different races at the TT. Essentially, everyone goes around the same track. The differences are the amount of laps and the quality of machinery.

The 'Superbike' is the king of the classes. It's basically a 750-1000cc machine running up to four cylinders that's souped up to go as fast as it can. There are two races at the TT, one at the start of the week – the 'Superbike' – and one – the 'Senior' – at the end. They both unfold over six laps. Both against the clock. Both against the finest riders in the world. It's the Senior that has the kudos. That is the blue-riband event. Even though the technology and the personnel is the same as on the first day of the meeting, what happens on the Friday is what people remember.

In between, you have the 'Sidecar', 'Supersport', 'Superstock' and 'Lightweight'. The Sidecar explains itself. The Supersport, known as the 'Junior TT', basically takes less powerful bikes than the Senior. These days it's four-cylinder bikes not above 600cc but over the years, like all the classes, the cut-off gets adjusted with the advances in machinery. Superstocks are production-line bikes with road tyres. The sort you can find in any showroom.

Then there's the 'Lightweight', which is pretty much how it sounds. Smaller, water-cooled engines, currently up to 650cc four-stroke twin-cylinder, sold for road use. Back in 1997, the limit was lower, nothing above 250cc. Unfortunately that was still too much of a handful for Dad for that length of race. Luckily for him, there was another class back then: the 'Ultra Lightweight', which let you run 125s. It dropped off the calendar in 2004 but for Dad's comeback it was exactly what he needed.

You can't believe how much pressure was on the man. Once again, the media had their microphones out for him. Back home I was grateful. The more interviews he gave, the more chance I had to hear him on the radio or, if I was really lucky, the TV. Dad was as good as gold with the media, but there was no mistaking what he was there for. He gave them boys their quotes, pulled down his visor and got busy with his left hand. *Moment of truth.* And what a moment. Four laps later he was being waved into *parc fermé* and told to pull up behind the banner marked 'Third'.

He'd done it. A podium finish on the track that had nearly killed him. In a race where the legendary Joey Dunlop had only finished tenth.

Now he was ready to talk to the media.

The rest of 1997 was steady but nothing mad. Nothing lived up to the TT; nothing ever lives up to the TT. There's an argument to say that the season begins and ends with those two weeks on the Isle of Man. People will do anything to race there. My dad was living proof.

North West 200 1998, he's flying. The clerk of the course isn't going to stop him this year. He has a point to prove with his favourite circuit, I assure you. But it goes tits up. Going into the link road, someone – Davey Lemon, it turns out – clips his handlebar and down Dad goes, sliding straight into a lamp post. He breaks his arm and his collarbone. When he comes home he's on crutches. And what does he say?

'Those boys at the TT had better not have seen this.'

This is the measure of the man. He's managed to find some new bones in his body that have never been broken before but all he's thinking about is making it to the TT. Call it grit, call it determination, my dad had no doubt he was going to make it. As long as the stewards never discovered how battered he was. But this was a boy who'd been hiding his pain for years. Another fortnight of secrecy on the Isle of Man was not going to tax him.

Anyway, over he went to the Isle of Man, all smiles and happiness when anyone was watching; he was allowed to race and he only went and won the bloody thing. That 125 and him were some partnership. It still makes the hairs on my arms stand up. I remember hearing the commentary and screaming at the wee radio. 'Come on, Dad, come on!' And he did.

Nine years old and in my mind, I'm taking the credit for the win.

If I'm honest, my dad struggled to maintain any kind of form. The records he held at the North West – his epic number of wins was only finally bested in 2016 – and elsewhere were mainly secured before the accident in 1994. Afterwards he had podiums and top steps here and there but nothing consistent. It hurt to ride, every single time. That brings its own problems. To his Number-One Fan, knowing how much he was struggling just made me want to watch him race even more.

I asked and I pestered and I begged but Dad kept saying no, he wouldn't take me. Said he couldn't take me.

He never said I couldn't take myself.

I don't know why it took me so long to come up with it, but the following year, ten years old, and I got myself a plan. More importantly, I got my friends to help. One of my buddies, Colin, was fifteen. Dad was racing at Monaghan, about two hours south. I sold Colin on the idea of going, you know, for the craic. Why should the olds get all the fun? He bought the tickets, and off we went. It was a school day. Even better.

I don't know what I expected. Rock up, find my dad, he's over the moon that I bothered to track him down, shows me off to the boys and I join the team. No more school. Job done.

Not quite.

'Michael? What the—?'

The man was furious. I'd never seen him so raged. I don't think he knew what to do. He's got his race brain on and the last thing he wants is a kid clogging up the works. It's too late to send me home and he's got no room in the van, so he finds a couple of spaces in one of his mates' caravans. Lovely folk they were, too. They let Dad get his head down and do what he did best, and sort of held our hand around the track.

We always had bikes around the house but seeing the paddock full of the things was an eye opener, I kid you not. The colours really hit me. My dad rode in all sorts of combinations, sometimes black and white, sometimes yellow, anything really. But we only had a black and white TV. The odd clip I saw never showed me the rainbow of him and the rest of the boys. There were blues and reds and greens and yellows and mauves and colours I never knew. Then the boys started up and the noise, I tell you, the sound was something else. That feeling of light-headedness I'd had when I got my wee tractor was the last time I'd felt something like that. It was magical, really. Thirty-odd bikes, all screaming to be let off the leash. It was more than I'd hoped for.

But that wasn't why I'd come. Watching strangers, however deafening and multi-coloured they were, wasn't the reason I'd bunked off school. I'd come to see my dad.

He didn't let me down.

Picking out one rider from the masses put the thing in perspective. They set off like a swarm but there's the fella you're interested in and whenever he goes by you can't miss him. It's like he's in colour and the rest are black and white. It was a good race. Real wheel-to-wheel racing. And my dad was the master at that. He was a different class. I honestly can't remember the result but I know whenever he passed me and Colin he was further up the road than the boys he'd been with on the previous lap. It was that fast. Almost too quick for the brain to follow. And he did it with the hand that I knew for a fact couldn't hold a pen. But on a bike he was transformed. He was the king of the 125s.

Afterwards you could see the exhilaration in his eyes. He'd got used to me being there, but even then, with the race gone, I was still the third wheel. He wanted to hit the wine with LB and the boys, not wet-nurse a couple of kids. He managed both.

I saw the way the paddock treated my dad and it made me proud. These days riders keep themselves to themselves. This boy's got his team, this boy's got his. They don't really mingle. They don't like to. It's all secrets and lies, winning at any cost. Back then, you saw everyone mixing it up. A real Dulux paint chart of colours, as this rider and that shared a beer and the banter. And there's my dad at the centre. Spinning the plates, keeping the wheels turning, smiling and laughing. No one suspected the pain he was in. Just shaking a hand made him wince, not that he let it show. But I knew.

That was the first time I went to a race, and my dad made sure it was the last. At least till I was old enough to be able to watch without a minder. But I had another plan.

I don't want to watch. I want to race.

The sport has changed mega. The only way you get to know what a few of the boys are thinking is by following their Twitter feeds. It's a joke really. Sad, too. Road racing started out as a bit of fun on the roads followed by a lot more fun afterwards. They've both gone now, to a certain extent. For most of the riders anyway. I do my best to keep the craic alive in my team. But then I had the best teachers.

My dad would have helped anyone back in the day if he could. Winning wasn't the be-all and end-all that it is to some. He saw the bigger picture. You need racers to race. You want to win because you're the fastest, not because your rival couldn't get off the grid. There was one fella he'd help out even if it cost him a win.

One day my dad was at the North West. He was the man around that track. Quickest in qualifying and tipped to win – again. It's one o'clock in the morning and my dad's asleep. Big race tomorrow. He's woken by a phone ringing. It's Joey.

'Are you all right?' Dad asks.

'My 125 isn't running right.'

'Oh shit. Okay, give me fifteen minutes.'

That's it, that's all it took. Dad got on the phone to LB and told him to get his arse up and out the front door. Poor Liam leaps up; he thinks it's race day.

'What's going on, Robert?'

'It's Joey. His bike's not working. We need to sort it.'

Two o'clock in the morning, those three boys are standing on Main Street, Ballymoney. They've got Uncle Joey's bike and my dad's and they just run the pair of them up and down the street for hour after hour, trying to work out what's holding Joey's back. After each run they take bits off of my dad's bike and bolt them on Joey's. Then they run again and make another change.

Who on earth would do that? At the very least, if you're riding at 200 mph you need to get a good night's sleep. But helping out the competition? The Dunlop bond runs tight. Those boys would have done anything for each other. That's how close they were. I like to think I have a similar bond with William. Even Daniel, the rare prick. You'd do anything for blood.

Dad was managing to earn a wage but it was down on the figures he was pulling in before 1994. Winnings were no longer guaranteed, although the lap money kept the wolf from the door. Either way, I knew the situation. I didn't dare ask for the one thing I wanted more than anything: my own bike. But I guess my dad was ahead of me. When I was eleven he handed me the keys to the kingdom: a bike of my own.

My God it was beautiful. It was a little motocross thing, and at only 85cc it wasn't powerful enough to pull the knickers off your girlfriend. But I loved it – until, that is, I got on the thing.

We went down to the beach, me, my brothers and Dad, and the closer I got to riding the thing the more nervous I was getting. It's stupid, I'd wanted one of these longer than I could remember and now I had it I was too scared to enjoy it.

Dad thought I was mental. I let William have the first ride, which everyone knew was very uncharacteristic for a selfish sod like me, but they let it go. When I said afterwards, 'Daniel can go next', that's when they knew something was up.

'Are you going on this bike or not?' Dad says. 'You know how much it cost me?'

But I was terrified, I'll be straight with you. Maybe seeing my dad's injuries put me off. I don't know. All I can say is I had no love for biking at that moment.

Dad started getting wound up. Eventually he virtually threw me on it, he was that annoyed.

'You can do this, son,' he says, and he talked me through the gears and the brakes. I nodded, pulled on my little helmet, and revved the thing. Then, with everyone watching, I took off.

And fell off about two seconds later.

I wasn't hurt, it was only soft sand beneath me, but I was spooked like a horse hearing a car backfire. There was no way I was getting back on that thing. I don't think I could have disappointed my dad more if I'd murdered someone. He was that irritated he would have chucked the bike in the sea if my brothers hadn't been all over it. The worst thing was watching Daniel bomb up and down. He didn't even like bikes and he was better than me.

But that wasn't the end of it. A few weeks later we went back to the beach and I had another go. This time I got the hang of it so well I wanted to ride the thing home. I think the bike would have struggled with one or two of the hills, otherwise my dad might even have let me, he was that proud. He could see it already, the day the four Dunlops – him, Joey, William and me – would take to the TT side by side. That was a goal worth having, wasn't it? That would give the boys at Joey's Bar something to celebrate.

It was a beautiful dream but it was never going to happen. We just didn't know it yet.

It tore the town apart, no word of a lie. Strangers were hugging each other and crying in the streets.

No one could believe that Joey was gone.

It was 2 July 2000. My uncle's racing over in Tallinn, Estonia, and the conditions are wet to say the least. These days the TT won't run if the weather's bad, but it used to, and so did the other events. No one really knows what occurred. It was nothing to do with not knowing the track, because Joey had already won the 750cc race and the 600.

He was going for the hat trick on the 125 when his bike left the road and smashed into the nearby trees. There were no spectators there. It's only when he didn't go past his next checkpoint that questions began to be asked.

Obviously they rang my dad. He was over with Joey's family like a shot. There was all the practical stuff to attend to. First things first, they needed to get the body back to the UK. Telling his mum was the worst. You should never bury your own children and that woman, May, had suffered enough with my dad's injuries and Uncle Jim's as well. The worst thing for her and Grandad Willy was having no time to themselves. It's all right lovely strangers commiserating on your loss when you nip out to buy some bread, but they had no time to grieve themselves. They were in the spotlight from the moment the news about Joey hit Ballymoney. It was well intended but not right.

Everyone was in shock. Even at forty-eight, Uncle Joey was flying that year. He'd recently won his third hat trick at the TT so you'd never say he was losing his touch. It didn't make sense. Whereas my dad was unbreakable – no pain, no accident could stop him – Uncle Joey just never crashed. He never had any of those moments that dot every racer's career. The boy just never made mistakes.

I remember the mood in the house being awful. No one spoke for ages. I think in case we started crying. It was terrible. Flowers kept arriving and you'd again be reminded why. My dad was not given to tears but you could see he was hurting worse than when he'd come off his bike himself.

The whole town shut down. Everyone felt they knew Joey. He'd done so much for them, they wanted to give something back. On the day of the funeral there couldn't have been a house with a soul in. Everyone turned out. And not just from Ballymoney. People travelled from all over the country to pay their respects. And of course, more than ever, bikers were welcome. Among the 50,000 mourners a good few were on two wheels.

The procession to Garryduff Presbyterian Church was like something out of a film. You'd think the Queen had died. My dad went in the main car. I walked ahead with my cousin Ben, Jim's son. We were dying inside but it was Joey's kids we really felt for. We'd lost an uncle. Those boys and girls a dad. I couldn't imagine how that must feel. All I knew is I never wanted to find out.

FOUR

Thick as Champ

EVEN TO A KID who's only really fussed about his own little world, you can see when your family's going through the wringer. For as long as I could remember it was one thing or another picking away at us. I'd never known us to have money, not really, so I never missed that. But as the years went by I began to realize we were never going back to Ballynacree. The days of the country mansion and all the playing space you could dream of were long gone. From where I was looking, our houses weren't a step up. They were actually getting worse.

From the wee cottage in Ballymena we moved to another dingy place on the other side of Ballymoney. Then, when we couldn't afford the rent on that, we moved in with my dad's parents. Their townhouse on Union Street was a decent size but it wasn't built for having another five bodies landed on it.

I liked it there, though. My gran is a lovely woman, very hospitable. My grandad was a brilliant man. People said he knew more about engines than any person alive. He could take anything apart and reconfigure it for the better. Rumour had it that he was running light bulbs and the like off a windmill-based generator he built himself years before the rest of the country acquired electricity. You could see where my dad and Joey learned the language of machinery. They were a good team, the three of them: shared interests and happy to socialize. Living in Union Street and taking a jar or two at Joey's Bar with the boys was pretty much all my granddad looked for in his later years. Though with one son gone he went out less and less, especially there.

After Union Street we went to Burnquarter, which is just outside Ballymoney. It's like my mum and dad were afraid to leave the area. Obviously with Joey gone, they felt they couldn't go too far. Wherever we did go, though, us boys would settle in as best we could. But you'd know that my dad wasn't happy. He'd had a dream of getting us the home we'd never want to leave and he'd come very close with Ballynacree. Probably, if he was honest with himself, that was as close as he was ever going to get. That particular dream, like his brother, was gone.

Eleven years old, I'm sort of on the periphery of all of this. I remember going to Joey's Bar with my dad. It was like a florists in there, there were that many flowers. The mood wasn't how I remembered, but even I could understand why. There were lots of toasts to my uncle. There'd be a decent buzz and then someone would catch a glimpse of one of the photos of Joey on the wall or his helmets and then they'd go quiet and the others would follow.

I still got to pull the odd pint, but without my uncle there was an obvious hole in the evening. Something was missing. My dad started going less and less. Only later did I begin to realize it wasn't just to do with his brother.

At some point my dad took a dislike to Joey's widow, Linda. I don't know if she did something or said something, or whether he did or said it first. It might have been related to the fact that after Joey passed, Linda asked for all her husband's belongings to be sent back over. All the bits and pieces in Dad's garage. That's fair enough. It's all her property. It's her right to do with it what she likes. But I know my Dad would have preferred to hang on to a helmet or something for old times' sake. What I can say for sure is that he was never exactly quick to rush over to the pub if he thought Linda would be there. Which meant I got to see my cousins less and less. Joanne I was the closest to, on account of us being the same age, but the others I always got on well enough with. William and Daniel were even closer to them. It was a confusing time.

I think Dad put it down to grief. Linda wanted as much of her husband's effects around her as possible to keep Joey's memory alive, which is natural. But I don't think Joey would have wanted things to turn out the way they did, with the families not getting on. He and my dad were typical brothers. They'd squabble and sulk, say things they regretted and poke fun at the same time, just like I do with William. I can be an arsehole to that boy, but at the end of the day we are brothers. There is nothing I would not do for him. Dad and Joey were the same. They were family, they were mates. Sometimes the best of mates, sometimes the worst. But always honourable. Always well intentioned.

Dad was haunted by the fallout from Joey's death for years. Luckily for him, he would never live to see the worst of it.

When it came to respecting Joey, no one did it in a more heartfelt way than my dad. Yet even he was blown away when, in May 2001, Ballymoney council opened the Joey Dunlop Memorial Garden in Seymour Street, just along from the bar. We went along to the grand opening but it was raw on all of us. Seeing the statue of Uncle Joey on his Honda was moving, even for a twelve-year-old. Although even that statue had its own helmet.

Tributes to the 'King of the Mountain' came in from all over. The biggest, for a racer, was having a section of the TT circuit renamed after you, in this case for the man who had – and still has – the record number of wins. What was the twenty-six-mile marker at Snaefell is now known simply as Joey's. Twenty-six miles, twenty-six trophies. Further down, at the Bungalow marker, there's another statue. And another helmet.

Having the family name attached to things like that is mind-blowing, really. If anything, it just inspired the young me to go even more. It's not that I was planning my future or anything, because at that age you're just thinking about your next girlfriend or, in my case, your next meal. But I knew bikes were in my blood. All I had to do was ride one of the damn things.

For ages I thought my 85cc was quality – right up until my dad got William a 125, the same bike he was a legend on. I was green as a frog with envy. And my brother? A dog with two dicks could not have been happier. Immediately he's badgering my dad for a ride outside the yard and eventually gets his way. Our road was as quiet as a grave so Dad took William up the top.

When they came back, William had this look on his face. You'd think he'd been to the moon and back. And, oh, the details. Every blade of grass he passed, every bump in the road, every gust of wind – he could remember them all. I know, because he wouldn't shut up about it.

This carried on for a couple of weeks. Every time they got the motorbike out I was at the window, foaming at the mouth. Sometimes I'd be in the yard with them, itching to go, but Dad always said, 'Your turn will come. Go back in the house.' I never did. I'd wait and watch William go screaming by.

Worse than being stuck on my Jack was waiting for the inevitable gloating from my big brother. Then one day my dad said, 'You want a go on this?'

It was like somebody had just given my mouth a dose of Viagra: I couldn't stop grinning. My head was clean spun, it was all freaking rock 'n' roll. *Me, ride the 125?* Is the Pope Catholic?

But it was nearly an instant failure. I was too small to reach the floor. No bother, William held the bike steady and my dad lifted me up on to the saddle. I had a wee helmet on – the old fella would never let us ride without precautions. Safety first. I knew the controls from the 85 but he talked me through them again anyway.

I'm listening but by now I'm itching to go. I just want to bite the bullet and show that road who's boss. I think my dad could see this was the case so he kept me there that wee bit longer, going over and over the maximum speed I was to reach and what to do about turning at the end of the straight, considering I couldn't reach the floor.

'Just lean and take it steady. Too fast and you won't make the turn. Too slow and you'll need to put a foot down and that's the end of it.'

'I got it, Dad. Let me go.'

He releases me and I'm that excited you'd have thought someone had given me a lifetime of sweeties. I've no idea if I kept within the speed parameters; I was just flying. I was a rocket. I was Joey, Robert and William Dunlop rolled into one. I was the man.

It was so tempting to go beyond the end of the straight and just ride and ride. But I knew that would be my last time in the saddle. So I braked, executed this fairly clumsy turn, then hightailed it back. My head was completely fuzzed. I had never known a feeling like it. When I slowed down by my dad, and he and William grabbed the bike, I was already babbling about the races I was going to win.

'I'm going to get more little ladies from the TT than Uncle Joey and you, Dad, put together!'

'Oh yeah?' William says. 'Big talk from a fat kid who's never set foot on the Isle of Man.'

I wanted to nut him, but the boy had a point.

I need to see this TT track.

I don't know how I swung it. I'm twelve years old and I'm allowed to go over the ocean – well, the Irish Sea. *On my own.* Well, again, not quite. My pal Colin was in my camp. By now he's sixteen and old enough to be trusted, so he says. Dad agreed the trip would be beneficial for my future. If, that is, my future was in continuing the family grip on the TT.

So here's the story: I'm Michael Dunlop, son of Robert, nephew of Joey. Those boys knew the Snaefell like the back of their hands. I would too. In time. But first I needed to do some serious fact finding. I was that determined about it.

The only problem was, I was twelve. Whatever higher purpose was on my mind on the boat over from Belfast, the second I saw the giant funfair I was gone. My head was jelly. I'd never seen anything like it. Rollercoasters, big dippers, big wheels – big everything. Normally it would have been the best day of my life. But on the way Col and I ate chips, cheese and gravy – big chips, big cheese – followed with every candyfloss and sugar sweet we could find. About one hour into the funfair the whole concoction got mixed in a way my constitution wasn't built for.

That boy running the Waltzer is probably still wiping it down today.

No lie, we were sick as dogs. Sicker than dogs. Sicker than dogs with mange. For three days we were greener than a dollar bill. And the amount of racing we saw was less than you see on the radio.

The TT for me was my Wembley cup final, my Hennessy Gold Cup, my Olympic gold medal. The dream. I'd always wanted to be there. And the one chance I got, I blew big time. Yes, I can say I went. But no, I can't remember anything. Not that it's my favourite story to tell. Life's a learning curve, right?

But I do remember this. The day I left I made myself a promise. A stupid promise that a twelve-year-old makes, but a promise nonetheless.

I'll be back. And next time I won't just be here to watch.
I'll be riding.

Big talk from a big kid. The truth was, I didn't even have a bike that was eligible. But William did, and more. You need a licence to race, at any level. I remember when William's came through. My mum said, 'Hold on, young man, you'll not be racing without my permission.'

And my dad said, 'He doesn't need it. He's got mine.'

I'm surmising they had a wee chat in private after that because not only was William allowed out to ride his 125 but Mum said, 'I'm not going to stop you. You'll get to eighteen and do what you like anyway. I'd rather you had your Dad helping you learn the right way while you're young enough to listen.'

He started out in the Clubman's series, a competition for beginners. You're not judged on age, just ability. They only put you against your own standard. So he was up with boys both younger and older than him.

When you're starting out, it's all about the racetracks. Proper circuits designed and built for racing with proper run-off areas and protective tyre walls and barriers. None of your street roads with lamp posts and telephone boxes shit. The biggest one in the area was Mondello Park over in Caragh, County Kildare. They don't come much better or more important. The only problem was, it was two and a half hours away.

My dad would drive William down any weekend he wasn't racing himself. But as soon as my brother passed his driving test, that was a different story. Dad got him this shitty van and he started to drive himself to the track. But he was never alone. I was there beside him every inch of the way. They were great times. Today William has a rare old style. Beautiful to watch, so smooth, like a ballet dancer on two wheels. I don't know where it came from. He was shit when he began riding bikes. He started slow, then he just picked up and picked up and started getting quicker and quicker, faster and faster.

It wasn't long before the road-racing bug bit him where it counts and suddenly he was off for whole weekends, again with yours truly at his side. The craic was out of this world. But there was also work. I tried to help out and I probably made more of it than was needed. I had a boiler suit and that was enough to call myself chief mechanic. I was the big dog. I did everything I could: change gears, jetting, scrutineering the bike. I did nothing, probably, but I thought I did everything.

My dad wouldn't ride an inch before he'd gone over a bike with a fine-toothed comb. William and I just fiddled about, and he would ride the bike as it was. If it stopped going or he fell off you would try to fix it. That was about the height of it. We didn't do much. We didn't know how. I wasn't exactly Grandad Willy when it came to engineering. That didn't stop me acting like the dog's bollocks around the paddock. I think sometimes I enjoyed racing with William more than he did.

A few of the races were right up the road and we'd sleep in our own beds. Others were a wee bit further, so we slept in the van. Us, the bikes, the gear. We had a mattress one side and the rest of the crap the other. If it was warm I'd take the front seats and give the racer his space. If it was colder – and even in fine weather the temperatures could plummet, believe you me – we snuggled up like sardines, two peas in a pod, just spooning to keep our bodies the right side of freezing.

I was proud of my brother from before he kick-started his first bike. My chest was puffed out the second we climbed out of the van. The further up the ladder he rode, the more my chest stuck out. When he got to the front you'd think I'd won the bloody race. It was the best of times.

On the podium they give you a wee thing that looked like an eggcup holder. To young Billy Bollocks here it looked like the World Cup. Then there was the fizz. I won't call it champagne. It's piss, that's what it is. But the boys would spray it and the brave ones would drink a sip or two. It looked good. That's all that mattered. It looked the real deal.

We'd put the eggcup on the dashboard and we'd rock our way home. That van was a wreck, no mistake. She was rotten. The chassis was in bits but after a good day racing we were virtually doing wheelies in it, chests shoved well out. We were idiots but thought we were the boys.

William was an obvious master of two wheels in the making. No question. Me? Right then, four wheels was about my limit. Licence or not.

That old van, hideous as she was, did me just fine for bombing around the fields. My dad showed me the basics – pedals, gears, clutch and even mirrors, whatever they were. Like everything, my dad wouldn't have let us have a go if he didn't think we were up to it. Believe it or not, risks weren't something he took lightly.

Maybe what he didn't know was that it wasn't just the fields I was driving in.

My brother is many things. But what that boy can do better than any other soul I have ever met is sleep. For Ballymoney, for Ireland, for the world. He can fall asleep upside down. He can fall asleep in the arctic. I'm not sure if it's a talent or a disease. Recently we had a thing for our mum round my place. William turned up with his girlfriend and my wee niece. He ate with us, said about four words, then fell asleep on the rug. That's him.

Coming back from the races he was diabolical. Two minutes out from the circuit he'd start yawning. Three minutes and it's, 'Hey, Michael, take over for us, will you?'

That's a request he doesn't need to make. I'm in the driver's seat quick as you like. The only problem is, I'm not much taller than a rat. I can get us from A to B but it's not pretty. I'm stabbing at those pedals with my short legs. We go forward like a kangaroo with hiccups.

In those days the police were a wee bit more lenient. On country roads they'd turn a blind eye to almost anything. To be pulled over you had to be weaving like Stevie Wonder behind the wheel. One or two times I figure I did just that.

One time I'm looking forward, high on the craic of just cruising the road. We're not speeding that you'd notice. The boy wonder's sleeping like a baby on drugs next to me. Suddenly there's the 'bloop bloop' from sirens, so I scramble a glance in the rear-view mirror and spot the boys in blue behind.

Oh shit.

They're lax round these parts but not exactly known for encouraging underage driving.

'William,' I say, smacking the boy round the face. 'William! Wake up.'

He cracks open an eye as I start to slow down.

'What is it, you idiot?'

'The police are all over us. You need to get across here.'

'Oh, right you are. Slide your arse over.'

So he'd manoeuvre himself one way and I'd go the other while we try to switch places and it gets a bit jerky for a moment so the boys behind think they've got a drunk driver on their hands. Easy ticket. *Happy days.* When we pull over they're straight in William's face, all over his breath, inhaling it for all they're worth.

'What's going on?' they say.

Sniff. Sniff.

'Sorry,' William says, 'just a bit tired.'

Sniff.

Which happens to be the gospel truth.

'Okay, son,' they say, trying to hide their disappointment. 'Remember to take a break, you hear? Don't want you hurting your wee brother now.'

'Sure thing, Officer.'

'Grand. Now on your way, lads.'

The police might have had a problem with me driving a vehicle – if not my actual driving – but my dad never did. He knew William as well as anyone. He knew me, too. It might have been my brother pulling out of the yard and pulling back, but the odds of Sleeping Beauty keeping his eyes wide open for three or four hours after a day's racing were slim. Slight. Zero, in other words.

He had his rules, my dad. My smarting backside was frequently testament to that. The things he'd punish were clear, though. Anything that wasn't obvious became a grey area worth exploring. Like school. I hated it. It hated me.

In later life, being a Dunlop is worth a fair amount. But kids don't like anyone standing out. Too big, too small, too fat, too ginger – too 'anything' and you're going to get it. There were one or two lads who had a gripe with me coming from such illustrious stock. Four days out of five there'd be no bother, then some idiot'd say something and that's it: fucking boom, lights out. I wasn't like Rocky Balboa or anything. I just tended to hit first and worry about it later. I'm exactly the same today. You make yourself a problem with me and I'm gonna lamp you before you get a chance to plant one on me.

I was big, that helped. Not obese but certainly on the chubby side. When you're surrounded by two dozen scrawny lads you seem even bigger. The PE teacher used to pick me for the rugby team because of my size. I'd get the ball and walk casually up the field and have all these slim jims bouncing off me.

It's possible my size made the fights look worse. Every time there was a dust-up I got a week-long suspension. Once I realized that was the punishment, I started to look for the aggro. In my book there was nothing better than not going to school.

To all intents and purposes, I left the education system aged eleven. I still attended after that. But mainly to save paperwork and stop my parents being arrested. I'd skip three or four days, then turn up for the next. Just for appearance's sake. Just to stop my mum and dad getting a rocket from the powers-that-be.

I've got no GCSEs, no A-levels, nothing. If you asked me to write down what qualifications I have, you'd walk out with the same blank piece of paper in your hand you came in with. There'll be nothing on it. I don't mind that. I'm not embarrassed.

I wasn't interested in learning anything that school could teach me. Every morning, aged twelve or thirteen, I'd climb in that old van and drive William and Daniel to school – then hightail it back home again. I really had no time for the place.

Let's be straight: I'm an idiot. I know nothing. I'm not great at reading, I'm not great at writing, I know nothing about geography, history or socio-politico-economics. I'm genuinely pretty stupid and that's the long and short of it. But I think you can only be as smart as you want to be. Everyone has the potential, I believe, but it's how far you want to let yourself go down a particular road. Everyone has a destination, a vision of what they want to be. That's why I was never too bothered about GCSEs and the like. I know my destiny. I've known it for half my life. And I knew I could get there without school clogging up my day. My Grandad Willy was a genius when it came to engineering and he was self-taught. My dad and my uncle spoke 'bike' better than anyone alive. They also made a few bob for themselves, which they never would have done chasing traditional qualifications. Those boys were smart in their own way, nobody could deny that. But the education system isn't necessarily suited to cope with their kind of smart.

Or mine.

I had a talent that the education system couldn't cope with. There'll be others like me every year. But I was lucky. I knew there was a place for me in the wider world. Everything is different today. Anyone thinking now of cutting out of education is screwed. You need a degree these days to get an interview at McDonald's. Just to get one foot on the bottom rung of the ladder you need to have Albert Einstein as a referee. For my dad and my uncle's generation, you could always get work if you were willing. I was hoping that would be the way the cards fell for me. Not that I was thinking that back then. All I really knew was I didn't want to be in school.

There's an argument that school is there to process the kids, get them to conform, prepare them for the Big World. That only works for the majority. I'm not sure it's for me. If I had children I'd have to analyse whether they were better off in mainstream education or not. Everything I know to this day I learned from my dad or off my own wits. I'm not saying it's for everyone. I'm not trying to be some Karl Marx revolutionary. But I couldn't have done it any other way.

Same as this boy in the town: like me, he effectively left school when he was eleven or twelve; he just started buying and selling cars and today he's a millionaire. Qualifications wouldn't have helped him any. These days he'd be lucky to get away with it. Too much politics, too many obstacles in the way, too many electronic paper trails for every bugger. I tell you now, there's someone in London who can check out all your details at the touch of a button. There's no hiding.

I think when my dad's generation used to skip school there was a bit of slack in the head teacher's response. When I was bunking off it had become a bit more of a problem and the old boy who ran our place was turning in circles trying to keep me in class. The truth is, he hated me. We would both have been happier if I'd not bothered turning up. But this was the era where his bosses were beginning to clamp down on truants.

I might go in on the days when we had a particular lady teacher. She was pretty tasty, I can tell you. I'd sit at the back drooling. Otherwise, I'd not see the point.

It got to the stage that meetings started being called between the school and my parents. My mum was a bit disappointed but Dad said he'd handle it. He knew the fella from when he'd been at school.

'You know, Robert,' the head says, 'your Michael has to come to school now. He needs to learn something.'

Dad says, 'What's the point? He's thick as champ.'

'Ah, come now, Robert.'

'Put it this way. There's none so deaf as those who won't listen. And believe you me, headmaster, this boy will not listen to anything any of you here have to say.'

The head looks at me and shrugs.

'Well, things are different from when you were at school.

There are laws now. It's out of my hands what'll happen to you if you don't send him in.'

We had a meeting like that every month or so. The next day I'd show my face at school just to keep the social services from coming down on Dad. Maybe I'd last two days if the hot teacher was there. The rest of the time I'd be dropping my brothers off and I didn't care who saw me. If any teachers were in the playground I'd give them a wave. When I saw the head I did a donut in my van. No wonder the guy hated me. I'd hate me, too.

The thing with my dad was, he knew I wouldn't learn anything in school. But that was okay. Right or wrong, he was confident that I would get through life on my wits. And by wits he didn't necessarily mean riding skill. Because by the time I was playing hooky at school, I'd already started my own motorbike-racing career.

And I was stinking the place out.

FIVE

Too Shit for an Airbox

I'M THE BOY, I AM.

I'm in Spain and I'm test-driving my dad's 125 and I am riding the tits off it. Or so I think. At twelve years old, you can be a bit up yourself. I was that far up I was coming down again the other side. But bombing round that track in old España you think you know everything.

And then you run out of road and you realize you know sod all.

By the time I lose control I'm going about 70 mph – not mad speed but fast enough that it's better to be *on* a bike than off it.

I'm going into a corner and I realize that with all the best will in the world I am not going to make that turn. Even as I'm braking, the road sort of just disappears to my right and suddenly I'm belting over the rumble strip. *Thoomp, thoomp, thoomp, thoomp.* Talk about tied in knots. Everything's jarring and bumping, my visor's up and down, my stomach and arse are being punched twenty to the dozen by a pneumatic drill, and I don't know where I am. Then suddenly the bumping stops.

Because I'm flying through the air.

It's probably less than two seconds since I missed the bend and I'm Superman-ing over the handlebars, flying without a cape. I've no idea where the bike's going. If I'm lucky, she won't be ending up the same place as me. It's bad enough falling off. Getting yourself run over in the process is not a story you want to be telling later.

That is, if you survive.

Even though it happens so quickly, you have all these thoughts rushing through your head. The word 'shit' keeps coming at me.

Shit. Shit. Shit. Shit.

It seems appropriate. I remember landing on my arms first. My helmet smacked down second and the rest of me cartwheeled over the top. Instinctively I tucked up into a wee ball and skidded a yard or more on my arse and side. The bike lasted a second or two longer. Then everything was silent. Even the cicadas were quiet. I lay still a minute or three, just the sound of my own heart bursting out of my chest to keep me company.

It's weird. I'm in pain, no question about that, but I have no idea where from. It's like you can feel every inch of your skin at the same time. It's all *alive*. That's more than your brain can process. More than mine can, anyway. I remember trying to work out the damage. I concentrated and managed to move a leg. Then the other one. Then my arms, then my head. Left, right, forward, back. Then fingers, toes, eyes, they all got a little test drive. Nothing appeared to broken, not even my helmet and that had taken a wild smack. What I knew for sure, though, was that as the other pains calmed down my arse was still stinging. And my overalls were ripped to shreds.

By the time my dad ran over I'd worked out I was okay, just a bit winded. He didn't know that, though. Maybe because I was still lying stock-still. His face looked like he'd seen a ghost. He scanned me up and down and said, 'Are you all right?'

'Aye. Just a bit sore.'

'Did you not see the bend? It's easier if you go round them.'

'Now you tell me ...'

We were booked to be in Spain a couple of days for Dad to put his bike through its paces. He spent a couple of hours fixing it up, getting it road ready again. Then he said, 'Go on, Michael, you'll need to be riding another lap before we go home.'

Ride another lap? Is he kidding me? I'm petrified. And I've got no skin left on my backside. What does he think I'll be sitting on?

But he was insistent.

'Ride this bike now or you'll never ride another bike again. That's not a threat – I've seen it happen to others, grown men at that. Trust me, Michael, you need to get back on the horse.

'And you need to do it *now*.'

I'd fallen off, I swear, because I was too small to control it. Big bike: small kid. Only going to end one way in my eyes. Dad's answer to that was just to go slower. 'And when you see those bits in the road where the straight part disappears, maybe think about slowing down again a bit more?'

He was right. I had no desire to get back on board, and the truth is, I was that shook up that I could already imagine never riding again. Only the thought of my dad going through his crash in 1994 got me thinking different. There must have been moments when he'd considered chucking it all in. When the bike became a bit of a bogeyman in his imagination. But he'd forced himself back out there.

If that man could drive virtually one-handed and in giant pain every day of his life, I was sure I could put a lap together. And I did. I went a wee bit slower than before and made sure I remembered where the bendy bits were. When I came back round to Dad I was buzzing. It's like I'd never fallen off at all. All my confidence was back. Of course, that gave the old man a new problem: how to slow me down again.

Each lap I did got a wee bit more hairy. When it was time to go home my dad said, 'You've done okay but if you carry on like that a broken bone or two won't be far away.'

It must be annoying to be right all the time.

I got the broken bone soon enough. But it wasn't from riding bikes.

That stupid way I had of taking risks on the track was just the same way I carried on in everyday life. I was out with couple of mates one day and we had nothing particular to do so we were hanging around in a playground. It was getting dark so all the wee kids had scarpered home. My mate and I, we're sitting on the kiddy swings and chatting. Next thing you know, we're standing up and seeing who can go higher. Backwards and forwards, backwards and forwards, we're flying through the air, yanking on those chains for dear life.

'First one to go over the top wins!'

'You're on!'

If you're looking at a clock, we were hitting ten, eleven in no time. But I wanted to go beyond twelve.

On the swings you have that moment where you change direction and you're suddenly falling. I loved that. But to get all the way over you need enough speed not to drop back down so I was throwing myself forwards at the beginning of every descent, standing virtually upside-down by the time I'd fall backwards. I knew I was close – and, more importantly, my mate wasn't.

One more, one more ...

It was going to be amazing. In my head I was going into the record books for acrobatics. Up, up, up I went and just as I was convinced I was going all the way over past twelve o'clock, I stopped moving.

Oh, Christ ...

I don't know if I hit the frame of the swing or if it was just the impact of landing tits up on the ground. But the net result was one broken collarbone. Not my finest hour.

The only good thing to come out of it was in giving us a comeback when 'concerned' parents and busybodies liked to point out how dangerous it was of Dad to let his lads ride motorbikes.

'Oh, you let your wee girls play on the swings, though, don't you? Believe you me, those things are more dangerous than my bikes. At least we wear helmets.'

It's fair enough. You can break bones no matter what way you go about your business. My dad, though, was never going to convince anyone that he could have got his injuries in any old walk of life. It's not exactly a risk of a banking job that you might lose control of your limbs one day. Or lose your life altogether. But you see the man's point. In any case, it was at least another year before I had another serious accident. This time I broke my wrist. By then I was used to it. And it meant I couldn't hold a pen in school, so that's a win in my book.

In skiing you can get coaching on the best way to fall to minimize damage to you and everyone else further down the mountain. It's not that straightforward on a bike. With skiing or some of those water sports, to a degree your crashes are going to be the same type. If you chuck yourself to one side that's probably going to be your best bet. On a motorbike it's all a bit different. When you're going too fast or you hit something or you've done a bad turn, trust me, that bike can put itself into five million different positions that can all throw you off. You just have to deal with it as best you can at the time. Putting your arms out, curling up into a ball, trying to swim through the air with your arms and legs. It depends on your situation. More often than not you're in a hedge before you know what's happened.

It can be dangerous, I know that. And it's healthy to be a bit scared now and again. But I can be walking down the street when someone blows their horn and that makes me jump more than any motorbike race ever will. I have the odd moment when you get your heart in your mouth, then you just swallow it back down and get on with it. It's a fine line between enjoying yourself, being successful and being hurt.

It was all stuff I needed to know, though, because from the age of twelve I was racing. William had been a later starter than me but it was the same process. I needed to apply for a licence to race and lucky for me my mum kept her powder dry this time. William was still breathing, maybe I'd be all right too. I think that's how she looked at the matter.

The MSA – the Motor Sports Association of the UK – take their job very seriously. To be able to race as a kid I needed to attend a school. Dad drove me down to Nutts Corner and I sat through a bunch of lessons that were infinitely more interesting than anything I'd endured at my own school, although the teachers weren't as hot. We went through all the basics of racing: what the rules are, what the different flags mean, how not to kill yourself or anyone else. I think there was even a little medical. For a chubby kid like me that's the only part that gave me any real concern. But I must have done okay. At the end of the day, this boy in charge shook my hand and gave me my very own B licence. I remember being so happy.

Now I'm like Dad, I thought. *Now I can race.*

Finally.

My dreams of setting the world famous TT alight were still a way off, mind. The races my licence qualified me to compete in were a wee bit smaller. They weren't even on the kind of bike I'd been throwing around the track in Spain.

The Mini Moto Championship was open to kids aged ten to thirteen, so I was at the upper end of the age bracket. But that just put me at a bit of a disadvantage on the bikes. A 49cc two-stroke is not going to go as fast with chubby here on board as it is with some skinny kid. Trust me, even as a kid I looked too big for them. But that was what I was allowed to race, so that's what I was going to do.

The season wasn't exhausting. There were seven or eight short tracks, at places like Nutts Corner, Aghadowey, Athboy, Midland and Bishopscourt. It was between seven and ten laps each circuit. My dad came down with me to the first one. Aghadowey is only up the road so we chucked my bike in the HiAce and off we went. I did all right. Heavy bastard or not, I was the only one walking off with the winner's trophy that day, I made sure of that. There might have been other boys who were quicker but did they want it as much as me? Were they willing to take a bend faster than they were comfortable with to snatch a position? On the day, no they weren't.

Dad never said too much but he was happy enough with the result.

'You'll need to watch yourself, though,' he says. 'Riding like that will test Lady Luck.'

Yeah, yeah, Dad.

Most weekends my dad and William were themselves racing, so word went round the family for anyone muggins enough to take me. Without fail, my cousin Kim, the daughter of Dad's sister, always said, 'Oh, I'll take him.'

She had a wee Ford Fiesta, the model that looks like a bubble, and we'd pack it to the bumpers. There was Kim, me, my bike, a jar of fuel, my leathers, and somehow her friend would squeeze in as well – there had to be someone sensible for Kim to talk to.

Fair play to the lass, she got the short straw in the family, no question, but she took me all over the place and never complained. I couldn't tell you whether she actually liked the racing itself. Her and her friend would be jawing away the entire meeting. But I couldn't have done what I've done without her and that rotten car of hers. When we finished the season in Whiteriver and I got a trophy for the race win and a bigger one for nailing the whole season, she seemed as pleased as I was.

Can you imagine what that did to my head? Twelve years old, winning my first championship. I already needed no encouragement to think I was the big dog. This was proof I was the Great Dane. Oh, the plans I had.

Get ready, TT. I'm coming for you.

When I'm old enough, anyway ...

I wasn't the only Dunlop celebrating. My dad managed to go the whole road-racing season unbeaten. *Motor Cycle News* was all over that. I remember the articles. For a boy with a button instead of a lever for a brake, that was a story that never got old. But things for Dad picked up even more a few months later.

Beginning in January when Dad was finally awarded compensation for his big smash eight years earlier, the year 2002 put a few markers in the family history. He'd never wanted to sue anyone, but I think he worked out that if he put a claim in against his old team and they put one in against the wheel manufacturer, it would square out for the pair of them. His legal team told the courts that at the time of the accident my dad was poised to become a major player in World Superbikes. Definitely top three. Carl Fogarty himself was lined up to give evidence to that effect. The judge praised my dad for the way he came back against his injuries and the way he dealt with the legal proceedings, but before he could give a ruling, the opposition offered a settlement and Dad was persuaded to drop the case. I think he was grateful, after so many years of fighting, to get the worry out of the way and happily took an offer of around half of what he'd been asking for.

Give a lot of men a lump sum of money and they wouldn't know what to do with it after the first dozen drunken nights. But my dad always had a plan for that money.

He was going to build a house.

My dream was the TT. His was putting a roof he could call his own over the heads of his family. By the year's end he'd found a piece of land, quite a chunk actually, about five minutes from the centre of Ballymoney, and got to work designing a house. Over the next two years he wouldn't just watch it grow – he'd make it grow. He was still working every hour during the week as a steel erector and racing every other weekend or so. But after work or on spare days he'd be out on that plot of land building the box, putting in the steel frame, getting the basics done. He had help from a friend or two but it was himself doing the lion's share or helping the specialists. When it came to the bricks, he had a friend in the trade who wanted help getting into the racing. Together they did all the brickwork, including the amazing redbrick round tower my dad had designed as the main feature of the property. A bit of eye candy, no mistake. For as long as I could remember, my dad had been in pain of one description or another. While this work was going on he was just shattered all the time. He'd do a full day's work, then have a bite to eat before heading out to the project and working through the night till he dropped. He was burning the candle at both ends and in the middle as well. He was a man on a mission.

I helped out whenever I could, whenever he needed mindless labour. I can shunt things here and there all day if you ask. Every weekend I'd chip in. That love of being

ow I started out. The round face on that boy went nowhere fast.

Above: Don't be fooled by me looking all smart here - this was on one of the few days I actually attended school.

Left: Dad's big crash in 199 left him in permanent pain and broke his leg so badly healed two inches shorter than the other, yet he'd stil make time for me.

Right: William, Daniel and me enjoying a moment together.

Below: Dad clearly had an influence on us lads!

I was keen as mustard to follow in my dad's footsteps and couldn't wait until I was old enough to get on the roads myself – as you can see below!

much as I admired everything my uncle and dad did on the bikes, Joey's ath in Estonia in 2000 shocked the family to its core and as a kid really ade me aware of the risks those boys took.

Dad's surgery in 2005 to lengthen his leg meant he could spend more time helping with my fledgling career, but it wasn't long before he was back on the roads – this time racing me!

I did it! My first big win on the Mountain Course – what I hoped was to be the first of many – here at the Manx Grand Prix.

around my dad hadn't passed. It didn't matter to me if he was tinkering with an engine or getting his head around some central heating system. I just enjoyed the man's company. The only downside to it all was that he never had a spare day to come and watch me race. I used to dream of him seeing me ride to victory.

Calm yourself, there's always next year.

Or so I thought.

I was expecting big things from 2002. I'd ridden my last Mini Moto and I was upgrading to some serious hardware: a 125. I don't know what the experience was of all the other competitors, ranging in ages as they did, but how many of those had done winter testing in Spain? In my eyes I was a pro. Those boys were going to learn a lesson or two from me.

And then we got to Race Day 1 and I realized the only thing any bugger was learning from me was how not to do it. I was awful. It was one extreme to another. On the Mini Moto I was arguably too big. On the 125 I was physically too small to wrangle the thing around the circuit. I needed arms as long as my legs to get comfortable. And once again, I still barely touched the floor. If the race stewards had noticed I'd have been hooked out. But I was pretty good at balancing. That was about all.

The thing is, the 125 wasn't your normal race bike. We were all riding Aprilias, basic road bikes. Not as powerful as the race version – sensible, being we were kids and all – but they were bigger. Bulkier. Designed for boys and girls a wee bit older than me.

Excuses aside, there is no getting away from the facts. I was awful. As good as I'd been the year before, I was as crap now. Worse, even. I still took stupid chances, going for overtakes that weren't there, looking for bits of tarmac that other riders couldn't see, but none of it was working. I fell off as often as I stayed on. It was humiliating, I don't mind telling you. And what made it worse was that my dad was there in the front row.

My lovely cousin Kim, she'd have driven me if she could, but the Aprilia was nearly the size of her Fiesta so it needed the HiAce to be shipped anywhere. With Dad on the building site and then racing with William and the big boys most of the season, that didn't leave too many opportunities for me to actually get to races, which meant I was never really getting the chance to practise and improve unless my old man decided to take a day off. Could I have driven any better with a bit more track time? Probably not. Did I admit that to my brother and father? Absolutely not.

It was not a time I enjoyed. I had more fun, more satisfaction those weekends I went away with William to play chief mechanic. I'd watch him do the business on the roads and think, *Yeah, this is proper racing. None of that circuit bullshit.* The craic was so much better when I wasn't the one doing the racing.

To be fair, when it was my turn, my dad could see I was struggling with the size of the beast so he kept his counsel. If I'd had any attitude, he'd have cut it out with his tongue. One thing Dad hated was a fake. If you talked the talk and didn't walk the walk he'd pull you straight. So for a year he watched me make an idiot of myself and he never said a word. He wanted me to sort it. The next year I tried. I'd had enough of Aprilias so I moved up to the 125 Grand Prix – a souped-up version in race trim. They're smaller and more powerful. Right up my street.

It was also the same bike William was racing, so he had more than a vested interest in my progress. Being a brother, nothing would give him more pleasure than seeing me fall on my arse.

He was not disappointed.

The Aprilia was built for the road, the Grand Prix was built for the track; they were completely different animals. But they were animals I could not take to. The other lads around me had it sorted. There was a guy called Mark in that championship who was flying. I'd look at him and think he had some kind of magic version of the 125. Mine was made of beans. I could not get things to click. About three races in, I really felt I should have made in-roads. If anything, I was going backwards. I remember seeing the shame in my dad's eyes. It's not just him looking at me; everybody in the paddock knows I'm his son. That reflected poorly on him. He knew, I knew. I tried to ignore all the whispers and the silences, but in the end the elephant in the room needed addressing.

'It's not working, Dad,' I say.

'Aye,' he nods. 'You are crap on that thing.'

William loves that, obviously. He's laughing like a drain. 'Yeah, you're shit.'

'Shut up, you idiot. Leave me alone.' Suddenly we're four and eight years old playing back at Ballynacree, not racers risking our lives at 100 mph.

I tell you, the boys took the piss out of me that year and I deserved it. Again. I was rubbish.

The next season was a little bit different. We finally moved into the house that Dad had been building. That was an honour. It had the space of Ballynacree with none of the creepiness. There was also plenty of space for the bikes. Dad's 125, William's 125 and mine sat side by side in the garage. Two of them were things of beauty. Then there was mine.

I'm not one to look a gift horse in the mouth. The reason I had a shit bike is that I was a shit rider. Dad needed to shell out on three of the things, so obviously he's going to prioritize his and William's. They're the boys riding the things properly. Mine wasn't actually shite, though, it was just bog standard. There were no trimmings. On William's, Dad had added an airbox and upgraded forks, bits and pieces like that. That's where mine was lacking. Obviously as the 2004 season got going and I didn't exactly impress I began to believe that it was holding me back, even though I knew my dad could have won on it no bother.

So I say one day, 'Dad, can I have an airbox on my bike?'

He doesn't need to think. He just says, 'No.'

'Why not? You've got four lying in the workshop. I've seen them.'

'You don't deserve one,' he says. 'You're too shit for an airbox.'

'Ah, come on.'

I start to cry. Yeah, Billy Big Bollocks can't help the waterworks when he doesn't get his way. Dad's not exactly impressed but he softens. A bit.

'Listen, work harder and you'll get your airbox. Right now, the way you're riding, the speed you're getting, it's not worth my time adding one.'

That was hard to hear. The only thing in my favour was that William hadn't heard. I'd never live it down if he did. But once the tears dried up and the humiliation died down I knew my dad had a point. I needed to put in performances on the track that would merit him spending a bit of time on my bike. And so I did. I knuckled down and I eventually started making some progress.

In the back of my mind I remembered William had started out in the same way. Slow, slow, slow, then he'd exploded. I was definitely making headway. It wasn't long before I was on a podium. Then came a win. That fake champagne never tasted so good.

The only downer was Dad still saying the same thing about 'Lady Luck'. I was fearless on the track, he could see that and he respected it. He might even have admired it, not that he was a man to say. When most people looked at the race circuit they'd say, 'Oh, this is an overtaking spot' or 'This is the only way you can take this bend flat out.' I'll tell you now, if a boy was in front of me and I wanted past, it didn't bother me where he was on the track. I was going up the side and round. There were a few dicey moments, let's say, when I'd go past someone and they'd turn in because they didn't expect anyone to be there. One or two near misses, and that's putting it mildly. Occasionally that'd lead to some juicy coming-togethers afterwards, sometimes from the boys I'd nearly hit, sometimes from their dads. It's all water off a duck's back to me. I do my talking on the track. As far as I was concerned, those boys should be looking in their mirrors a wee bit more. Then they'd see me coming.

But as my dad said, 'The reason they're not looking in their mirrors when you go past is because no idiot's ever been stupid enough to try to overtake there.'

I don't know if that was a compliment or not but I took it as one. I'm smiling, but Dad says, 'You're going to have an accident soon enough because these boys don't expect you to be there.'

I says, 'I don't expect to be there. How can they know?'

If I've got a style it was definitely beginning to come through back then. I race as fast as I can and deal with what occurs. I don't plan a race out like some fellas do, with their strategies and their pet manoeuvres, little tricks they have for getting past someone and favourite places to do it. Some of these boys needed their lucky pants and the stars in perfect alignment before they'd blow their nose. I just dealt with what I found at the time and hoped for the best. Especially on the last lap. I didn't care if I fell off, and believe you me, I did plenty of times. I was rash. But I wasn't going to finish a race thinking I hadn't done enough. So mostly what happened was I either made it work or I went down trying. What my dad was saying about me being reckless, about my luck running out one day, that was still the case maybe. But I was no longer taking risks just to come home twenty-fifth instead of twenty-sixth. I was starting to fight for victories. In my book that's always going to be a prize worth being reckless for.

If I'd just continued winning everything straight from the Mini Motos onwards, I'd have enjoyed it less than I did by having two years of feeling lower than a snake's arse. Or maybe I wouldn't. But the point is, after the hardship, if you like, the occasional victory tasted sweeter than a bag of Starburst.

After my fourth podium finish in a row I asked my dad for an airbox.

He looks me straight in the eye and says, 'No. You're still not riding hard enough.'

'Ah, come on!'

But I went away and I just pushed and pushed. Mark was still the boy to beat, and race after race I ran him nearer and nearer. For the rest of the season it was either him or me on the top step. I swear I was flying. I was riding harder and harder and getting closer to the lap records wherever we went. In my own mind I was riding the wheels off that bike. The truth is, my dad's standards were on another level. I'd probably never reach them. There was no point kidding myself I ever would.

Come the end of the year, there's the big one, the 'Sunflower', the race where all the major players come out of their hidey-holes for a shot at glory. All the fast boys from the roads like to drop in and show us track crawlers what real riders look like. I liked the attitude, I'll admit, but it pissed me off royally that I was one of those being looked down on. Especially when you consider that William was one of them looking down.

There was a bit of a buzz around the house in the days leading up to the Sunflower. William's swanning around like the big cheese, gloating that he's gonna show me how to race. I'm calling him all the names under the sun. I know it's probably true, everything he says, but it's my duty as an annoying little brother to cause him as much grief as humanly possible.

Dad spends a day or two in the workshop making sure William's bike is tip-top. That's normal for him. He's spending more and more of his weekends now looking after my brother than actually riding himself. Nothing made him prouder than giving William a bike that he then goes out and wins on. I dreamed of making the old fella look as proud of me one day. Maybe the Sunflower was going to be the place, because when he'd sorted William's machine my dad says to me, 'Let me see your bike now, Michael. I'm gonna give her the once-over.'

That was music to my ears because my dad never gave anything the once-over. A 'quick look' for him was his shorthand for a forensic search, basically stripping down the whole bike, fine tuning every single aspect. A major exercise for anyone. I'd seen him do it plenty of times on his own machines. I'd seen him do just about everything over the years, so I thought I knew it all. I thought he couldn't surprise me any more.

Then he wheeled my 125 out to the van on the Saturday morning, and there it was. I had an airbox.

I was like a kid at Christmas I was thanking him so much.

If I hadn't noticed, he'd never have mentioned it. That's the man. He thought I was ready, so he'd done what was needed. There was no sentiment. I'd reached the threshold he'd set and this was the consequence. It wasn't even a reward in his mind. It was just the next step.

So, race weekend and we pile both 125s – and their airboxes – into the HiAce. There's sleeping stuff as well. All three Dunlops will be kipping side by side tonight. The Sunflower is held at the track in Bishopscourt, just outside Downpatrick, County Down. It's a few hours' drive, just far enough away to make it worth staying over.

I can honestly say now that I have no idea if the airbox made a difference. But lining up for my first practice, my first qualifier and my first race, I was convinced it was the secret ingredient that would send me to victory. And it worked to an extent. I placed in the first race and finished third in the second. But the one we were all waiting for was right at the end. That was the one all the grown-ups hooked up with. All the road racers. There I was, for the first time, in the same race as my brother. I was sitting a row back but that was closer than I'd ever been. It damn sure beat being 'chief mechanic' and waiting in the paddock.

Nothing would have given me greater pleasure that day than to beat William. But he was a class act. Whatever he'd learned on the roads he made work twice as well on the track. I had it in my mind that if we ever got wheel to wheel I'd best him because I'd want the corner more than he did – that was my mentality – but I never got close. He took first place at a canter and made me and Mark look average to say the least. As a competitor I was pissed off. As a brother I was beaming so widely you'd think it was me up on that podium.

We argued all the time – of course we did, we were brothers – but we had each other's backs. And the truth of the matter is, William was a different class to me on two wheels. He'd made the leap from circuit racing to riding on the roads so effortlessly. That was the dream but I knew that even once I was old enough – and you needed to be eighteen to get a road-racing licence – I'd be like Bambi on ice for a season or two. Fast as I was, I didn't seem to be the quickest learner. Maybe that's why I never got on with school. But I'd get there. And when I did ...

On the circuits I was proving the point. Aged fifteen I won the Clubman's championship, aged sixteen I did it again. Dad and William were there to wave me home. As far as I was concerned I had the whole formula nailed. There was nothing those lads riding against me could do. The wins came that easy I didn't even have to do anything stupid. Although there were always exceptions.

Recklessness was an accusation that stayed with me. I'm not sure I've shaken it off yet. One weekend I was at a loose end, my dad was racing, so I say to his mate, Ronnie Shields, 'I'm thinking of going down the Aghadowey for the meeting. Do you fancy driving me?'

Ronnie was like a rat up a drainpipe. Of course he'd do it. Try to stop him.

Aghadowey is a short circuit right round the corner from our house. I just stuck the bike in the back of the van, no warning, no nothing, and we went down and enrolled on the day. No sooner do we pull up than it starts to get a wee bit drizzly out in the paddock, then a bit heavier, then the heavens really open. We've just got Ronnie's van, nothing else. There's no space to work on the bike or even stretch your legs without getting a deluge from Niagara Falls. But given the rush we'd come out in, the 125 needed a few bits and pieces replaced, so I had to go through with it, rain or not.

I'm barely out there five minutes when this boy across the road gives me a holler. He has a large lorry and an awning running along the length of it. He's out there with his mechanics, his son – who was racing – and his family. They're all dry as a bone.

'Hey now,' he says, 'You want to come over?'

That's a welcome you'd be happy to hear, awning or not. So Ronnie and I wheel the bike over and we do our tinkering and generally get ready for the first race.

It all goes like a dream. I manage to win from pole and I'm set up right for the second outing. There's a bit more spice to this one because the lad whose awning we're sharing qualifies on the front row next to me. It's no bother to me. I know I'm faster.

Maybe it's cockiness but after a strong start I begin to drop back and a few boys go past. I'm not having that. I try to shit out the cobwebs and go hell for leather at it. One by one I pick the leaders off. Suddenly I'm in second and there's just the boy with the awning ahead of me.

Let's put things in perspective for a second. His dad's a diamond. His kid's a decent enough fella himself and more than okay as a rider. It's no shame coming second to him. In fact, there's an argument to be made that I should allow it to happen. The last thing I'd want to do is cause a ricket for either of us. Imagine going back to the awning if anything like that were to occur.

I think all this for maybe half a second. Then I think, *Fuck it. I'm having him.*

It's the last lap and I've been running closer and closer

to the boy and I know I'm nearly out of time, so I just run up the inside of him. There's no plan but obviously one of us is going to have to go off-piste if we're to avoid an accident. One thing's for sure.

It's not going to be me.

Twenty seconds later, the boy's still trying to find his way back on to the track as I cross the finishing line. Ronnie's slapping me on the back but that's about the only friendly face I see. At the awning Ronnie had to separate the lad from belting me. His dad let me have both barrels of verbals. Obviously it was not one of my more magnanimous moments. But a win is a win, that's how I saw it. That's how I see it to this day. If you have a chance to win you owe it to yourself to take it. The record books don't remember the good guys. They just remember the successful ones. I come from a family of record breakers. Can you blame me for wanting to join them?

By the end of 2005 I'm thinking the records I want to break aren't on stupid short circuits. *There's no way I can stand another year of this. I have to get on the roads. That's where the real action is. That's where I need to be if I'm racing the TT. That's where my brother is. All the boys.*

But not my dad. For as long as I could remember he'd been fighting the pain in his arm and leg caused by the accident in 1994. He'd smile his way through it when he was in public, but when he thought he was alone you'd see the grimace as he lifted a mug or stood up from a chair. People were concerned. My dad was loved all over the country. Maybe more so since Uncle Joey had gone. He was someone the region could not afford to lose. I remember seeing that one fella had even written to the Northern Irish Assembly to get them to persuade him to stop for his own sake. I don't know if that was the tipping point but in 2003 he said that the following season would be his last.

When politicians are talking about you, you know you've made it. But Dad was serious. He finished the season as promised, then in 2005 he signed himself up for surgery to fix his busted leg. How he'd lived eleven years with one peg two inches shorter than the other was beyond me. The surgeons broke his right leg and reset it longer. By the time he was up and walking again he was balanced for the first time I could remember. It was incredible.

'You don't look drunk any more,' I says.

'Looks can be deceptive, Michael.'

It was good news for all of us. And it just got better. Now Dad had time on his hands he could really get behind William's fledgling career. I was happy for my brother, of course, but not as happy as I was the day the postman brought this letter:

Dear Michael,
Please find enclosed your A licence.

Well, what do you know? *Michael Dunlop: 'Road Racer'.*

I liked the sound of that.

SIX

Don't Fuck It Up

YOU'VE NEVER SEEN so many microphones. Everywhere I looked there was someone sticking a recording device or a camera or both in my face. And muggins here was loving it.

'Michael, how does it feel to follow in the footsteps of your Uncle Joey?'

'Michael, how does it feel to follow in the footsteps of your dad?'

'Michael, are you scared of letting down the family name?'

'Michael, what's your favourite colour?'

'Michael, do you like cheese?'

Thick and fast the questions were coming. Me, the chubby kid from Ballymoney facing the bloody BBC, Ulster TV, everyone. They all wanted a piece of me. And why is that? Because I'd just planted my bike on the front row of the grid? Because I was the quickest boy around the track?

No, although that was all true. It was because of my surname.

But that's all right. I'm not ashamed of my family name. I was only on that grid because of them. All of them. I could talk about my dad and Joey every minute of the day if they wanted.

And that was the problem. There I am telling another journalist what it's like being Robert Dunlop's son when a lad taps me on the shoulder.

Not now, I'm thinking. *I'm live on the Beeb.* But he's persistent, he won't go away.

'Michael,' he says, 'you need to come on. You've missed the start of your race.'

Saturday 29 April 2006. The Cookstown 100. The start of the road-racing season. Believe you me, I had been counting down the days ever since my A licence had arrived in the post. My dad was counting down too. The idea of his lunatic son bombing around a road course in the same cavalier style he'd pursued on the track circuits was turning his hair grey. He trusted me, of course he did, but he was scared as well.

'You're gonna have to tone it down when we get there,' he kept saying. 'Road racing is a different kettle of fish to track racing. You'll hurt yourself if you carry on the way you do.'

It was the words unsaid that I heard loudest.

Remember your Uncle Joey.

But my response was the same. I was an arrogant prick, still am probably. As I'd said so many times in the past, *Yeah, yeah.* I was untouchable, I honestly believed that.

Unbreakable, too. I was going to show the road boys how to suck eggs. That was a promise.

I don't know if my dad was happy or sad that my first few goes went well. I think privately he hoped I'd have a bit of a scare and settle down and play safe, or at least not be a wanker. But the Orritor course at Cookstown suited me right from the off. I did one exploratory practice lap then the second one I put the hammer down. By the time we were pulled off I'd got the whole course memorized. It wasn't hard. It's only 2.1 miles and it's basically a wobbly square. As long as you can turn right you'll not go far wrong.

I was lining up in the Junior Support race, the first on the race ticket. There were sixty of us newcomers and, by the look of it, I was just about the quickest. Ah, fuck it, I knew I was the quickest. I was that cocky.

What made it all the more special for me was that I was riding a bike I'd never seen before in my life.

This is the way sponsorship works in road racing. It's not like Formula 1, with Vodafone, Marlboro or Texaco pumping in millions per race to get their name out there. In my sport it can be as much or as little as a guy buying you a set of tyres for a particular race – or in this case, a lad asking me if I'd do him the honour of riding his bike.

Ronnie Shields was the fella, the proud owner of a 250cc Yamaha, which needed riding. Ronnie himself had a sponsor, Shaun Catterall. Between them they came up with the cash for the wheels, the fuel and the stuff I had no idea about. Basically they put me on two wheels and told me to race the hell out of them.

Sitting there, waiting for the marshal to let me go for that first few metres of practice, was among the most intense moments of my life. I'd always had this vague dream of the TT. I never really thought of the inches on the map or the route to getting there. Until that day. Cookstown was the first step. I realized that in spades. The problem was, about fifty-nine other boys were thinking the same thing.

For the weekend, a prize pot of £10,000 was on offer, to be shared across the thirteen races for winners and lap leaders. I did not have a pot to piss in but I can assure you the money did not enter my brain for a second. I just wanted to win. At any cost.

So, practice came and went. Five laps where I got to know the bike as much as the circuit. Then the next day was qualifying. Somehow I managed to hook it all together and I did the best time of anyone.

'Congratulations, Michael,' my dad says. 'Pole position on your first race. Don't fuck it up now by being a smart ass.'

The man was worried, and with good reason. Maybe it would have been for the best if I'd struggled to get halfway up the pack. I arrived thinking world domination was mine for the taking. Getting pole didn't exactly dent my confidence. That night I was buzzing. The things I was going to do in the sport.

But I remember my dad being a wee bit on edge because riding the short circuits I was wild. Over the edge plenty of times, on the limit all the time. I would ride the wheels till they fell off. But short circuits don't have lamp posts and brick walls to find you if you make a mistake.

So he was nervous, but at least he was no longer calling me 'shit'. I can't put my finger on when it stopped but it had. I'm not sure he ever meant it, not literally. He just wanted me to do well and he would say or do whatever it took to get me on the right track. Me? I guess I'm the sort of character who would rise to the bait if someone comes telling me I'm crap. Horses for courses. My dad was there for William in the way William needed him to be. And for me he said what he thought I should hear. But as he told my old headmaster, was I really a boy who was prepared to listen?

Race day came and, unusually, I was hit by a wee bout of nerves. I'd only done five laps of practice. A lot of the route I remembered but there were gaps. I was pinning my hopes on the warm-up lap to fill in the gaps. Otherwise I'd be riding round a lot of the Orritor blind.

Maybe it's the nerves that make me gabble on so much to the journalists. Maybe it's just my ego. But when suddenly I get the nod that the race warm-up is underway, it's like someone's dropped a brick on my head. How can I have been so stupid? I need those laps under my belt if I'm to stand a chance in the race.

I'm sweating like a pig when I get down to the paddock. There's Ronnie and his precious Yamaha waiting for me. I can't say sorry enough. There's no time to say anything, in fact. I have to catch up to the pack. I throw myself on board, I'm about to hare off and this marshal appears in my way.

'Come on now,' I says, 'I'm late already!'

'You'll not be racing today, son.'

'What? You're having a laugh.'

'Aye, you wish. You missed the start of warm-up. No warm-up lap, no race. Them's the rules.'

Talk about a kick in the teeth. My very first road race and I'm on pole and I'm not going to get to enjoy it. You couldn't write a worse story for a debut. Knowing it was all my own stupid fault just made it worse.

But it's at times like this you're proud to be a Dunlop. My dad goes steaming in, telling the boy to change his mind because (a) rules are made to be broken, (b) he's got a fucking Dunlop waiting to race, the biggest publicity that meeting is getting, and (c) he's denying the public their pole sitter. He's a man on a mission. The fact there's a bloody BBC camera hovering in the background helps. In the end we get a compromise. I get to race.

'But you'll be starting from the back.'

Well, that's just great ...

That wasn't the only punishment. For some reason the bosses said they wouldn't give me my interval splits. Cookstown is a timed race. You didn't have to overtake anyone as long as you were quickest. But that wasn't for me. If I wanted to win the race I had to do it on the road, not on the clock. There were twenty-two of us lining up who'd qualified. That meant overtaking twenty-one bikes in ten laps. I rated myself highly, don't get me wrong. But all my planning, as little as I'd done, had centred on me having clear air ahead of me. It hadn't even occurred to me I'd have one bike's exhaust to look at, let alone a couple of dozen.

Even my dad's never seen anything as ridiculous as what I've done. But he's by my side all the way, William too. They're as steamed as me.

'You can do this if you take it easy,' my dad says.

William's more direct. More *Dunlop*. 'Don't be too much of a wanker and you'll be grand.'

A ringing endorsement, but I knew what he meant. Anyway, I didn't have time to dwell on it. There wasn't much time left till the warm-up was over. After an age I heard the field come back round. Everyone was on their markers on the grid. Row after row. When they were all settled I was waved out and given my own berth at the back. No one on my left, no one on my right. Ahead of me the entire lot of them.

I was annoyed, no doubt, but I was happy too. Yes, I'd royally cocked up before I'd even started. But in a few seconds the lights were going to go green and I'd tick something off the bucket list. I'd start my first road race. I couldn't wait.

Suddenly it's time. Enough talk. Visors down, time to focus. The race is the Support 400. Everyone's racing 250ccs, 650s, 400s. It's race one, the Enkalon/Loanends, the crowds are itching for some action. Ten 2.1-mile laps. That's not a lot of tarmac. I just needed to do what I do best. And, as my brother said, not be a wanker.

I was so far back I was round a corner, by the crossroads. When the green light came, I was oblivious. It was only the sound of twenty-one engines that gave it away. A few seconds later and the boys in front of me roared. Then I got the tap and away I went.

Already the boys at the front were out of sight. They were beyond Gortin Corner, already hammering up towards McAdoo Bends. I had some serious work if I didn't want to win the wooden spoon.

My dad said hold it together. *Yeah, Dad, and come home a loser? Right.*

I remember the start at Braeside. You go off the line, first, second, third gear, then back to first at the end of the road, then there's a wee bit of a straight into fourth gear, then back to third for a left-hand, then immediately back to first for a right hand, then up the hill you go to fifth over a jump with the turn, then you go down the hill breaking into first, turn right, first, second, then into a right/left chicane, that's third, fourth, then fifth over a jump, through a fast right with a jump on it, then into a road end with second gear and another jump. Then you go into fourth, then back to second for a right/left chicane on to the start/finish. By the time you're coming through the finishing straight there's 130 mph on the clock. I'd never done speeds like it. If I hadn't seen the dial with my own eyes I'd not have believed it. All around me were lamps, phone boxes, driveways with cars and people everywhere. And despite the speed, despite the red mist in my brain forcing me on and on, I saw every one of them. It was like the world had slowed down, not speeded up.

They say that the best footballers have more time on the ball than the average player. During that race I had that extra time. I was seeing everything so clearly. It helped that the weather was perfect. I didn't have to worry about grip.

By the first turn on lap one I'd gone past three backmarkers. After that it was roughly another three each corner. By the end of the lap I'd got past the whole last section. Fair enough, on paper that's how it should have been. The second batch of three was going to be harder. They were fifteen seconds up the road and they were that much quicker individually.

The second group were a different calibre altogether. I managed to close the gap and get past one but not as quickly as I hoped. I had to be content with picking them off one by one, not in bunches like before. See them, catch them, pass them; see them, catch them, pass them. That was the plan. With five laps down I managed to get past the last of the second group. Then it was on to the real challenge.

There was no other way: I rode hard and took every chance I could find. There were boys turning in on the apex and they'd get me zooming up the inside even if it meant pushing myself into the greenery at the side of the road. There were boys overtaking each other, tussling and then I'm thundering through the middle, catching them both by surprise. I'm taking no prisoners, I'm screaming over grass verges, white lines, bumps and divots. I'm not even bothered if I take out myself. But I am not going home without being able to say I tried my very best.

The feeling of messing it up for myself wouldn't shake off so I just rode harder, taking risks no sane person should consider. Going across the start/finish there's a left-hand bend in the road and I was all over the grass every time. The boys were standing there, Dad shouting at me to back off, shaking their heads, all of them thinking, *This is not going to end well, this is madness*, and it was. I'm riding the wheels off a bike I had no experience of. I wasn't equipped for the things I was demanding of myself. The bike certainly wasn't built for what I demanded it do. I should never have been riding that hard but when you have what's yours snatched away – my position on pole – you don't think straight.

Eight laps down and there are three boys ahead of me. One by one I pick them off. Then it's just a lad called Paul Newton on a Honda 250. He's going great guns but I nail him when he least expects it. Very quickly there's distance between us and by rights I should hold back, take it easy. But that's not my nature. When you've overtaken twenty-one bikes, especially when you should never have been asked to, there's an adrenaline rush you can't explain. So instead of cruising home, I put the throttle down and eventually finished twenty-two seconds ahead of Newton with a time of 16.30.

How'd you like them apples? My first road race, my first victory, a lap record to boot. And I'd done it in style from the back of the grid.

Oh, happy days. Happy days.

After Paul there was a gap back to 17.06, with a bunch of dudes piled around that time. So I'd done okay, whichever way you looked at it. Or so I thought. My dad found another way to see it.

'Well done,' he says, 'but you're asking for trouble out there.'

'Come on, Dad, I won.'

'So you did, and how much hedgerow did you bring home with you?'

It was no good arguing. My arms were green with bush juice where I'd gone too close to the sides.

'One branch could have had you off,' he says. 'Next time you won't be so lucky.'

'Ah, you always say that.'

'And one day I'll be right.'

I know he meant it for the best. William was more on-message.

'Good ride, little man. I didn't know you had it in you.'

'Aye,' I says, 'you wait until tomorrow.'

I was that full of myself I wasn't listening to anybody. That didn't stop Dad trying to talk sense into me.

'At the left/right bend at the start/finish you did it in third gear, but there's no room,' he said. 'There's a big house and a fence, and you were brushing the grass before you got to it.'

'Yeah. So? That's exactly how I took it every lap.'

'I know. Just because you got away with it ten times doesn't mean eleven won't catch you out and you'll not end up in someone's front room.'

'Come on, Dad,' I said, 'I was plain last. I had work to do.'

'Aye, and that work could have written you out of the rest of the season. Or longer. Remember who you're talking to here, boy.'

He was insufferable to listen to but my dad was never wrong. It just sometimes took me a wee while to appreciate it. Problem was, I wasn't in the mood to appreciate anything right then.

Even as I mulled over my first road race victory, part of me was already planning my next outing, this time on the 125, airbox and all. And I'd need every advantage I could get because this time I wasn't just up against strangers. I'd be racing William and, even more excitingly, someone else.

Dad's surgery to lengthen his leg had been so successful he was making a comeback. He'd had a run-out or two at the end of 2005. When it was time to line up for the 125s, the press were all over him like they'd been swarming around me. The only difference is he was never going to miss the start of his race.

Aside from me, Dad and William one of my cousins was also racing. It was a Dunlop royal flush. And I bet each one of us thought we were going to win.

When it came to qualifying, I'd already had fifteen laps around the Orritor, not including the latest practice. I thought I was the king of the track. Then we went out for qualifying and I virtually proved myself. There were only three boys ahead of me out of a field of twenty-four. My dad, William and, in pole, a fella called Nigel Moore. I had to admit, there's no shame coming behind them.

The race itself set me alight. Ten laps, real quality talent. There was so much wheel-to-wheel and a fair bit of to-ing and fro-ing but when it all shook up I finished exactly where I started, in fourth, just ahead of a great rider, Mark Curtin. My dad hadn't moved either. But William, the jammy so-and-so, he was top dog, pipping Nigel Moore.

I had to be happy with fourth. My brother really was that good – he still is. Lining up against him was never going to be a fair race. And my dad always had enough in his pocket to keep the likes of me far behind him. When the dust settled I was actually just proud to have stayed as close to them as I did. This was my first senior road race, don't forget. I'd done a junior event, which is basically the same race but lower standard entries. This was the first one against serious opposition.

Some people would have buckled under the weight of expectation. Make no mistake, being a Dunlop around a road-racing paddock was a big deal. A journalist or two asked me how it felt to be continuing the Dunlop name. I said, 'There's nothing we can do to improve what my dad and my uncle have already done. The best we can hope for is if we don't fuck it up.' I'm not sure they printed the exact quote.

My dad was satisfied enough with my performance, although he mentioned again and again the risks I'd taken out there. In my defence, the road was dry and I knew what I was doing. In *his* defence, he had his brother and his own accident as evidence.

Speaking of his brother and himself, there was one thing –
no, two – they had in common that I could not argue with.
And it wasn't accidents and pain. It was their reputations
and their records. My dad and Joey shared the 'most wins'
honours at just about every road event in the country.
They'd been over to Macau and Germany and stamped
their names – the Dunlop name – into the international
annals as well. I was at the start of my career but I wanted
some of that. And badly. I wanted my name to mean
something. And to achieve a sniff of it I needed to make a
mark where it really mattered.

The Isle of Man.

Only one wee drawback. In 2006 the TT – the hallowed
Tourist Trophy – did not have a category for anything as
small as 125 or 250s. They weren't accepting any two-stroke
engines at that time and, since that was all I was riding with
any purpose, it meant I was not eligible. But that didn't
mean I couldn't race around the Mountain Course.

Not while there was the Manx Grand Prix.

SEVEN

The Problem is You

IT WAS A MAGIC YEAR FOR ME, 2006. I rode at Cookstown and I won. I rode again at Cookstown and I came fourth – and I did it behind my brother and my dad. Two of the three men in my life that I would ever call heroes.

I went on to do the rest of the season as well as I could. Mostly 125s but occasional 250s as well, the availability of Ronnie's bike permitting. There were one or two wins, one or two lap records, and three or four – or more – spills. The crazy ways that my dad warned against on the mini circuits and at Cookstown just wouldn't go away. And can you blame me? I rode the way I wanted to. No one, not even a living legend, not even my own dad, was going to knock that out of me.

Case in point was a wee little race in Tullyallen. It's not on the calendar any more; it was cancelled. I remember it was damp so everyone's riding within themselves. Everyone except me. My dad was sitting third, I was in second and William was out in front. On the last lap I got closer and closer, then on the final corner I chucked the 125 up the inside. We were side by side for a while going round the bend, and we're seriously motoring. One tiny wriggle and either one of us would take out the other. But I managed to hold it on the tarmac and eventually I felt William throw in the towel. He knew I was never going to let up. He knew I'd rather crash than let him back past.

Nothing beats the feeling of winning. Doing it over your brother and dad is the icing on the cake. I knew, though, that both them boys were holding back because of the conditions. Dad could have blitzed us both if he'd been of a mind to. But you can only play with what you've got and at the end of the day I wanted it more than they did.

After the race one or two people said I was crazy. One boy says, 'You drove like you wanted to crash.'

I put him straight as a die.

'I don't know what you're doing out there,' I says, 'but I'm racing to win.'

Nobody wants to fall off a motorbike, myself included. But I'm not that fussed about risking it. Right from the start, I'm prepared to push it as far as it will go, and maybe others aren't. Why? Because that's where I get my buzz. It doesn't always mean I'm going to be the fastest. But it does mean I'm the boy giving 100 per cent.

Scarborough was proof of that, I suppose. We were all together at the start. It was me, Dad and William, and it was tight as anything from the get-go. It's about two miles. It's very tight and twisty. Not really my cup of tea but not my dad's either. The old fella struggled at road ends for the simple reason he found it hard to get his hand round to the throttle again because he didn't have as much grip. I knew this so I took advantage. We were coming up to the hairpin at the top and I barged up the inside and just braked later, knowing he could not match it. Then I kept it going until I won the race.

Afterwards my mechanics are all slagging Dad. 'Ah, Robert, your boy smoked you.'

'Maybe it's time to retire?'

'Aye,' he says, 'we'll see next race.'

It was all good fun, as well he knew. Just like I knew what he was capable of. To be honest, I think he was more interested in my and William's careers than his own. He was only in Scarborough for the craic. But the boys winding him up put the fire back in his belly and the next race he just left me for dead. Obliterated me. It didn't matter I was good on the brakes, the old fox just finished me without breaking a sweat. When he came in, he laughed to himself and went to the pub, not a word said, but bragging rights well and truly his again.

Class will always tell. My dad and William have it in spades. What I realized I had was a desire that maybe outweighed my ability. But I made it work for me as best I could. I was the same all season long. Always on the limit. Tandragee and the North West 200 in May, Athea, Dundalk and Skerries in June, Walderstown, Kells and Faugheen in July, they all came and went. Every circuit I thought I was the boy, at least until I went for a move that ended with me sliding on my arse. But you know, every race I did was fine and fun, fun and fine. I can't fault any of them because they were road races and that's what I wanted to be doing with my life. The truth is, they were only ever building up to one thing. One place. One event.

August Bank Holiday, that was the target for me. Monday 28th, the Newcomers' Race around the fabled Mountain Course at the Manx GP. It was the TT in all but name. Some people consider it a warm-up for the TT. Not me. It's the same course, the same challenges, the same chances of feast or famine. I could not have been more excited about going. If I'd have had two tails I'd have wagged them both.

But the Manx is different to everywhere else. It has one rule from the old days of when it used to be called the Manx Amateur Road Race – namely, if you've raced at the TT, you can't race at the Manx. It's a way of keeping the meeting for the amateurs or the juniors. But it's why it doesn't have the same prestige. What it does have is this charm. There are boys who compete there every year, one or two of them in their seventies. The atmosphere is very much like a big friendly family. When they do let TT riders in, it's to take part in the 'Classic' bike race. They change the definition all the time, but basically your professional riders aren't turning up on the latest Superbike.

Anyway, because I considered that the TT was going to be huge in my future, I knew I had one chance at the Manx, one shot. I needed to make it count.

Even so, because I was mad keen on doing everything in my first season, I was still at the Ulster Grand Prix in Dundrod when the practice started on Saturday the 19th. But that was all right, I figured. There's no riding on the Sunday and then I'd still get the full week.

Like the TT, the Manx runs over a fortnight. The first week is all about practice. Getting to know the course. The second is when you get the races: Saturday, Monday, Wednesday, Friday. I was that fired about my own chances that I didn't think I'd miss an extra day learning the circuit.

What a prick.

I had the full complement going over with me. My dad

and William weren't eligible because they'd done the TT, so they were specifically coming as my crew. We went in William's van. He had a Mercedes Sprinter by then, the model with the wee bed up high in the back. It wasn't a four-poster but it was better than we were used to. The bikes were down below and there was a sofa. Then there was Ronnie, who really knew what he was doing when it came to the pit stops. He drove over with his then wife Valerie. If there was a boy with better support, I'd like to meet him. Even Valerie was out there selling cakes and running events to raise a coin or two for me. Lovely lady – mad as a brush, so perfect for the team.

We got the boat over to Douglas and it's about two miles from there to the pits where we were based. I'd done those two miles as a tourist and that was exciting. This time there was no fun fair as a distraction. The pits is massive – it's basically a giant field. Being a couple of days late, we didn't get the prime spot by any means, but I didn't mind. Everything was a wonder to me. The drive up from the port, seeing the signs, noticing the fans just meandering around, it got the hairs on the back of your neck standing up.

The first bit of business is getting the bikes checked out. As well as the Newcomers, I was entered in two other races, so I had my dad's white Honda 125 and a white 250 he'd got hold of for me as well. Both two-stroke, both non-eligible for the TT, but just what I needed. And more than I was used to. That 125 was still warm from winning the Ulster GP the day before. It had also helped my dad win his fifteenth North West 200 title a few months earlier. Whereas my 125 was pretty much standard issue, Dad had built his bike from the ground up, hooking up his own exhaust pipe and cylinders. He was not his father's son for nothing. No one could get better performance out of a machine.

I was touched the man let me anywhere near it.

Ten minutes after I started her up, I think he began to regret it.

That Sunday, as soon as we arrived, with the roads still open to the public, Dad took me out in the van to get me the feel of the place. Driving at 30 mph in a stodgy Mercedes is a wee bit different to going five times that speed on two wheels. But you can see the houses, the lie of the land, get a sense of where the bends are, where the straights are, the street furniture that looks a bit trickier than the rest. Being on a public road, though, you have to stay in one lane, so there's no point looking at apexes and that. Not until you can use the full width.

And all the while we're going, Dad's pointing out where to look out for when you're on a two-stroke. He's not going to bother telling me where to brake or overtake; that's a rider's prerogative. If you need to be taught that, you're no rider. But engine management on a demanding course is something that you can pass on with experience. So, going up the end of Sulby Straight, he says, 'Make sure you're not revving too much here.' You don't want to rev the tits off the machine so it's important to know where you can lift off and where you can push. 'Going up the mountain you need to watch out for the symptoms of being too lean or being too rich.'

We did two laps, each just under an hour. Then it was back to the paddock, to the van and William. We had a bit of food and then turned in. My dad was good as gold. He just climbed in with me and my brother. There were no airs or graces. The next morning I felt for him, though. The injuries, the surgery, maybe some early arthritis, they all took their toll. The agony was written on his face just getting out of the cot, and it took a small while to shake off. But he never mentioned it. All anyone was focused on was my first taste of the circuit, which was coming up that afternoon. I couldn't wait.

The Snaefell Mountain Course is 37.7 miles long. It's got more than 200 turns, taking you from Douglas through Braddan, Union Mills, Glen Vine, Crosby, Greeba, Kirk Michael, Ballaugh, Sulby and Ramsey. There are stretches with houses butted against the road, others where it's just you and the mountain. At its highest part, at Hailwood's Height, it's some 422 metres above sea level. At your top speed you'll be doing around 200 mph.

All these facts you sort of know before you arrive. The stats of the circuit are legendary. The most important of them being that my Uncle Joey won there twenty-six times. With every minute that went by I got more buzzed about following in his and my dad's footsteps. I'd read and heard what I was up against from both of them over the years. But getting out there and experiencing it for yourself is a whole different story.

If you get it wrong it could be a very short story as well. More of a paragraph. That's why no newcomer at the Manx gets to ride a single mile without a marshal showing them the route. It's called a 'sighting lap' and the idea is to bed you in with the route before you are let into the practice laps. Obviously the marshal has his speed that he thinks is safe and appropriate for everyone to have time to pick out the obstacles, the hotspots, the turning points. It's more about health and safety than helping you go fast. It's definitely not the opportunity to go bouncing off the hedges – which is exactly what some prick was doing.

I'm so hyped about getting going for real I'm leaving my mark on everything. You're out there to acclimatize and I'm dropping back, snail's pace, letting the pack get out of sight so's I can floor it for a few seconds and catch them up at full speed. I didn't have a clue where I was going. I must have found every bush and kerb but in my head that's what's needed. That's what Joey did. That's what my dad did. *This is what it takes to win.*

Seriously, why didn't anyone give me a slap?

I was terrible the whole lap but one thing stands out. I'd dropped back so I could get a good run at the fourteenth milestone. The problem was, I wasn't at the fourteenth. I was at the thirteenth. A completely different story. I wait until they are all out of sight and I open the throttle and I'm flying when suddenly there's this big left-hand bend that I didn't know was there. I'm thinking, *Shit, I'm not making that, I'm not making that.*

I entered the bend flat out. I probably would have got away with it if I'd known where I was going and had the right line, but I ran out of road and went up the kerb. I stayed on the bike but I pulled the hedge up; about three foot of it was stuck to the bike. I stopped to check everything was all right. The bike was but I don't think the hedge is there any more. Later, when my dad asked about the scratches, I said the truth: 'I didn't know there was a thirteenth.'

Bloody prick, really.

Anyway, no harm done as far as I knew and it didn't

dampen my spirits. That's how thick I was. I couldn't wait for the lap to be over so I could get out there in practice and show everyone what I'd got for real. I was the man. I was going to blow everyone's minds if I hadn't already.

After we crawled into the pits there was a boy in a bib come right in my face. Inside my helmet I'm beaming like the cat that got the cream. I'm waiting for him to say, 'That was the best riding I've ever seen from a newcomer', and I'm gonna say in return, 'You ain't seen nothing yet.' Everything's grand.

I switch off the engine, take off my helmet.

'Michael Dunlop?' he says.

'Aye.'

Here it comes, the 'You're as fast as your dad and uncle' speech.

'Son,' he says, 'you're wanted up in the race office.'

Up I went and inside there's a guy who introduces himself as the clerk of the course, the top man, and about six or seven others. I literally have no clue what they want. The Manx is different to the short races, so I assume this is just something they do.

'Michael,' the clerk says, 'I'm sorry to tell you we don't think you're ready for this course.'

'What's this about? Is there something wrong with my bike? We can change it.'

'There's nothing wrong with your bike. The problem is you. The way you're driving. You're too dangerous to be let out again.'

I can't believe it. I'm a newcomer. I think I've just shown that track who's boss. And this wanker's telling me I'm not allowed to race? He starts going on about 'we're doing this for your safety and everyone else's' and 'we have rules in place for a reason', all this shit. And I'm just standing looking at that arse there, thinking, *What's he slapping on about?*

I just wanted him to stop talking. I'm a kid, I'm an idiot. I'm not listening to some old prick telling me how to ride. Every word that comes out of his mouth I'm thinking, *Dickhead. Dickhead. Dickhead.*

The poor sod's being deadly serious and I'm nodding but I'm not even listening. I'm amazed I never told him where to stick his head. But when he did finally shut up I told him I was sorry and that I'd learned my lesson, and I came as close as ever I've come to begging for another chance.

The boys had a word and then the clerk says, 'Okay, you've got your chance. But we'll be watching you.'

'Ah grand, you won't regret it.'

Then the next day out in practice I drive ten times worse.

Being around the paddock and the pits with my dad was like turning up to a party with Beyoncé on your arm. The boy was a superstar. Even though he was so small there wasn't a person there who didn't look up to him. Junior races rarely got someone of his calibre anywhere near them. At the big races the competitors were too embarrassed to admit they thought he was anything special, because they're meant to be on the same level, some crap like that. It's all about the ego with those fellas. Everywhere I'd been with him doing the wee races that year, you had the odd chap coming over for a chat or a photo, but at the Manx, where there were so many amateurs, so many fans and students of the sport, there wasn't a soul who could hide how much they admired him.

I went back to the paddock once to look for him and found him sitting in this old boy's awning drinking this fellow's red wine. They'd never met before in their lives but this fella, I promise you, thought he was entertaining royalty.

It was great to see. I knew my dad's history full well, I lived with the tragedy and the comeback. I didn't know what it was like to walk in his shoes exactly, but William and I'd got as close as anyone could. Just seeing that it wasn't all for nothing – all the suffering, all the hard work – gave you a warm feeling. Hearing more than one stranger tell me that my dad could have gone on to smash Joey's records if he hadn't had the accident was like music to my ears. What he won in the time that he won, he'd definitely have had a chance. But then maybe Joey would have kept riding forever without his accident. You can't compare what-ifs.

Maybe some people would be jealous of their old man getting all the attention. *I'm the one racing – why aren't you looking at me?* That kind of crap.

I never cared about that. William's exactly the same. In any case, people were looking at me *because* of my dad.

'Oh, is this your young boy, Robert?'

Walking around with him meant men and women who'd never heard of me were sizing me up. I had a lot of nice conversations with person after person just because of who my dad was. But I could feel a wee bit of the pressure rubbing off, too. It's like you can hear what they're saying to each other.

'Is he going to be any good?'

'He's a big lad. Is he going to make it round?'

'Is he going to let his dad down?'

'Is he going to embarrass the family name?'

We'd soon find out.

The Manx organizers try to keep the roads open to regular traffic as much as possible. For practice week they're closed about 6 p.m. and we go out fifteen minutes later for maybe an hour. Basically you have a whole day of waiting to get going. By the time quarter past six rolled up I was chomping at the bit. I was a coiled spring. And I fucking sprung.

Just the chance to go 140, 150 up those famous roads was not an opportunity I was going to pass up. And there's no point in going slowly. If you don't get around at a decent lick you'll not be allowed to start any of the races.

The next day at practice I was at it again, finding every single blade of grass, rubbing shoulders with fences and foliage alike. I knew I was getting faster. I could feel it. I was passing boys on the roads where they least expected it. Going past anyone is a grand feeling. But the smile was soon wiped off my face. Waiting again in the pits when I came home was a marshal with the same message as before.

I knew I was for the chopping block, so this time I made sure to take my dad with me. He didn't say a word on the way up the steps to the office. The first words he spoke were inside. The room was packed, every marshal and steward had turned out to see me get what was coming. That's what it felt like. My dad knew most of them by name, so he went round with his hellos, how are you doings, etc. Classy man. Like everyone else, they all thought he was a prince, remember. He saved the warmest welcome for the clerk of the course. Really shook his hand, did a wee bit of reminiscing about when he'd done the Newcomer's race way back when. Proper nice to listen to, actually.

By the time we got down to the nitty-gritty, I think my dad had already extinguished quite a number of flames. The clerk still went through his speech and said they had no alternative but to eject me on the grounds of me being a danger to myself and others. While my mind was full of insults for every man in that room, my dad was obviously listening. When the clerk finished, Dad explained how fast I'd been without a single incident. How I'd won various races this year on the short circuits. How I just needed to find my way and, with the right encouragement, I'd go out and make them proud to have another Dunlop bringing press attention to their event. He ended by giving a cast-iron Robert Dunlop guarantee that he'd keep me on a tight leash.

I honestly never knew the man was capable of such bullshit.

My dad, though, was a great thinker. A quiet man but he knew the workings of people the same way he knew the workings of an engine. He pressed the right buttons and, after the end of a pretty intense grilling, I was allowed to stay in the event.

There was no mood of celebration as we walked back to the van. Dad only said what needed to be heard. When we started walking back to the van, away from prying ears, he said, 'This race will bite you, Michael. At the end of the day, the choices in life are what people make for themselves, but there is a fine line, remember that. You have to know where the edge is.' The naive, young idiot part of me is going, *Yeah, yeah*, but the racer in me is listening. It has to. He's no bureaucrat in a suit. The man's track record speaks for itself. People would pay money to have the advice I'm getting for free. I know that.

'I can only teach you so much off the track,' Dad says. 'On the track you have to find your own way. I'm not going

134

to say you have to slow down. I know what it's like your first time around here. It's all boiling up inside. You're desperate to get going. But you need to calm down. You've got nothing to prove to anyone except yourself. Race a good race, don't put yourself in unnecessary danger for the sake of showing off. Because if you do, they'll take away your licence. They can do that. They can stop you racing for good. And then you'll be screwed.'

It was about the longest speech I ever heard him give. Then he was silent the rest of the journey and we never spoke about it again.

My dad could have called me an idiot or an embarrass-ment. He never did. He treated me like a man. Let me make my own decisions based on knowing the consequences of those decisions. I loved him for that. Not that I deserved it, perhaps. But then maybe he didn't deserve to be cooped up like a junior mechanic in our van in the state his bones were in. Luckily, someone else agreed.

At the end of the middle week a fella called Martin Marlow came into the paddock with his wife, Maria. Martin was a friend of my dad's. He rented Dad a garage down in Douglas whenever he raced. This was his first opportunity to come over and find him.

I didn't know the fella or his missus but they were nice enough company. They were as intrigued as everyone to see if I'd be a chip off the old block or a chip shop. From the size of me it wasn't obvious one way or the other.

'How's your boy getting on?' he asks.

Dad says, 'He's okay. I reckon he'll be all right.'

They go on a bit about old times, then Martin says, 'Are you not using our garage this year, Robert?'

'I didn't like to ask since it's not me racing.'

'Ah, get away, you fool. You're working in this mud and shit when you can call me?'

135

He turns to me and says, 'Michael, bring everything you have up to mine and you work as long as you like on those bikes in the garage.'

Then, turning to Dad again, he asks, 'Where are you staying then?'

Dad says, 'I'm kipping in the van with the boys.'

'For God's sake, man. I tell you now, there'll be no more of that. From now on you're staying with us up at the house.' He looks at me and William.

'And that goes for all of yous. And Ronnie, too.'

Martin and Maria had two properties back to back. They'd already got a fella in the spare house for practice week so they offered us their spare room and the sofa in their lounge till the other place became free the next night.

I say, 'That's very kind of you, Martin, but Dad, you, Ronnie and Valerie make yourselves at home. Me and William will be all right in the van.'

And we were. We ran an electric cable into the garage and me and William watched TV in the van, lived like kings really. In the morning, Maria brought us breakfast. I didn't think it could get any better. But then the other house came free and my brother and I moved into there. What with Maria feeding and watering us, it was like a five-star hotel. Going down to the pits each day felt like we were slumming it after that. Even so, I couldn't wait to get there.

That's where I was going to make my name.

Or ruin it forever in trying.

EIGHT

Badly Built Snowmen

BANK HOLIDAY MONDAY. It's finally come round. I'm jacked. I'm like a bunny rabbit on helium; my head is totally gone. I. Can. Not. Wait.

We go down to the pits, then on to the track. My dad's there, William's there, Ronnie's there. It's a four-lap race and there'll be one pit stop for fuel. The boys will be over there by the time I come round. I'm sitting on my bike – on my dad's bike – and I've got my shades on and my chest is puffed out that far you'd think someone had shoved an airline up my arse. And why not? I was the cock of the walk. I had the best mechanics on the grid, a great bike and I'd done all right in practice. I was averaging 105 mph around the track. On my class of bike, there was no one quicker. I was given number 45 – first in my category. Proof, as if I needed it, that I was going to be the boy to beat.

The Manx, like the TT, is a time trial. You're racing the clock, not the boy ahead of you. One rider goes, the next one waits ten seconds, then he goes, and so on. In the

Newcomers there are three classes of machine, so three separate races going on at the same time. I was only racing the other 125s. We were C class; we would go off last. The A class was the 600s – the big boys. They'd be the first group out. Then the B class, the 400s and 250s. The way it's set up, you might overtake a bike or two if you're at the front of your group, but if they're on faster machines, like I was going to be running behind, that's unlikely.

The 125 was my best bet, no question. But it was also, if I'm honest, looking a bit small under my bulk. Doing four laps in anger was going to leave me sore, I could guarantee that. But that did not wipe the smile off my face.

Sitting on the grid waiting to go I was like an old boy injected with Viagra. I was rock hard and ready – so pumped that Mike Tyson could have taken a swing at me and I'd not feel it. He'd break my neck – but I'd not feel it. I'd just laugh. That's how hyped I was.

As the moment of truth came closer, I began to calm down, to chill. I was the fastest boy in my class. I needed to remember that. My dad's 125 was the best in show. We were the dream team. If I kept my cool I knew I could do it.

I had on my yellow overalls that match my own 125. For the first time that week you could see them. At the Manx the newbies have to wear bibs during practice to identify themselves to the other maybe more experienced racers. Going out there in my own colours felt right.

Fifteen minutes before the start of the race there was a klaxon. That's your cue to get organized and to get your people, your mechanics, off the circuit. Up until that moment there were hundreds of people milling around. Ronnie said, 'You've got this, son.' William wished me good luck and my dad looked me in the eyes and just nodded. He'd done all he could. Whichever way it shook out, it was up to me now.

Five minutes to go.

There was another blast on the horn. I move forward into the holding area with everyone else from my time band. We are all in groups of ten.

Three minutes.

Getting near crunch time. I pull on my helmet, flip down the visor and try to get some focus. I'd managed to fool the boys and myself that I was cool as a cucumber, but inside I felt like a pneumatic drill gone rogue. If I didn't calm myself it could all be over before the first corner.

Suddenly, even above the engines and my heartbeat, there was a cheer and I knew the first boy had gone off. Now shit was getting real. There's no big frantic start like in a wheel-to-wheel race. At the Manx everyone goes on their own, ten seconds apart.

One after one after one … The process is relentless. Every ten seconds another lad goes off. It's like a human centipede getting longer and longer. Like a freight train in the American Midwest – one of those that never seem to end.

As each group of ten is called forward to the release area, the rest of us concertina forward, all revving, all thinking the same thing. *I just want to get going.* The organization is like a maths project. Ten riders in each wave. Ten seconds between each rider. I was number 45. My group was the fifth wave. I would go out 440 seconds after the first lad. It doesn't sound long but it felt like forever.

With all the constant edging forward, you can't relax. But you can't get going either. It's damn frustrating. You're like sixty moths banging your head against the same light bulb. What you want is just out of reach and it's doing your brain in trying to get at it.

Four hundred seconds after the first bike, my wave of

riders finally reaches the starting area. *Three more to go.*

The guy at 42 is away. We all shunt forward a position. *Two more to go.*

Finally, the last of the second class of bikes is gone, away up the road, and I'm beckoned forward. The first of the 125s. There's a man on the start line with a flag and a watch. When he waves the flag, my ten seconds' waiting time is over. But I'm not really watching him. There's another boy standing next to me. He's got his hand on my shoulder. It's his job to watch the flag. When it's my time to go he'll give me a tap.

I'm counting down in my head. *Nine, eight, seven, six ...* I'm revving like crazy. If I don't get going soon, my dad's bike is going to explode. *Five, four, three, two ...*

And there's the tap on my shoulder.

I wish I could say that all the anxiety, all the palpitations I'd had on the grid, just washed away and some calm, serene driving God took over the bike. But that did not happen. Those final ten seconds, I was so excited to get up the road and ride hard that my head was full. I don't know what of, but it was just full. The anticipation was killing me – and nearly the bike. When the tap on my shoulder came, I nearly ripped the clutch out to get off the line.

I tell you now, that release when you finally pull away is overwhelming. Mind-blowing. The thing I'd most dreamed of, of racing the Mountain Course, was right at my fingertips, and I couldn't tell up from down. It's funny: it's like a dog barking at a car, that's what you feel like. You're chasing the car, you're chasing the car, you're chasing the car – and then it stops and you don't know what to do with it.

It only lasted about three seconds. But three seconds at 60 mph is 264 feet. If you don't sort your brain out quickly, you won't make 265 feet.

I felt something click. Like a flame on a cooker being

turned off. And suddenly I could see everything. The emotions were gone. Reality was giving me a kicking. My head for just about the first time that day was clear. *I know what I have to do.*

I wasn't there just to have a bit of fun. I wasn't tearing down Bray Hill, Braddan Bridge and Union Mills because I wanted to see the scenery. I was there to win a race. Plain and simple. There was nothing else in my head.

To win the race I just had to beat my class. I'd been quickest in practice; it should pose no real problem. But in time trials you never really know what the boys behind are doing. If the bike that's gone out sixtieth is overtaking everyone, unless he comes near your mirrors you wouldn't know that up at the front. So I did the only thing I could and drove the wheels off that bike. I brushed every hedge, pushed harder and harder, and when I started to close up on the group in front I took no prisoners. The way I saw it, those boys were on more powerful machines. They should not be letting a 125 get anywhere near them. They deserved what they got.

For all my ego, I knew that my engine could not compete with the 250s and 400s in a straight line. So the straights were out. But when those boys lifted for the corners, I didn't. I just said, 'I'm coming through. Like it or not.' Even leading the race, even having so much to lose, if you change the way you drive, if you start second-guessing yourself, that's when mistakes happen. I threw that bike through gaps that didn't exist. I swear, some of those boys' overalls were browner on the inside than the outside. You can hear them thinking, *You're not meant to overtake there.* They never saw me coming.

On the straight they could get me back if they wanted to. One or two had a go. But a few of them held off. If they overtook me I'd only get them back in the corner – and none of them had enjoyed their taste of that medicine.

The pits at the Manx are towards the end of the course. After two laps the bike is running on fumes. The tyres are beginning to thin. I pulled over and there's my team. I'm buzzing. They look like they've got the weight of the world on their shoulders. Do they know something about my times that I don't? Am I not out in front in my class?

'You're leading by a good stretch, so just chill your shit out,' William says.

Translation: I've watched you ride like a lunatic for two laps. You've got the win in the bag. You don't need to take any more chances.

Aye, I thought. *But where's the fun in that?*

Ronnie finished the refuelling. William wiped my visor between lectures. Then I was out.

Coming down the Nook and Governor's Bridge two laps later I knew in my head that I'd won the race. There's no way anyone behind could have made up the difference. But in my heart it was a different story. You can't shake off that feeling of 'What if?'

'What if I slow down too much?'

'What if some boy back there stitches two of the best laps of his life together?'

You just don't know.

I was a young lad, remember. Nobody gave a shit about me. Nobody was holding a board up at the side of the road with my position. But as I crossed the finish line I saw complete strangers clapping and waving. People I'd never seen before in my life were cheering me. I couldn't hear them over the engine but their faces shouted volumes. As I slowed down, I heard applause and I let myself begin to think, *They know. They know the result ...*

But still there's that tiny space for doubt in your head. It was only when a boy with a hi-vis bib on flagged me down that I knew for sure. While most of the pack park up in the main *parc fermé*, as it's called, the top three from any race get hauled off to one side. I was told to head that way. There in front of me were three signs: '1st', '2nd' and '3rd'.

And a guy beckoning me towards the 1st.

After 150 miles, an average of 104 mph, and 75 minutes in the saddle, you're such a taut wire physically and mentally. Then you stop and your brain is still racing at 150 mph. Even as I switched off I think it was only just sinking in.

I've done it. I've only fucking done it. I've won the Manx Grand Prix.

Even though I'd been saying to anyone who'd listen that I was the boy, actually putting the words into action felt massive. I was the youngest ever winner, obviously. That added a few degrees of extra pleasure. I hadn't done it alone, mind. Getting me there, getting me a bike that was half-decent, getting me not chucked out of the meeting, had all come from my family. Speaking of which, William was over the moon. Ronnie was like a dog with a bone. And my dad? Well, my dad was my dad. He came over, looked me in the eye just like he did at the start, and shook my hand.

He never said a word. He didn't need to. We both knew what it meant to each of us. He couldn't have been prouder. And I couldn't have been more relieved not to have tarnished the family's reputation.

I was led through the winners' enclosure and out on to the platform for the prize giving. When your name is called as the winner it's a grand feeling, but you don't know what to do with yourself. You've got the wee trophy, you've got the laurel wreath around your neck and you've got your bottle of bubbly. You want to throw them all in the air like a student with his mortar board.

I can honestly say I've never been happier. Being in the bosom of my family really was the icing on the cake. William was my idol when I was growing up, and to have him there helping me was big news. He was my big brother and best friend. I actually got more of a buzz from working with him than from riding myself in the early days. So to have him there returning the favour was one of the nicest moments for me. And my dad. What can I say? I was the proudest man around to have those two at my side. It was only right that we all went to celebrate. And, oh boy, did we? It was full on. I got sick in my eyes. Sick. In my eyes.

Bottle-bank green I was. We got that drunk in the beer tent afterwards that no way should we have gone on anywhere else, but we stopped at the chippy – there was about twelve of us: Martin and Maria, our supporters, Ronnie, Valerie, my dad, William and me – then staggered on to Colours sports bar, as it was called at the time, in Douglas, and got absolutely rubbered. By the time we emerged we were walking like badly built snowmen.

As you can maybe imagine, the next morning wasn't too pleasant. We weren't in great shape and I don't think Maria's house was much better. She didn't give a fig. She and Martin are always up for the craic. I don't think you can be part of my team if you're not.

So my first experience of the circuit could not have gone better. Of course I wanted more.

Before I went to the Manx all I craved was to win a race. But winning for me is an addiction. No word of a lie, before I'd even downed the first pint after the race, part of me was thinking of Wednesday's Junior Race. So as soon as our heads started clearing we were in the garage getting Dad's white 250 ready to go. In this race we'd be up against more powerful classes of bikes. We needed to squeeze every drop out of her.

Come the second race, my dad was there, William, Ronnie – the usual suspects. Same boys, same setup, same pattern, same procedure. To get going it was the same start, the same flag, the same hand on the shoulder. The only difference really was my mood.

Setting off the second time was a bit more subdued. There were none of the topsy-turvy emotions. I definitely set off with the arrogance of a winner. I knew from practice that I was going fast enough to make an impression in this race as well. Even though we were up against some serious 600s, I thought, *You've got enough. You can do this.*

I knew we had to go quicker but I knew we *could* go quicker. When you have faster bikes ahead of you the gap is theoretical. The reason they're ahead of you is because they started earlier. Not because they are quicker or better. They might be, but you can't assume that. When you set off, that ten seconds puts them out of sight, regardless of how good they are. You just have to ride as hard as you can. You're not watching the speedo. You ride to wherever your brain thinks it's capable of going. That's the be-all and end-all of it. And I have to say, my brain was capable that day of going bloody fast.

Even though there were many quicker bikes, as I came off the third lap, going into the last, I was pretty sure I was doing enough for a podium in my class. I'd passed that many people. William was encouraging at the pits. I never allow myself to take the foot off the gas, even when I think a victory is in the pocket. I probably do the opposite.

And that was the trouble.

I was halfway through the fourth and final lap, just coming off the mountain, and a piston broke. The old girl just stopped. I'd likely been revving too hard, just like my dad had warned against. Either that, or maybe too many birthdays and not enough presents. I managed to keep her ticking over and I got back to the finish, at least five minutes down on where I should have been.

We were back down the pub that night, and I was sick again. But for a different reason this time. I was disappointed, but there was still another race to come on Friday. And this was the Lightweight, so I'd be riding a bike that had already won. That had to be another victory virtually in the bag.

For my final ever race at the Manx (probably), I was excited again to get going. There was a little bit of that nervousness I'd had on Monday. Maybe it was knowing that people were beginning to notice me as a rider to be reckoned with. As I waited for the boy on the line to tap me, I thought, *This is where you step up. Even against 400s in the same race, you can do this.*

I got the tap and I was away. I did 107 mph average from a standing start, which on a 125 is really good. Then, on the second lap, into Kirk Michael, about the fifteen-mile mark, it was *déjà vu*. Something didn't feel right and I noticed the temperature gauge going up and up. It would turn out to be an insert broken somewhere inside the head. It had cracked and was leaking water so it started to overheat. That would be the forensic explanation in time. All I knew at that moment, on that track, was that my race was over.

Once again, it was my own fault. I knew I'd pushed too much in my desire to show them 400s who was boss. Those boys were just so much faster in a straight line and I'd refused to give up the places I took off them. There was no way it was any fault of my dad's. He'd gone over every last detail. The cylinder had been fine before but I'd just done fifty-odd miles and they run at such high temperatures anyway, they're like wasps in a jam jar. You over-rev and you run the risk. I knew all that and I also knew that if I rode on, all I would achieve was melting the cylinder. To replace one of those is upwards of five grand. Money I did not have.

So I did the only thing I could: I pulled over at Kirk Michael, right by somebody's house. I stuck the bike against a wall, and was standing there when a couple came out from the house.

'Ah, how're you getting on?' the man asks.

I say, 'I'm all right.'

He says, 'You're the young boy who's in the race?'

I say, 'I think "was" would be the word you're looking for.'

'Ach,' he says, 'these things happen around here. Would you like a drink?'

Maybe today's not so bad then.

Because I was sick as a dog, I say, 'What's the strongest thing you have?'

A few minutes later I'm sitting on his front wall watching the bikes roaring by. I've got a beer, a sandwich and a wee radio. I'm that disappointed at not being out there that I'm only half paying attention to the commentary. But I definitely hear, '... and Michael Dunlop has crashed. Rider airlifted ...'

Ah crap, I thought. *William and my dad will think I'm hurt.* I was so pissed off with myself, I hadn't given them one thought.

All the bikes are fitted with a wee transponder that gets read three times round the circuit. I would have gone through Glen Helen but never shown up at Ballaugh Bridge. So they would have known I wasn't riding any more well before I failed to appear on the start/finish line. And naturally they would have been worried shitless, especially given the way I was riding. I could hear William's thoughts: *That fucking prick's probably come off up the road.*

I knocked back on the couple's front door.

'Excuse me, can I borrow your phone?'

A minute later I get my dad on the other end.

'Where the hell are you? Are you all right?'

'Oh, I'm at Kirk Michael. The bike broke down.'

'Ah shit,' Dad says, but he's almost smiling he's that relieved. 'We were told you were airlifted.'

'Aye, I heard that on the radio. But I'm fine. Just annoyed. Will you come and pick me up?'

'No bother. But it'll be after the race.'

I was there maybe another hour, hour-and-a-half. It felt like a month. Long enough to gather my thoughts, anyhow. I was gutted, I really was, that I'd been in the lead in two races against vehicles above and beyond the power I had underneath me. If it weren't for my own recklessness, I could have left the Manx with three trophies, not one.

By the time my dad found me, I'd put it all into perspective. I'd gone to the Isle of Man. I'd taken part. I'd even won a race. There were 200 other riders that week who never got that lucky. So really I was a happy camper, especially when I realized the great experience it had been in preparation for something around the corner.

Next stop, the TT itself.

NINE

I Want to See Bob Jackson

THESE DAYS, IF YOU TAKE a look at my overalls, it's like picking up a book. You can be reading an hour. I'm blessed to have a fair number of sponsors who want to be associated with me. Marlow Construction, Around A Pound, Robinson Concrete, Jordan Road Surfacing, Frey Daytona, Paintbox, Street Sweep, Den Motorsport, MTEC Graphics, Gortreagh Printing, Hunts, James Jamieson Construction, HolTaj, Roadside Garages, Angus County Windows, Paul Kirkpatrick Plant Hire, Arai, Monster Energy Drinks, Furygan, Pogo Loans and Automatic Fire Control – these are the boys keeping me running today.

When I started out on the roads in 2006, my clothes and bike were a blank page – but that was soon to change. Before I went to the Manx, one of William's and my dad's sponsors, David Glover, gave me a few pounds to buy some fuel. His company's name, Solitude Motors, was already on the side of my dad's bike, so maybe he felt obliged! William had never let him down, so he might have been hoping for the same from me. But mainly I think he did it because he was just a good bloke who wanted to help out.

He wasn't the only one.

I have been very fortunate in my career to run into really good people. I got to know Gerard Rice and his wife at a meeting early on and they gave me a couple of pounds. It was nothing massive. But then, I didn't need anything massive. It didn't take much to run me then, not racing 125s and 250s. Three or four hundred quid, enough to buy a set of tyres or pay an entry fee, something like that. Since then, Gerard has stumped up a fair bit more, and his business, Around A Pound, the discount store, has been on my overalls for ten years now.

Another boy came in at the start, a sponsor of my dad's. Adrian Fegan ran Crossan Motorcycles. He actually owned the yellow bike of my dad's, and when Dad got a new one Adrian says, 'There you go, run away with it yourself, Michael.' So that's how I came to start wearing the yellow leathers. It didn't stop there with him. He was good to me like he was to my dad. I got what Dad didn't need. New tyres, bits and pieces, fuel and the like. Adrian was really generous.

And then you have Martin Marlow. On top of all his and Maria's other kindnesses during the Manx GP, their company, Marlow Construction, have been sponsors ever since. Without them all, I'd still have survived my first year of running on the roads, but there's no doubt it would have been harder. Superbikes, on the other hand, they are cash guzzlers. Those big bikes really soak up the money. I know that because, in 2007, that's what I decided to race.

It's pretty obvious why. By the end of 2006 I'd done a year of road racing on the 125 and occasional 250. Neither of those was eligible for the TT and that, more than anywhere else on the planet, was where I wanted to be. So

Superbikes it was – whether I was ready or not.

And I was not.

A normal step up from a 250 is a 600. Adrian gave me one to ride, a Yamaha R6. Then my dad got hold of the Big One. He found a boy down the road who was selling an ex-racer Yamaha R1. It was beautiful: red and black, it had all the bells and whistles, and it was only two years old. The boy had bought it as road bike and added the extras himself. New, it was a 40k bike. It cost us around seven grand – or rather our sponsors. My dad got a couple of lads to look after it for us. It was a sweet deal and a none too shabby bike. I just needed to get the maximum out of it.

The final piece of my jigsaw puzzle, the final part of my plan for world domination, also arrived that year. If you're going to be at a meeting anyway, you may as well ride everything you can. I now had three bikes that I wanted to race, but no way of transporting them, so I bought myself an old van, an old 98 Mercedes Sprinter. Mine wasn't as well kitted out as William's was, but I was getting there. It suited me just fine.

As far as I was concerned, all the pieces were in place now for an assault on the mountain. Or rather, almost all of them. I still had to learn to master two new bikes.

Mere detail ...

When you're chasing your dream, nothing's going to stop you. Not if you want it enough. And I seriously wanted to race at the TT. So much so that I risked my life and almost everyone else's by riding the Superbike at Tandragee. It made sense: there were only a couple of races before the bike world headed off to Douglas and I needed to get some serious miles under my belt. But in all honesty, I was not ready.

We were a three-van-family by the time we got to the season opener. Even though Dad was racing, he was still on hand to work on my bikes and my brother's. Whatever extra bits and pieces we needed, he found somehow, either by borrowing or paying for it out of his own pocket. He couldn't have done more on the bike front – nor on the riding front either. Even though he couldn't physically race the bigger bikes any more, he knew all about getting the most from my new toys, so he was a font of knowledge on all fronts. But did I listen?

Actually, I did. I just wasn't good enough to make it happen.

I was hideous. I dragged the 600 around the course and then the Superbike dragged me round. The difference in quality is like night and day. A 125 will put out about 45 horsepower whereas the Superbike will put out about 195. It's a wee bit different. If you're wild on a 125 you can get away with it, but being wild on a Superbike is a different story. A different ending, anyway. We're talking death wish.

My riding style, if I have one, is aggressive. I want to dominate my machine and make it go where I want it to go. I'm not one of those racers who lets racing lines and convention dictate their movements, and I certainly won't be bullied by a bike. Not any more. But in 2007 I was that Yamaha R1's bitch. It owned me. I could not control it. That didn't stop me trying though – at 180 mph. Yes, we were wild, we were out of control. But it was necessary. I couldn't go into the TT cold.

The big one before the Isle of Man is the North West 200. Now there's another course where my dad couldn't move for backslapping and autographs. He was riding the 125 as usual and I took a ride in that race, too. He and William kept me well in my place. The same with the 250. I was disappointed but not too much. The meeting for me was all about the 600 and the Superbike. I desperately needed those miles.

The 600 was never a thing I could coax magic from. But it was better than the Superbike. I couldn't even coax a finish from her. Two Superbike races, two DNFs (Did Not Finish). It was not a weekend to be remembered. Hopefully the TT would be better. It had to be, right?

Going back to the Isle of Man was a wee bit less exciting than my first visit in anger. But that was good. I didn't want nerves to betray me. Or ego. Nothing like that. I wasn't playing with the amateurs any more. I was about to come up against the big boys, the seriously big boys and the boys even bigger than them. I was a nothing rider at the time, and in that company I was destined to be an even smaller fish in a bigger pond. Unless, that was, I could find some magic.

These days, the Manx GP is a bit of a poor relation to the TT. Back then it was a wee bit more prestigious but it was never going to eclipse my first TT – not because I was showing my face but because it was the hundredth anniversary of the first Touring Trophy. If you're going to pick a fortnight to debut, pick that fortnight. Everyone was there, everyone wanted a piece of potential history. The place was rocking with supporters and riders as well. It was madness. The difference in crowds from my last visit was like the support of Manchester United versus Ballymena.

All the boys were there. The Superbike riders tend to be the superstars, and for those races the likely winners were very familiar names: you had John McGuinness, Bruce Anstey, all the established riders. You'd forgive me, as a fledgling Superbiker myself, for being a wee bit star-struck. But I'm a Dunlop. I've grown up with the greatest riders ever. No Billy Come Lately is going to impress me on their name alone. They need to earn it on the track.

Apart from William, my Uncle Joey and my dad, there's only ever been one motorcyclist that I've cared about. I was about twelve when my dad said he'd take me to a meeting. That was a rarity, I promise you. But I'd been once before and there was a name I remembered. So I says to my dad, 'I want to see Bob Jackson.' Why I was a fan of the man I don't know. He was just a normal man, good going in his day, but I got well excited. 'Can we meet Bob? Can we meet Bob?' I remember my dad saying, 'Okay', and he took me over to meet him. That was rare. I had nothing to say to the man. Why would I? I was a kid. I don't even know why I liked him. I would've seen him on a wee road race somewhere. I probably just liked his colours or one particular manoeuvre. Whatever the reason, I remember vividly idolizing that fella. Apart from my dad he was the bee's knees.

After him, nobody really floated my boat. Definitely not the boys I was lining up to race. So I just walked by them. It wasn't a big deal to me seeing any bugger. It certainly wasn't a big deal to them seeing me, either. I was shit off the shovel to them. I made no difference to their lives in any way, shape or form and they made no difference to mine. The only thing that piqued my interest at all was their bikes. John McGuinness and the boys, they were all on the top factory machines, and that, from what I'd read, was worth more than a few seconds per lap. So when others looked at them with envy and said, 'I'm coming for your title', I wasn't interested in that. I didn't even want their reputations. I just thought, *I'm coming for your wheels.* I want the best materials available to maximize my chances of winning. Because that is all I care about. Winning.

But you can only play with the toys you have.

I did not happen to have a factory Honda like John. I was not blessed with a team of Japanese specialists stripping and rebuilding my bike in a factory somewhere hot. But I had the next best thing.

In preparation for the TT you work on the bikes at home. I was doing a lot of the engine work myself, trained by my dad. He was helping me, as well as looking over William's bike – a 600 ZX6 this time. Basically, every minute you can spend checking a bike over, you should. You're never truly done. You have to make sure this is right, that is right. You can go over and over these things. It never stops. Then, when you get to the paddock – or in our case, Martin's garage – you just do it again. You can always find something to do. And that's before you do a mile in practice.

Sometimes your best is not enough. On the first day of practice, my 600 blew up. No one saw it coming, there was no reason: the engine just gave out. We could have chased around for a replacement but that was a lot of work and I had other pies with fingers in. Namely, my Superbike. I'd just have to squeeze the most out of her.

It doesn't matter how prepared or smooth or experienced you are, things still go wrong. William took a sizeable knock one day in practice. It was his second year there, he was trying to find his ball bearings around the place, and he fell at the waterworks. He hurt himself a wee bit but he was all right to ride again. He just ran out of road, got a bit trigger-happy. It was only first or second gear, but he took a tough hit and that was it.

I'd be happy with pilot error. I was left with a Superbike to run, and between you and me it was turning into a bit of a pig. But it was my pig, that's the way I looked at it. I was already down one bike. So one way or the other I had to make the best of it.

I was incredibly lucky with the support I had. Ronnie and Valerie paid to attend the event out of their own pocket. She was always doing things to raise a penny or two for my riding. Ronnie was older than my dad, but he was young at heart and what he didn't know about stripping bikes, especially Yamahas, was not worth speaking of. He'd been with me since I started. I never lost on that 250 he ran. That's how good he was.

And then there was my dad. I felt for him, I really did. The bikes he was able to race weren't eligible for the TT but, hand on heart, I'm not convinced he was that worried about it. I saw how he physically struggled around some of the longer short races. The TT was so demanding I think he worried that he'd not last the course. I knew the man. If he'd thought he could ride that circuit he'd have picked a bike that was allowed. The fact he didn't spoke volumes. We never had the conversation but in my mind he was just on the edge of how strong he was going to be. Would he be able to last the race distance? Was he fit enough – mentally fit enough? That played a lot on his mind. I think he probably knew that if he took one more knock it would probably finish him. As a racer or as a person. Or both.

He had nothing to prove to anyone. He was at the

TT every year after his accident until they removed his category in 2004. He never found it easy. But he said, 'The thrill of competing just outweighed the fear of hurting.' So in the end, it was a question of maths.

It's remarkable how resilient the human psyche can be – my dad's and mine. For all the technical worries on my doorstep, I still had this unerring confidence in myself. I'd go as far as to call it arrogance. I was the boy who'd turned up and won his first race on the Mountain Course. And I'd nearly won two others. Was I really going to be that out of my depth at the TT?

The answer: an almighty 'yes.'

Amazingly, I hadn't miraculously learned how to control the bike since the North West 200. I could barely ride the bike up the lane, I was pure shite but for some reason I still thought I was the boss. The truth is, there were flies on visors that went round quicker than me. I was a tractor on two wheels. And the reason was that I just could not cope with the power. My usual approach of throwing the bike around, going for holes that aren't there, and generally being 'wild', was right out the window. I was struggling to hold on. And the pain – nobody mentions the physical agony of stepping up to the big bikes.

It's easy riding around when you're going one, two, three, four gears, stopping to turn, go up the road then turn right. This time, you're in fifth and sixth flat. That's an experience your body doesn't get used to in a hurry, I tell you. And all those wee tiny kinks in the road that you barely register as you bounce over them on a 125, they become regular knee-in-the-dick stuff because you're carrying so much more corner speed. You're thinking, *Shit, that's quick. Shit, shit, shit.*

What was fun or at least manageable on a 125 is wall-of-death time on an R1. You cannot imagine how much you will shit yourself going flat out through the streets until you do it. In practice I scared myself every other corner and every third straight. You don't understand how quick the bike is until you're on the roads going flat out. I was stupid, bouncing off trees and hedges and banks, basically running through the repertoire I performed last time I was there. But that was when I was in control. On the 125 you can put your bike anywhere. On the Superbike it can hurt you. I came home and my leathers were green and brown from hitting hedges. In my own mind I thought it was pretty cool but I knew it was going to end in tears. There's only one ending to this episode. This is a day for the men in white coats. There is a fine line obviously. You're trying to be fast but you need to be safe. And I wasn't achieving either. I was being slow and scary.

There's always the option of stopping. Some people take it. I'm never going to do that. Not out of choice. Sometimes, though, the bike makes the decision for you.

Bearing in mind the 600 was a write-off for the week, that put a lot of pressure on my R1. In the first race, the Supersport, we had a mechanical problem and I didn't finish. In the second race, the Superbike TT, it looked like going wrong again. We had an oil leak, it was running on to my boot, and I was probably more concentrating on that than on the bike. Being distracted by anything at 200 mph is not a good idea. In the pits we shoved a sponge up the leak to stop the stuff going on to my foot. That was all we could do. It wasn't a catastrophic thing, but because of the size of the engine it just blew a bit of oil. There was no way I was going to make a name for myself in that contest, but the idea of stopping never crossed my mind. That race, the one before and the one after, they were all about getting miles in, learning the circuit. I was playing the long game. Getting ready for a proper onslaught on the TT the following year. Or the year after. Or the year after that. All I could say for certain was that success on the Mountain Course was in my future. That much I was sure of.

At the end of the week I'd ratcheted up the grand sum of two DNFs, several non-starts (on the 600) and one twenty-fifth place. In hindsight, there aren't many teenagers who achieve even that much first time out, the course is that demanding. Not many teenagers even attempt it, in fact. To put it in a bit of context, it was still one place better than William's debut the year before. When you think he's four years older, maybe it shows how ahead of schedule I was, which was either a good or a bad thing. But I had the arrogance of youth, and twenty-fifth was not exactly something to tell the grandchildren. I wanted to win. It hurt me when I came nowhere close.

You have to look for positives. On the plus side, at least I looked the part. For the start of the season, I upgraded my overalls to a white and red Arlen Ness design: right dandy. I even changed my helmet. A year in and I'd begun to see the mythos behind the hat. Your helmet is your stamp, your helmet is your brand. At 180 mile an hour it's your identity. It's a very personal thing, choosing the design. The only piece of flesh on view is your face behind that wee visor. At the time, my dad was running a black and white combo. William took that design on and switched the placing of the colours round. They're both heroes to me, so I just did a half of each design. I ordered an Arai helmet half black, half white, to honour them both. Keep it in the family if you like.

The helmet cost about 750 quid, and then to paint it was about another five or six hundred. Totally worth it, though. For a biker, designing your own lid is a rite of passage. But then people started taking photographs and I realized: I had a big fat head on me. It's true. It was just from eating too much. I remember looking at a picture of myself and thinking, *Shit, you are some size. That is not a good look.* It was as though the Michelin man off the TV was trying on my clothes. While you're at the back of the grid and being ignored by the world and his wife, you can look however you want. But if you then start winning and the photographers begin taking an interest, having eight chins and three stomachs gets you noticed for the wrong reasons. Trust me, I know.

Uniform and track miles aside, the only other real positive I could take from 2007's TT is that I had no injuries, no accidents. A miracle when you saw how I was riding. I took a bit of the local flora with me. I ripped a few hedges out. But that's the long and short of it. Others were not so lucky. Marc Ramsbotham lost his life in the Senior TT I was riding in. His Suzuki went down at the twenty-sixth milestone, an incident that sadly also took two spectators' lives. Back in the paddock you hear things but, heartless as it sounds, even though he's a brother on the circuit, and these are fans who have paid to see you, you have to make sure it doesn't become your problem. You can't look at it as a normal human would, otherwise you will scare the shit out of yourself. It sounds a bit callous but you have to believe racing is a positive. For the duration of the meeting, at least, you have to say, 'It's not my problem. Nothing to do with me, guv.' It's not the most pleasant or respectful way to carry on but it might save your life. Doubts on the circuit cause mistakes. You have to be committed.

So there it was. My first TT, aged eighteen. I can't say it lived up to my dreams but, in the light of what the Ramsbotham family were going through, I suppose I had to be glad to survive. That's aiming pretty low though, in my opinion. I learned things, no question. Number one: put me on a Superbike in 2007 and I'll embarrass you. That's a guarantee. I'll trim your hedge more than win you a race.

For the rest of the season I didn't much improve. But I was on a mission. I signed up for every race in every category that I owned or could find a bike for. I wanted to become the complete rider or as close as I could get. My dad had been able to ride anything, same as Uncle Joey. They were the benchmarks. Unfortunately, early on I was more about skid marks.

It was 07/07/07. A mystical date for sure but not a great day for me. I fell at Skerries attempting to grab the lead of the B race. I was on Adrian's 600 and I committed a schoolboy error: I tried to win the race on the first lap. To do that, I went on the grass, on the outside of a flat-out right-hander. It was a nuts thing to do. I went down the inside on the kerb, there was a bit of track where it was somebody's front yard, not even a kerb by then. How I got up there I don't know to this day, and when I came out of it I ran on the grass, went straight through this bush and bounced back on to the road again. Me and the bike. I slid for what felt like a mile on my backside. The bike tumbled into the road and another racer smacked into it, breaking it clean in half. Not my fault. Adrian saw it differently. The things he threatened to do to me if I tried another stunt like that. I didn't care. I wasn't listening. My arse was too much on fire to concentrate on mere words. My backside and hands were red raw. I knew my sores would be bad when I got back to the pits, and managed to take my leathers off without undoing a single zip or fastener. I just stepped out of them like a banana skin they were that ragged.

People accused me of not caring about myself or others. They said I didn't think of the consequences. They were right to an extent. I never thought of the negatives. I always assumed I'd be all right. But living for weeks afterwards, unable to move without being caked in Sudocrem and Vaseline, unable to escape the feeling I was lying in a bed of nettles, that was a lesson I'd not soon forget.

Not when you'd go for a shit and you couldn't sit down. Again and again. Weeks, that lasted. And I brought it all on myself.

It's fair to say my luck was up and down most meetings on the small circuits. Earlier that day I'd come second to William in the 250 race. Mark Curtin was third.

Kells that same month was another good one. In the 250 race there were six of us leading at different times. Guy Martin was up there, Darren Burns, John Burrows of course, Ian Morrell, William and myself. But I was the one who left it latest to have a turn. Guy slipped off, John had a mechanical issue, which left three others in my way. I got two of them and thought I'd have to settle for second behind William.

Who am I kidding?

Typical big bollocks, on the last corner I rolled the dice one more time and threw everything into one of those kamikaze passes every bugger hates being on the receiving end of. I trusted William not to do anything reckless. That was *my* job in the family. This time I made it stick and nicked the win. I got the 125 victory as well. Dad retired from second on the last lap, giving it to Mark Curtin. My cousin Samuel inherited third.

In Killalane two months later I won the Junior 250cc, again from my brother. Seven laps and I got him by a couple of seconds. That's pretty big in my head. Darren Burns was third, Mark Curtin fourth. Mark was a good rider. He gave as good as he got. He proved that when he trailed my dad home by a mere second in the 125 Championship. Sam got fourth in that one. William didn't enter. I did but I lasted less than two and a half minutes, which no one would be impressed by. At least I did twice as well in the 600 race. I got close to a full five minutes under my belt in that one. William was second again, this time to Conor Cummins.

Travelling around the country, the three of us and sometimes my cousin, it felt like a family reunion every weekend. If there wasn't a Dunlop on the podium I began to take it personally. Between the lot of us there was a great deal of talent. But I was more potential than finished article, as a few boys found out.

Because of my style, I was always going to have dust-ups with someone. When you're going for gaps that don't exist except in your mind, there'll be the odd miscalculation. And the odd coming together. And the odd broken bone or sore arse.

I've had a couple of real good dices with William, especially on the 250s – real good races. He is great to ride with. You see, with William, I can ride wheel to wheel with him. Him on the brakes, me on the brakes, no bother the two of us. We're like synchronized swimmers on wheels. We can run centimetres between each other because he's so smooth: his lines and his style are just perfect, so you always know where he's going to be.

The same can't be said of me.

We were at Killalane and it was wet. William was better than me on that circuit. He was better than everyone. Even when he didn't win a race he more often than not got the fastest lap. He was the boy, that's the long and short of it. But on this occasion I was sticking in, clinging on to his tail for dear life. I remember I passed him just before the start/finish and he got me back on the straight. He went to brake and went tight. I'm thinking, *I'm going to do him here. You're for it now.* If he was going to go tight, I'm going even tighter. We're on the last corner of the last lap, and big bollocks here decides to do something. I'm *boom*, like a cannonball. Whether I can brake or not is a different matter.

I went so tight I was on the grass with the front wheel and I took the two of us out. Bang, down we go, spinning and sparking. We were only doing fifty miles an hour. But when you hit the tarmac at that speed, it hurts. I think William broke his brake lever. He could have had mine. I never used them anyway.

I don't think he was impressed. I saw he was okay and then, being the good brother I was, scrambled to get back on my bike. Partly to get back in the race. Partly to get away from him.

You can't run forever though. He caught me back in the paddock.

'What're you fucking playing at?' he says.

I go immediately on the defensive. 'You shut the door,

you fucking arsehole.' I'm blaming him, straight up.

'There was no space, you moron.'

'Plenty of space if you knew what you were doing.'

'When have you ever known what you were doing? You're a fucking lunatic.'

It was totally my fault, and against anyone else I would have admitted it. But against my brother it was instinctive to deny, deny, deny, just like I did when we were kids. William had taken plenty of slaps for me then. One more as a grown-up wouldn't hurt the boy.

We were fine the next day, like we always were. William was good like that.

Someone else who can tell the difference between business and personal was John Burrows. I have a lot of time for John and I like to think it's reciprocal, although I think he likes me a lot more now he's retired. I have one of his helmets in my collection at home, he was that good. He runs his own team now but when I was starting out on the bigger bikes he was the boy to beat. And so that's what I tried to do, any which way I could.

And he hated it.

One race stands out. We were at Tullyallen in September. I was going against him on William's 600, his Yamaha R6, and he freaking despised me, he loathed being anywhere near me. Three times I nudged him – actually hit the side of him – at maybe 100 miles an hour. It was intentional. He was in my way. I'm thinking, *I want to get past and if I can't see a space I will make one.* That was my style back then. Wild and stupid. Just like it is now, some people say.

That day he got the better of me, second to my third, but the ding-dongs happened a few times and he fucking hated it. Hated *me*. I know that because he told me.

I wasn't too bad at the front of the field but John

would've been one of the front runners most days so if I'd had a bad qualifying he knew I'd be coming up eventually. After he retired he told me, 'Nothing good ever happened when you were behind me. If there was a space on the left you'd go up the right. It was horrible. I used to hear your bike coming and I'd be dreading it.' In fact, he says, 'The day I retired was the happiest day of my life because it meant I didn't have to look at your fucking face.'

A great man, John.

My wee battles on and off the small circuits were great fun. I was all about collecting miles at that stage. But as the season came to a close there was only one thing on my mind – same as now, actually. *What are we going to do about next year's TT?*

Realistically I knew I was nowhere near ready for a win, so showing that I'd taken a step forward was the real goal. And I wanted my dad to see it, too. He had so much faith in me. I wanted to make him proud. I'd got the six-incher from the Manx GP. One of them flying ladies from the TT would suit me just fine.

TEN

Burn the Bastard

THE STEP UP FROM 125s TO SUPERBIKES was gargantuan not just in terms of power. The costs were hideous also. Everything cost ten times more. I was fortunate, then, that people continued to be impressed enough by the trajectory I was on to take a punt.

Early 2008 we were over in Spain to test a bike my dad had found for me. It was a new Yamaha R6. A beautiful thing, red and white. Like everything we did, the trip was on a budget. But we were lucky enough to bump into some other lads over there doing the same.

Gary Ryan is now one of my closest friends. But honestly, if he was a dog, you'd not know whether to tickle his tummy or put him down. He's that frustrating. He has a company called Street Sweep, based in Dublin, and for the craic he sponsors races and riders he takes a fancy to. At the time we met, he was the money behind a racer called Martin Finnegan – The Flying Finn they called him. But the boy he was out there with during our time was Michael Sweeney.

Like a lot of conversations, our first one took place in a bar over a couple of *cervezas*. Gary observed that I'd been running round for the last few hours on thinning rubbers, so he says to my dad, 'Get that young lad a set of tyres.'

My dad says, 'Tyres cost dough. We've got one set and he's stripping them bald.'

Gary takes a sip of his pint and has a think.

'Who's looking after the lad this year?' he says.

'Well, Martin Marlow's helping him out.'

'I'll tell you what – I'm gonna help the wee bugger out as well. I've seen the way he's riding. Imagine what the fella can do on wheels that grip the surface.'

And so Gary came aboard and soon he was the main man for my 600, which meant I had more cash to throw at the Superbike as and when.

Over the years Gary has become more intrinsic to the team. I run my own operation in the main these days, so I do the hiring and firing. I'm not sure I've ever hired Gary but he won't go away either so we're stuck with him. He knows I'm joking. The guy is a legend. A massive support to me – and all the boys in my team, actually. Both with his time and money as a sponsor, there is nothing this lad won't do. Without Gary I don't know where we'd have got to. He has a way of looking at the world that is either hilarious or impressive, so it's win-win for anyone lucky enough to be near him. I suppose you'd call his job on the team these days 'manager'. There is no one better at sorting stuff out.

'Gary, can you handle that?'

'No bother, boy, I'm on it.'

And that's what he does. He gets things done. When I'm on track at the TT or the practice is going on, it is very hard for the boys, because I'm the boss. Everything revolves around me. So if someone has a question or a problem, they have to wait until the Big Bad finishes driving round in circles. That's where Gary comes in. When I'm on the track I can't tell the boys what to do, but he can. Gary is fantastic at getting them to work in a way that he knows I would want. He tells the boys what needs doing and makes sure it's done. He knows exactly what's what. He's class at that.

But the thing he excels at is making us laugh, sometimes intentionally, sometimes not. We were racing at Skerries one day – or meant to be. My bike broke down on the grid and I'm ready to punch someone. Or something.

'Leave it to me,' Gary says.

He takes a stroll up the back of the grid and finds a bike he likes the look of. He tells the boy on it, 'You're not quick enough for that bike. Why don't you give it to someone who knows front from back.' And he just takes it.

I'm saying, 'Gary, you can't do that.'

'Ah, it's wasted on that fella,' he says. 'You'd be doing the bike a favour.'

He has a way of problem solving, I'll give him that. He helped me out a while back in getting a lorry to replace my van. It was a smart thing, big, one careful owner etc. etc. When I decided to drive it to a race in Scarborough I'd not had a chance to check whether Gary had got it registered or any of that. All I can say is there was no obvious paperwork in the vehicle. I didn't see the tax disc or the insurance papers. There wasn't even a UDP leaflet under the windscreen wipers.

I pulled off the boat the other side and I'm heading to the paddocks. Just as I'm approaching a roundabout the lorry lurches and then cuts out. I manage to wrestle it under control without hitting anyone but by the time it stops I'm mounted on the roundabout. In rush hour.

'Well, this is a fucker.' I grabbed my phone and called Gary.

Sometimes the man surprises you with his wisdom. This

was not one of those times. The first thing he does is laugh. For about two minutes. I says, 'Come on, Gary, help me out. I haven't even got a licence to drive a vehicle this big.'

'Okay, boy, I know exactly how to get out of this. Just do exactly what I say.'

'Agreed. What shall I do?'

He says, 'First, you need to get everything out of the lorry.'

'Right, I can do that. Then what?'

'Burn it.'

I says, 'What?'

'Burn the bastard. That lorry's given us nothing but trouble.'

'Gary, I can't do that. It's rush hour. There are people here. What if someone recognizes me?'

'Can you not put your helmet on?'

Honestly, the man's a piece of work. It was back to vans after that, although it wasn't the end of our problems. We were doing a race down in Dunmanway at the far end of Cork. We're driving along there and the van was packed with stuff, jerry cans of petrol, everything. I had my four bikes and the bike of a boy who used to go racing with us. All this gear, she was low at the back she was that full. I'm driving – with a licence this time – Noel my tyre man is in the middle, and Gary's at the side by the window because he's smoking away. That boy never stops smoking. He would kill you and himself with cigarettes. We're going along, we can't see for the smoke in the cab, he's choking to death, and I say, 'Gary, give them up.'

'What for?' Cough, cough, splutter, splutter. 'I'm fine.'

Anyway, the van starts vibrating and he's saying, 'Ah, lad, that's your driveshaft hanging.'

Great.

The next thing, I'm looking in my wing mirror and I see a

wheel coming up alongside us. It overtakes us and rolls up the motorway in front.

'Ah, lad, I think you've lost a wheel.'

'You don't say, dickhead!' By now I'm clinging on to the steering wheel to try to steady us up so I can brake. Suddenly Gary's climbing over the top of Noel to grab the steering wheel as well.

'Don't you let go of that, son,' he says.

'Get off, you clown; you think I'm going to let go of it?'

He's so busy leaning over that his cigarette touches the seat and *whoof*, that starts to burn. We have a fire in the passenger seat, smoke pouring out, Noel wetting himself, and I'm doing ninety miles an hour – on three wheels. And all Gary has to say is, 'Well, boy, if we have an accident now with this petrol in the back they're going to need CSI to pull us out.' And he just laughs and laughs and laughs.

I could go on and on about him. On his day Gary is as funny as two left feet. The boys love him, he's such fun. Of course, you have to take some of his stories with a pinch of salt. The clue is if he says, 'No word of a lie' or 'I swear this is the truth.' But he really makes it worthwhile running your own team sometimes. Without characters like him, I don't think it would be worth the bother.

No word of a lie.

So, 2008: I'm poised for a step forward. I've got enough money to run four bikes and, after Spain and 2007, I'm thinking that the TT is getting closer to my grasp. Ten months after I last raced there I can still see every bend, every pothole, every bump. I remember everything. From launching two wheels off the ground every single time I fly through St Ninian, to that pillar box, that farm wall, that telegraph pole. I can picture it all.

I can also remember the bruises and the aches and pains from wrestling my R1 around the course. Those kicks in the nuts linger long in the memory.

It's fair to say that these days my year hinges around the TT. It's a pity, in my opinion, that it comes so close to the start of the season. All your plans hatched over winter can go out the window if you don't get a good few races in first. Which is why, come 25 April and Cookstown, I'm there in full effect. I'm entering everything. That was quickly going to change.

I like the Cookstown. Arriving, I actually still had the lap record for the Junior Support race, set in my debut year, 2006. But this time around I was driving something a wee bit bigger. I'd been loaned a Suzuki to get a run-out. A K6 I think it was, a 1000 Superstock bike – basically a road bike with treaded road tyres as opposed to the souped-up bells-and-whistles 'Superbikes'. I was excited, of course I was, to start the year on a big bike. I started okay in practice; I felt I had the thing under control compared to feeling like a passenger the year before. I was going great guns, actually, then I came to the jump out the back, and the frame broke in half. Just snapped on landing. The only thing that held it together was the throttle cables. I thought, *Shit, I've got to stop* – only nothing but the throttle was working. And that's the last thing I wanted. I went up the slip road but I couldn't stop, not until something stopped me. That wasn't the most pleasant experience and it fucked up the rest of my weekend. No races, no wins. It got me thinking: did I need the hassle of driving a Superbike on these wee courses? I'm not normally a conservative thinker where safety is concerned but I didn't want an accident that would write off the TT before I even got there. When you're looking forward to something so much, you sometimes have to be sensible. Even me.

So, believe it or not, I thought, *Maybe I'll just ride 600s and 250s from now on.*

And it worked out. I started to get steadier on the 600. Going around in circles seemed a bit more reliable; I started to get closer to the top of the pack more regularly. Still not setting the world alight, often in my dad and William's shadow. But closer than I had been, no question.

It's a funny thing to say, but accidents are a way of life for riders. I've come off my bike so many times I've lost count. You look into the history of any racer and there'll be broken bones somewhere down the line. But the mad thing is, we always get back up, get back on. There's only one thing that stops us. One thing that *can* stop us. And that's the thing no one talks about.

The second meeting of the year was Tandragee, early May – somewhere else I held the lap record on that Yamaha 250. The Dunlop boys were there, plus the usual suspects. I qualified second on my Honda 250 behind Ryan Farquhar. Dad, of course, tied up pole position for the 125s. We were set for Saturday.

Then the unthinkable happened. Gary Ryan's boy, Martin Finnegan, had a bike malfunction in the Supersport race. The later inquest said it was a bolt loose. Ryan, who was behind him, says he saw oil on the boy's rear tyre. Whatever the cause, the Flying Finn's rear wheel took off and threw Martin against the bank.

However hard you tried to put his death out of your mind, for your own wellbeing, it doesn't work. Martin was a friend and, more than that, Gary was his sponsor and mentor. That madman was in bits, I promise you. The whole event was scrapped out of respect for Martin, his friends and family, a decision you have to support. There was a cloud over everyone. As riders, you're completely in thrall to the machinery, and if something did go wrong with Gary's equipment, as the coroner believed, there's nothing anyone could have done. It's one of those things. But it hurts. It hurt all of us. Somebody's life's gone; it's shitty. It's hard to get over that.

Later that month 2,000-odd bikers turned out for his funeral in Lusk. In his honour, the TT introduced the Martin Finnegan trophy for the fortnight's fastest Irishman. I don't want to spoil anything, but I would become very friendly with that particular title further down the line.

Picking yourself up after a loss like that is difficult, but you have two choices: sink or swim. Callous as it sounds, Martin wouldn't have wanted anyone else to suffer. That wasn't his way. None of us would. The show must go on even if we don't. I truly believed that. What I didn't know was that the black cloud was going to follow us.

The TT was only two meetings away. My preparation wasn't exactly going as planned but I felt good in myself. Going into the North West 200 in mid-May I was pretty confident I'd put in a performance or two.

We all set off that week as competitors. Me, William and my dad. The three of us were in the same race, the 250. The way it works at the NW is that there's practice on the Tuesday and the Thursday and racing on the Saturday. After the Tuesday, people were tipping my dad for the win.

He was the record holder, after all. Either him or William were the favourites, they were the two boys to watch. I wasn't really on their level, I was too busy making noise just behind them. I had the odd visit from the stewards but that's about as memorable as my week was turning out to be. John McGuinness was the only real opposition to the Dunlop crown. In fact he went on to take pole by a sizeable margin. Christian Elkin, the British short circuit champion, he was real quick as well.

Thursday practice came round. I was riding for a German duo. Two fellas, Norman Rank and his partner Rico Mendel, had a Honda 'Burning Blood' 250 and they'd asked me to ride it that meeting. It looked a decent beast so I was happy to. For some reason there was a delay and we finally got going around eight o'clock. It was late by our standards. I wasn't sure we'd get the full session in.

As it turned out, we didn't.

We set off in groups according to ability. William, my dad and Darren Burns – if my memory serves me right – were away first. William broke down at University Corner, so that left the three of them. I was a group or two back.

I was going okay on my first lap when I got round Ballysally Roundabout. I'm getting to grips with the bike and surface, minding my own business, when suddenly I notice the marshals are waving red flags. *That's not good.* For a moment the black cloud from Tandragee popped into my head. You just knew something had happened.

Sometimes under a red flag you're told to stop where you are. Other times you can pootle around until you get back to the pits and you can stop there. On this occasion we were waved on but slowly. Up I come through Islandtasserty, still none the wiser about the flags, through Maddeybenney. Only when I get to Mather's Cross is there any sign of action. I can see right up in the distance there's a bike in the road – bits of bike actually. I'm thinking, *Shit, something's gone on here.* As I get closer I see a man lying next to what's left of his bike. I slow even more, of course, and crawl closer and closer to the scene. That's when I notice. That's when it hits me.

The man lying next to the broken bike is my dad.

And he is not moving.

ELEVEN

I Had to Do It for Him

SHIT. SHIT. SHIT.

You're flying on adrenaline and that's all your brain can come up with. I screamed to a halt, threw my bike against a bale of hay and ran over to my dad. He was alone. There was no one with him yet. But at least he was alive.

It's all a bit of a blur. I remember trying to undo his helmet. I could see he was struggling for breath. He was making signs that he was hurt. I grabbed his hand and told him, 'I'm here. You're gonna be okay.' But what the fuck did I know really? I'm no medical man. I hate hospitals. I looked up the road and saw two bikes screaming their way towards us. It was Dr John and his colleague Dr Fred. You could not wish for better medical attention than those boys will give. I stayed right where I was until the doctors were ready to take over, then I moved back ten or so feet to give them the space they needed. It was 15 May 2008. And I was watching my dad die.

I just didn't know it.

Everyone thinks their dad is unbreakable. I knew mine was. He'd tried enough times. The man was Robocop, no question. As bad as he looked on the ground – and there was blood everywhere – I was convinced he'd pull through. He always did. The man was a boomerang. He kept coming back. And he would again, that's what I kept telling myself. I could see full well how serious it was but you can trick your mind into pretending everything is all right until you are told otherwise. That's what I did.

It seemed like forever before two ambulances pulled up, for my dad and the other fella involved. The doctors climbed in after them. I was not invited nor did I ask to go. I wanted no distractions for them. I wanted all their concentration to be on helping Dad fight the fight.

I've fallen off my bike many times and occasionally seriously damaged myself. But none of my injuries hurt me more than standing there helpless watching that man in such obvious pain. I totally forgot where I was. I was numb. This is where the human body is a marvellous thing, because I'm holding it together on the outside but inside I am shocked, I'm scared, I'm completely drained, empty of emotion or energy. I've switched off. Nothing's coming in or out.

I have no recollection of how I got back to the paddock. Whether I drove or got a lift or fairies carried me on a carpet. I was so far gone that, whatever happened, it happened without me contributing. My body was on automatic pilot. That's the only way I can explain it.

The next thing I remember with certainty is arriving at Coleraine hospital about ten minutes away from the track.

I got out of a car, still in my leathers. It was probably a taxi. I have no recollection of paying or not paying. I hope the meter's not still running.

William was just walking through the entrance when I got there. I followed him and a nurse told us that my dad had been taken straight to surgery. She also said my mum had been contacted.

'You'd better call my gran as well,' I said. Pure autopilot, that response.

'Aye, we've done that. Don't worry yourself.'

She directed us to a small waiting room but I took one look at that tiny, confined space and I thought, *Those four walls are not going to help.* I needed to be outside. William got there before me. He had a couple of his people with him, I was on my own. I stood where I was for a few moments and he did the same. We didn't say a thing to each other. What can you say? There were no words. He had that look of emptiness in his eyes, like me. You wonder, looking back, why you didn't hug or say something, but we were not operating properly. The lights were on but no bugger was home.

When you're in that vacant place, time has no meaning. I could have been standing there seconds, minutes or hours when the door opened and a doctor came out. As soon as I saw him, I knew what he was going to say. You know by the expression. His mouth was moving and you're not really hearing what he says, but it doesn't matter. He doesn't need to say a word because you've grasped everything from the face.

He went back inside and I just stood there like a statue. What else was I going to do? My dad, my best friend, my hero had gone. What was the point of going anywhere? Nowhere I went was going to bring him back.

It's funny, you stand there and you have that news and

it hits you like a wrecking ball in the stomach, and all you can think of is the 'what if?' scenarios and the 'why didn't I?' questions. Oh, and the regrets. They came flooding into my head. Just about every row I'd ever had with my dad in my entire life flashed into my brain. Stupid things popped up. Like when I'm working with him during the week and I'm being an arsehole. Usual teenage wanker behaviour. He'd say, 'Bring me those ten-mil sheets' and I'd say, 'They're five mil' and we start going at it and I'm arguing the toss and he's right of course, they're 10 mil, and I'm just spouting garbage like a prick. At seventeen, eighteen, nineteen, you're on that very fine line between turning into a man and still being a teenaged idiot. To simple things like, 'Can you take the wheelie bin out?' I'd come back with, 'I don't want to take the damn bin out.' Stupid, stupid arguments that meant nothing just kept coming into my brain.

It makes no sense to me. I worked with that man, I rode with that man, I lived with that man. We drank wine together, we shared amazing times that a lot of fathers and sons never do, so why was my brain just thinking of the shit times instead of the hundreds of thousands of brilliant moments? You're standing there and you just remember every harsh word that you said because you were being a dickhead and you know you didn't mean it and you know he knew you didn't mean it and you just want that one chance to say sorry.

But it's too late.

I couldn't have felt worse if I'd killed him myself. Or so I thought. Then I saw my mother arrive with my gran. They still had it all to come. It broke my heart knowing that they were about to have their lives turned upside down the second they stepped inside that building. But the truth is, they knew. One look at me and William and the others, and they knew everything. I tried to force a smile for my mum and she nodded and took Nan's arm, and in they went. They sat inside a small room for a while. I suppose they were gathering their thoughts. It only takes two seconds to ruin a life with the truth.

I don't remember how long I stood there. I had nothing on me. No phone, no wallet, no clothes. Eventually I got a ride back to the circuit to get my things from Norman and Rico's lorry. Baseball caps were invented for moments like that. I stared at the floor and basically ignored every person who wanted to commiserate with me. If you were one of them, I apologize, but I hope you understand. I grabbed what I needed, then got another ride home.

I don't remember sitting down with my mum, but I do remember the things we talked about, so we must have done so at some point. She was distraught, obviously, like the rest of us. But she also wanted to be a mum and help her children. That's some sick shit. She needed to grieve the same as anyone else.

But we spoke. She said she'd thought my dad would live forever. 'He was the Six Million Dollar Man. They rebuilt him from scratch. I thought nothing could stop him.' She couldn't get her head around how he could walk away from the 1994 accident and get done by this one. They were as fatal-looking as each other. She believed, like I do, that many, many people would not have survived that accident at the TT. It took a Superman to get up and do what my dad did. He rose like a phoenix. We couldn't understand why he wouldn't rise again.

At some point I must have gone to bed. It's part of the blur that I don't remember. The next day, Friday, was open house. It was also open casket. Dad was there, in his box, in the upstairs room. Mourners came in their droves to pay their respects. This is when my mum showed that she was the strongest of us all, because William took himself out to the garage for the entire time and I disappeared out into the fields. The wilderness surrounding our house matched my mood. I'd tried to be a man and help Mum out but I saw too many faces walk through that front door that I knew full well hated my dad and they hated us. Arseholes, the lot of them. Making no bones about loathing us, then coming to our home and pretending to be sorry? Two-faced people make my blood boil and I would not stay in the same building as them. Not then. Not on that day of days.

It sticks in the craw, it really does. When you're grieving you're expected to let any Tom, Dick or Harry into your house, but I couldn't stomach it so I left. Don't get me wrong, 99 per cent of the people who came in were genuinely great people who loved my dad. We had Valerie, we had Annie Twaddle, Dad's sisters, friends, lots of great people who just wanted to make things as comfortable for Mum as possible by helping around the house, whatever they could do. They worked like dogs, making tea and coffee and sandwiches for the guests. It was special. But that tiny percentage of wankers soured it for me. Maybe I was being a brat. Maybe I should have stayed. But I think – no, I *know* – I would have said a word or two to some of those folk and it would have upset my mum.

The thing is, my mum had been around racing for a long

time. She lived it 24/7, my dad told her everything. She knew exactly who the dickheads were. No one was pulling the wool over her eyes, don't worry about that. She was in control. No one ever got one over on my mother. Not even my dad.

When everyone had gone, that's when I went in to see my dad. I couldn't grasp it. I've been to plenty of funerals. People always say, 'Don't they look lovely? Don't they look peaceful?' No, they don't. They look like shit. There's no life in them. It doesn't matter what's on the outside, there's nothing coming from inside.

I feel bad saying it, but that wasn't my dad. He was dressed in a suit, he looked smart. He had no visible injuries. The boys at the embalmers had done a good job. But it wasn't him. I knew it because I sat there and I chatted to him and he said nothing back. And that's not my dad, believe you me. He probably would have told me to shut up. Especially when I'm apologizing for stupid things I said or did when I was eleven or fifteen or six years old.

The funeral was set for Sunday, two days' time. Mum didn't want to hang around. You hear about people waiting two or three weeks for slots these days. The name of Robert Dunlop still carried some weight. Fortunately, Mum had about a hundred friends happy to help with the arrangements.

I wasn't looking forward to it. Funerals seem so final and I still didn't want to believe he was really gone. They never truly capture the person anyway. The funerals I'd been to never did the deceased proper justice, not in my eyes. And where my dad was concerned it had to be perfect. I wanted truly to honour that man. And I knew exactly how.

It did not involve funerals.

Late Friday I texted William.

'What are you doing tomorrow?'

He says, 'I'm going to race.'

I says, 'That's no problem. I'll be right beside you.'

We had barely spoken since the accident. We'd not mentioned one word about the race. But in both our hearts we knew that's what my dad would have wanted. He wasn't someone who'd demand you put your lives on hold on his account. Get out there, enjoy yourselves while you can – that was the Robert Dunlop guide to life. And William and I, we were going to honour it.

All day Friday I was walking around the hills, thinking about my dad and mulling over things. I remembered him making me get back on the bike when I fell off. It was the right thing to do. At that moment I never wanted to see a motorcycle again but I knew in my heart that Dad wouldn't accept that. If he were there he'd say, 'If you don't ride tomorrow there's a good chance you will never ride again.'

That was a genuine fear. The state I was in, I was prepared to chuck the whole lot in the sea. It was the same for William, I imagine. You have to bite the bullet or the bullet will bite you.

I remember calling Norman Rank. He was the boy with the 250. Gerard Rice, my sponsor, had paid for him and Rico to come over from Germany with their bike and they had been like kids in a toyshop. I was probably the only Dunlop they could get hold of, otherwise they'd have approached my dad, I reckon. Either way, I'd been honoured to have them want me. I rang Norman to see the lie of the land. He was good as gold.

He says, 'I'm not going to tell you what to do, Michael. You are your own man. But what I will say is that if you are here on Saturday you will have a motorbike to ride. We will have it ready, I promise you. If you're not here, no hard feelings. We will pack the lorry after the race and go home.'

Come Saturday I had my decision. But I wasn't the only person who'd made one. I remember getting to the circuit and the organizers saying they didn't want us to race. The stewards had had a meeting and they'd decided we were mentally unfit to be in control of a vehicle. The clerk of the course came over and tried to talk to us like we were wee boys. He just pissed on my chips, if I'm honest with you. He pissed on William's as well. I wasn't having it.

'Are you kidding me? My dad died on this circuit. He holds the record for the most wins around this shit hole. You asked my mother if you should cancel out of respect and she gave you permission to go ahead. I'll be racing today and that's the end of it.'

Or words to that effect.

I don't think he was my biggest fan before and he definitely wasn't after.

But the boy stood firm. We were not racing on his watch, that was the end of it. I wanted to lamp him, I really did. I was that emotional I could have done. But what I didn't know was that the matter was being taken out of his hands. William's bike was already on the grid and mine was on its way. Norman Rank is one tight man. If I was ever in a fight and it was just me against a thousand people and I wanted one man, I would choose Norman. I would punch myself in the face before I let him punch me. He's not big, he's just wiry. I just knew from looking at him that he wasn't taking any nonsense. Not one person is getting in the way of him. Then there's his friend Armand. A digger wouldn't shift him. So while I'm arguing the toss with the course jobsworth, Norman and Armand are pushing everybody out the road and getting that Honda on to the grid.

Obviously everyone around us is coming over, offering their condolences, just letting us know they're thinking of Dad and the family. And that puts the stewards in a tricky position. They'd already banned us but they knew if they got heavy handed and tried to take our bikes off the grid, there'd be a mutiny. I already despised them. This weakness just made it worse. Either have the balls to back up your own decision or get out of my face. Don't go throwing your weight around like some spineless playground bully.

I think maybe someone down the line told the boy in charge that me and William being there was gold dust. The North West is the largest sporting event in Ireland. One hundred and fifty thousand people turn out to watch. They knew that the record that day would be broken. But only if the Dunlops were allowed to race.

The media was mental. No one expected us to turn up but when we did, it's boom, all systems go. Cameras, microphones, shouting and hollering. I squatted behind the bike, on the road, hiding under an umbrella, and

Norman, Rico and Armand stood in front so that no one could get near me. I was front row, easy pickings, between John McGuinness and Paul Robinson. William was behind with Christian Elkin and Paul Owen. The press can smell a story. Dad had only just died, he was still on the front pages, so no matter what happened, my brother and I were the headline of the weekend.

While I was down there, I couldn't shut out the noise. No one was saying anything other than kind words but I didn't want to hear them. It was too much. I just wanted to be alone, actually.

Finally the klaxon goes and I get on the bike and put my helmet on. The silence is deafening. It's beautiful. The bullshit around me just disappears. It was as if somebody had just lifted all the weight off my shoulders. It was like being given a shot of general anaesthetic. Everything faded away. All the drama was over. Now I just wanted to get on to the warm-up.

Off we go. I'm suddenly aware of being on a bike. It's the first time I've known where I was, really, in forty-eight hours. The words I imagined my dad saying to me about getting back on the bike never sounded more true. I needed to race, I realized that now. It's the one thing I can be in control of. I couldn't control my dad's life or his death. I couldn't control the media or anyone who came to visit our house. But I could point that bike where I wanted it and I could make it sing.

When I get back round to the grid, Norman comes out. 'Are you all right? Everything okay with the bike?'

'No bother,' I says.

'Remember, you're the man. You can do this. We're all behind you.' That's what this German bloke I barely know says to me. It's just what I need to hear. It's what my dad would have said.

Then Ronnie comes over. 'Michael,' he says, 'William is out. He broke down again on the warm-up lap.'

Ah, shit.

The boy's gutted. I know that without speaking to him because I know how I would feel in his position. We're there to honour our dad. How can you do that if you don't race?

Normally part of me would think, *Epic*, because William is more than capable of blowing me away on this circuit. (The next year, 2009, he wins it, as well as the 125. Point made, I would say.) But that wasn't the plan for today. *Fuck, I'm on the grid here on my own. Where is my brother? I need my brother. We're meant to do this together.* It felt like I was caught with my pants down. But it's too late to fix anything. William leaves and, *bang*, we start.

I'm nineteen years old, I'm raring to go, but somehow I'm only second off the line. Power down, the back wheel skids. For the first ten yards my right leg trails the ground, just in case. It's over in a second, the uncertainty. First gear, second, third, fourth while I'm still in Millbank Avenue. Tucking down for the right-hander, then left again at Primrose Hill.

At least that's what it looks like. The truth is, I have almost no recollection. You can find the race online or on DVD. That's the only way I know what happened. I remember nothing until the last lap. Zero. Zip. Nada. I'm just sitting there, coasting. I've never raced like it before. I'm on autopilot. I don't think I even noticed going through

Mather's Cross. If I did, I can't recall. My dad was in my head, in my heart. That's how I remembered him. Not lying by the side of the road.

What I do know is, I won. I beat that old warhorse John McGuinness, and if he was going to be beaten, on that day he wanted it to be by me. Christian Elkin felt the same. And Paul Robinson. As the BBC commentator says, 'That's the result that everybody wanted.' There's nothing complimentary in that about me – they just respected my dad. I was doing it for him. Everything I ever did in my life was done for him.

As I pull up at *parc fermé* John and Christian give me slaps on the back. William comes over, all the boys do. I know this because I've seen the footage. I have no recollection. I've watched myself on the BBC climb off the bike and I just stare, like a zombie. There's nothing in my head. Just pain, I think. That's what the tears say to me.

I climb off the bike and drop down, hiding behind it like I'm praying. My legs don't have the energy to keep me up. My heart doesn't have the strength to hear all the well-wishers tell me what I already know: that my dad would be so proud. At some point my visor comes down and the floodgates open. No one can see it but you know it's there.

The man from the BBC sums it for me. 'This was more than a race.' He had that right. This was everything I could do for my dad. It was the best way and the only way I could pay him a tribute. Everything I have I owe to him.

Weirdly, I do remember Norman coming over. He was happier for me than for himself. He knew what it meant to me. Before the race he'd been so worried that I would try too hard and fall off. But I held it together and I have to thank him and Rico for giving me a fantastic bike to do the job I did. I will be forever in their debt.

Eventually I manage to calm myself. The helmet comes off, the yellow cap goes on – 'Dunlop', of course – and I do my best to prepare myself for the TV cameras and their questions. It's all I can do to stay upright when there's a microphone in my gob.

'Going into that last lap, I says, *Screw this*, I have to do it for him. And I done it.' I'm fighting my tears with every word. I can't even look the interviewer in the eye. I manage to thank everyone at home looking after my ma. Then the man from the Beeb says, 'You've done yourself proud. You've done your dad proud. You've done Northern Ireland proud.' And you know what? I think I did. In any case, I couldn't have done any more.

I went home. It didn't sink in what I had done. To this day I don't think I really believe it. To go out and drive two days after your dad has died – who does that? When you win a race you normally get a back page. This time we got the front pages as well. That's how big Dad was.

The way the world revolves, you can't always control it. That week of sadness at the North West set me up for a lifetime of greatness. I'm convinced of it. I don't see any other way I would normally have been able to beat McGuinness and Elkin on the track. I felt for William, I really did. He deserved the win as much as me. I wonder sometimes what would have happened if I'd broken down and he'd won.

Garryduff Presbyterian Church, near Ballymoney, was where my father was due to be laid to rest. It's the same place Joey ended up. It makes sense. It's what they both would have wanted. More than 5,000 people turned up in the village to pay their respects. Ian Paisley and Martin McGuinness were among those that made it into the church.

I was one of the coffin bearers, along with William, Daniel, Uncle Jim and Dad's sisters Margaret and Helen. His other sisters, Linda and Virginia, walked behind.

Knowing who I was helping to carry was a rare feeling. It was surreal, really. What really brought me back to reality was seeing my gran, though. You should never bury your children. That woman had already lost one son. Now she was saying goodbye to another.

However you look at it, Mum and May, my gran, suffered the most. Don't get me wrong: I'd lost the most important person in my life. He was my dad, my hero, my friend and my boss. In a way it was like I was losing four people. But Daniel, William and I were young. We had our lives ahead of us. Daniel already had a wee girl and William was in a relationship. Our futures were going forward. Mum and Gran didn't have that luxury. The gap that Dad left they would never be able to fill.

Dad's old mucker Liam Beckett got some giggles from the mourners with his tales of Dad's vanity, but the Reverend John Kirkpatrick, chaplain of the Motorcycle Union of Ireland and the same fella who'd conducted Joey's service, summed my dad up best.

'We live in a world where not many people finish what they start. Not all persevere in adversity or push themselves to their potential and this makes those such as Robert stand out from the crowd. Beneath that determination was a man of depth and sincerity, a man clever and skilful. He believed that you should do something with your life and he was always at something.'

As they all spoke I had a rush of my own memories and this time not just the bad ones. Silly stories kept popping into my head. Like the day he'd taken a horsebox to a race because he was going to pick up a nag for Mum on the way back. I'd driven the lorry with the beds in, and that night, because it was cold, I expected we'd be snuggling up together in the wee cot to keep warm. All three of us did that regularly, I'm not ashamed to admit. Dad never saw me and William as anything other than his little boys.

On this occasion he didn't come to bed, so I went looking for him. I found him in the horsebox, sound asleep on a bale of hay. Honestly, airs and graces were wasted on that man. He just got on with stuff.

But you know the biggest tribute I can pay? I'd say my dad made a difference, a positive difference, inside and outside his own family. A lot of people, I'd say most of them, can influence those near them, but they never reach any further. But he did. And there are thousands of people who would agree.

I didn't honestly care, though, what he was like outside the family. I only cared what he was like with me. And all the grateful people in the world wouldn't bring him back.

idn't get any better than when all the Dunlops were racing together.
ey were some of the happiest times of my life ...

... But reality came crashing down with the death of my dad at the North West 200. Two days later I returned to win there in his honour in what was the most emotionally charged day the sport had ever seen.

I finally done what
I always dreamed of,
getting my first TT win in
'09 in the Supersport.
My God, it felt good.

My dad got his own memorial garden (below) to complement Joey's (above). They were two of Ballymoney's finest and their legacies will live o

Pulling out the moves on my way to a total of four TT wins in 2013, including my first on the big bike.

Below: Battling for the lead with Guy Martin, a constant thorn in my side at that time.

I won four TTs in a week again the following year, getting the big one, too: my first Senior TT.

Top right: 2014 also brought the premiere of *Road*, the documentary of the whole Dunlop dynasty, which William and I attended.

The wins kept coming at the TT, and in 2016 I was the first man to go under seventeen minutes there, pulling out the fastest ever lap and race records.

The road goes ever onwards, and I'll be on it, racing – and winning.

TWELVE

Give Me a Sign

FOR DAYS, WEEKS, MONTHS, PROBABLY YEARS, my dad was everywhere I looked. I'd be in the middle of the most mundane things and a new memory, completely unrelated to anything I was doing, would pop into my head. Like this one. I'm cleaning my teeth one day. Out of nowhere I found myself remembering the time Dad and William started playing golf. That was their thing they did together. But I couldn't handle that. I was like a jealous ex-boyfriend. *Hang about, we're the Three Musketeers. You're not going without me.*

I was fifteen, sixteen, and going through the Clubman's series at the time. I had plenty of things on my plate but I could not bear to be missing out on 'Dad time'. Not if William was getting it.

'But you don't even like golf,' William says.

'Aye. What's your point?'

I'd follow them around their stupid long walk and at some point I'd find myself diving into the pond to see if I could find some golf balls to sell. So I had a nice time and made a bit of dough. Stuff like that – stupid things – kept coming into my head. But they're all bittersweet. They all reminded me of what we had and what we'll never have again.

We were meant to be together forever, that's how I saw it. We were the 'Dunlop Dynasty'. We were a team. Even though we were three men at different stages of our lives there was this bond, this friendship more than kinship, that we had in common. Me, William and my dad actually led separate lives – we were different personalities. Three different characters. But our circles come together in the middle. Sometimes I would sit down and drink red wine with Dad and Uncle Jim, but other times I'd think, *Look at these old farts. Who wants to sit with them?* We were so close and yet so far away at the same time.

But whatever we were, it all ended in May 2008. And William lost a golf partner too. Add that to the list.

The truth has a funny way of coming out. The rumour mill after Dad's accident said a dozen things. Dad had accidentally hit his brake button at top speed and gone over the handlebars. The front wheel had locked. The pistons had seized. There'd been an engine malfunction. Further down the line there was an inquest. All these boys gave evidence about Dad not being happy with the way the bike had been performing; he'd come into the pits just before the accident to try to get it sorted. And then the coroner concluded it was Dad's fault for hitting the brake.

I suppose they need an end to the story, don't they? If they blame the course you can sue someone. If they blame the bike you can sue someone. If you blame the rider the story ends. You know what I'm saying?

At the time of his death my dad had the most wins at the North West. (It took until 2016 for someone to overtake him.) He'd got most of them between 1989 and 1994, which just goes to show how much he could have dominated the sport if he'd not had his accident. Even after that, there was no boy who knew the Triangle like Robert Dunlop. So, for me, the likelihood of pilot error shrinks with every hearing. But what do I know?

In those days and months afterwards you want to lash out at someone. There was another person involved in the accident. Dad had just overtaken Darren Burns when he came off. Darren had no time to react, no time at all. He smashed into Dad and seriously damaged himself. In my darker moments I think, *Why was he there? What was he doing?* But he was racing. Someone like my dad comes past, you probably want to be as close as you can to get a half-decent lap. And the truth is, it could have been anyone. If William hadn't stopped at University Corner, maybe he'd be the one behind Dad. You just don't know.

He can't be blamed but I'm grieving and I need a target. To this day I have never spoken to Darren about it because I might get angry. I don't trust myself not to and that's sad.

You have to know your own mind and I'm pretty thick with mine. I went along to the inquest but I couldn't stick it out. Nothing anyone in that room said would change a thing. William was the same. I didn't care what anyone said. I knew my dad and he knew bikes. I didn't want to hear what some wanker thinks happened. I didn't want to know about the injuries in any more depth than I already did. And I certainly did not want to see footage of the accident. The fella leading proceedings was good enough to warn the family when they were going to show film taken from a helicopter of my dad coming off. Not everyone had those manners.

In 2014 there was a documentary made of my dad, Joey, William and me called *Road*. It's a cracking film. We contributed to it. I was followed for a year with cameras. I took time off work, gave up pay to do interviews. I'd never say, 'Don't watch it.'

But I don't think the producers played us with a straight bat.

When it was finished, William and I went over to Coleraine for a private screening. I was looking forward to it. I thought the footage they found about Joey was really moving. Then the story moves on to my dad and I start twitching in my seat because it's uncomfortable seeing him up there. It was just wrong. He should have been sitting with us watching it.

I knew they were going to cover the accident because I'd been interviewed about it. What I didn't know was that they were going to show it.

This was 2014. I'd gone eight years without ever seeing the moment that took my dad's life. And there it was fifteen feet high on a fucking cinema screen.

Call me naïve but I didn't expect it. They showed the air helicopter camera tracking my dad and we just assumed they would get to the crucial point and it would stop. There was big swelling music going on and we expected *boom*, then the screen would go black. But they showed the accident and *then* it went off.

I was poleaxed. I was furious. You know, I don't mind that they included it. If they think that's what's going to make a better film, that's up to them. They're the experts. But they could have warned us. It was too quick for us to turn away. And to this day I cannot get those scenes out of my head.

Would it have been too much trouble for someone to say, 'Hey, boys, just to give you a heads up, in around forty minutes we show the accident.' You know, we could have prepared ourselves or even left the room.

William was just as knocked out as me. But then he says, 'What about Mum and Nan?'

'Oh fuck, they saw the film this morning.'

And they hadn't been warned either.

The fallout from something like a death is seismic. It goes in waves. After I won the North West, people assumed I'd be gearing up for the TT. Nothing could have been further from the truth. Racing that Saturday had been cathartic. It was an itch that needed to be scratched. I didn't do it for myself; I did it for my dad.

But carrying on now, after everything, well, that seemed disrespectful. And I don't think my mum would have been keen, either.

William was in the same frame of mind. He decided to let road racing take a back seat, maybe for a while, maybe forever. He even sold his 600 to John Burrows. John's a good guy, he knew the lie of the land. He said to William, 'If you ever need to borrow it back, just pick up the phone.' Words he'd come to regret ...

Gary Ryan, my sponsor and the owner of Street Sweep, was another one who couldn't see the way forward. Don't forget, before he lost Dad as a friend we'd just said goodbye to his boy Martin Finnegan. Gary was straight on to his other protégé, Michael Sweeney.

'Michael,' he says, 'there'll be no more roads for you. Not if you want my backing.'

It was a black time for everyone.

I remember being out in the garage: I was clearing stuff up but mainly I was trying to keep busy. Everything I'd done with my life had been with my dad. Without him I was a bit directionless, a rudderless ship. Everywhere I looked there were these reminders of the races we'd done. It got the blood stirring and I had to admit to myself that I wanted to go to the TT. It just came upon me. What held me back was how it would look. You can't just carry on as though nothing has happened, can you?

Mum was in the house. We still had friends in and out, checking on us. It had only been a matter of days. We're all coping as best we can. I says to her, 'Mum, I think I want to go to the TT.'

'Are you sure that's a good idea?'

'No, I'm not. But I'm worried if I don't go I will lose my love of bikes forever.'

And bikes, as far as I was concerned, were a direct link to my dad. If I gave them up it would feel like I was giving up on him.

I was all over the place mentally. That in itself should have been enough of a clue to knock the plan on the head. But when the practice week came round a few days later I found myself sitting in the garage listening to the radio. It was torture. I rang Gerard that night.

'I want to go, Gerard. Is that wrong?'

He says, 'You have to do what you feel is right. You'll always have my support.'

He wasn't the only one in my corner. The next morning this van pulled into the driveway and it's Gary Ryan. At this stage I didn't know him that well.

'Are you all right, Michael?' he says.

'Aye.'

'I hear you're going to the TT.'

Christ, news travels fast. Gerard must have rung him.

But I says, 'Aye.'

'I'm having no more to do with the roads,' he says. 'But I promised your dad I would help you and I am a man of my word.' He took me to the van and there's ten drums of fuel and fifteen sets of tyres. 'There you go,' he says. 'I keep my promises.'

And that was it, he drove off again. In fairness to the man he went out of his way to go and get that fuel and tyres, even though at that point he'd washed his hands of road racing. He refused to go anywhere near the TT that year, but it wasn't long afterwards that he came on side and he has been with me ever since.

This was Tuesday 27 May. Practice is on all week. But I still hadn't decided. It sounds daft now but I needed to know my dad would be all right with me going.

Just give me a sign.

While I waited for divine intervention I rang Paul Phillips, the organizer of the TT.

'I know practice has started but is there any chance you could let me come over?'

I've had my run-ins with Paul over the years but he's always been straight with me. He answered, 'Normally no, Michael. But special dispensation: if you're here by Thursday practice I promise I will let you out.'

'Thank you. Thank you, *thank you.*'

That was it, my mind was made up. My next phone call was to book a crossing, but there was no space on the ferry. Of course there wasn't. It was TT week. The busiest time of the year.

I looked at the heavens.

Is that the sign, Dad? Do you not want me to go?

I decided, no: he'd want me there if I could get there. I was desperate now so I rang Gary Ryan.

'Gary,' I says, 'you've a boat down there, haven't you?'

'Aye. Why?'

I says, 'Can I take it?'

'Er, I suppose. Where are you thinking of going?'

'Isle of Man.'

He says, 'You're not right in the head.'

For Gary to say that, you know you're going down the wrong path. Thing is, he did have a boat, but it was about the size of one of them you play with in the bath. That's all I could think of, though: I needed to get across the water. If the ferry wouldn't take me I would make my own way.

I clearly wasn't thinking rationally. All I knew was that suddenly I had to get to practice. I would have swum across if I could have done. I don't know what was driving me. It was something bigger than myself.

The thing is, by the time I decided to go on Wednesday morning, the weather had turned evil. Going down to the beach where Gary had his boat, it was tipping down. I barely noticed it. Just like I didn't notice the boat was not fit for purpose. Aye, it would take you around the coast for a spot of fishing. But you wouldn't want to lose sight of land. There was no cabin or anything. It was only a step up from a pedalo.

In my logic, I just needed to get me and a bike and enough fuel and wheels for practice over there. There were spaces on the ferry for the next day so Ronnie would follow with everything else in the van. It all made total sense to me.

To his credit, Gary was alongside me, helping me get as much fuel and wheels on board as would fit. He helped me dismantle the bike, too, in order to squeeze it in. But what he wouldn't do is step on board himself.

'Have you not seen the weather?' he says. 'You'll be sunk before you get out of sight.'

But I knew I had to get going. If I missed practice that was it. Game over.

I promise you, I was a man possessed. How else do you explain doing something so mad even Gary wouldn't entertain it?

I got about an hour out in the boat and, no word of a lie, Jaws would not have been in that water, it was that fierce. I had more water inside the boat than outside and eventually I had to turn round.

When I got back to the shore Gary was still there. He knew full well I'd be back. 'To be honest,' he said, 'I never expected you to last so long.'

I was gutted, I really was. We unloaded the boat in sombre silence. I felt in my heart I'd let my dad down. We'd just finished and Gary says, 'Tell me, Michael, how were you going to find your way to the Isle of Man, anyway? Got a map have you?'

'Don't be soft,' I says. 'I was using that satnav you've got.'

He looks at me, he looks at the boat, he looks back at me. 'That's not a satnav, you idiot. *That's a fish finder.*'

So even if I hadn't drowned I wouldn't have found Port Douglas anyway. Although I might have caught a nice bit of dinner.

Sometimes in life you just have to admit defeat. And I did. Thursday morning I was beat. I was down. I had my hands in the air. That's when I get a call from Ronnie.

'Michael,' he says. 'The weather's been shit.'

'Tell me about it. I'm still wet through.'

'No, listen. Not here – over on the island. The rain was so bad they had to cancel Wednesday practice.'

'So?'

'So, they're running it tonight. Get yourself down to the ferry. We're going to the TT.'

I'm not one for religion but I looked up to the sky and I said, 'Thank you, God.'

That was it. That was what I had been asking for. That was my sign.

Dad wants me to race.

I was only taking Dad's 600. I'd had my fill of Superbikes the previous year. But when I arrived, Paul Phillips came over. A team had lost a rider in an injury during practice.

'There's a Superbike going if you want it,' he says.

In a rare moment of humility I said no. 'I rode an R1 last year and I didn't really get going.'

'That was last year,' he says. 'But okay, I just thought you might want the extra laps.'

'Well, if you put it like that ...'

My whole plan with the TT was long term. No bugger ever just turned up and won straight out of the box. You needed practice, practice, practice. I may not have believed that once but I did by then.

In practice I got the Yamaha three miles up the road and it stopped. The fuel pump went. By the time I got back to the pits there was one lap of practice left. I should have called it a day but I rode in the race anyway and I came tenth. On the 600 I went better and claimed an eighth.

Prize money had never been in my sphere of observation before. But the TT works by paying you for every lap you complete plus a bonus for finishing in the top, say, fifteen. They change it from time to time. What I do know is that in 2008 I trousered £2,800, which is nothing to be sniffed at. Not for a first proper attempt.

More importantly though, I won something else. A bit of family history. Leslie Moore, editor of *Road Racing Ireland*, came up to me afterwards. This boy knows all the numbers for everyone.

He says, 'Congratulations, Michael. You just did a one hundred and twenty-four mile-per-hour lap.'

'Aye, thanks.'

'You know what that means?'

'No?'

'You are now officially the fastest Dunlop ever to ride the TT.'

I knew it. I knew I'd made the right call to come. The sign was right. Any thoughts about putting my racing on the backburner disappeared in an instant. This was the message I needed to continue. For my sanity, for myself and for my dad.

This is just the beginning, I promised myself. *Next year I'm coming back to win.*

THIRTEEN

I'm Gonna Finish This

FOR A WEE MAN, HE CAST A BIG SHADOW.

Not having my dad at my side at the TT was eerie. There was a genuine hole. Aye, Ronnie could do the mechanical side of things and William was over with me, but all those supportive nods and handshakes were missing. And just knowing that in your corner was a guy who'd won all around the place was a huge boost. Who else had that?

I know it's a one-man sport but behind every rider there's a team. You can't do it on your own.

I wasn't short of help. Martin and Maria were sensational. Like Gary, they'd felt – wrongly – that they owed me something because of my dad. They couldn't do enough for me. Not just financially, but being there, hosting me, making sure I was settled in my mind. Age-wise they are the same generation as my dad. They don't have children of their own and I'd probably put them off for life, but I think I was a kind of surrogate son to them. They couldn't have done more for me if I'd been their own flesh and blood. I know that over the years if I've ever had to turn to somebody, Martin is the man. I can rely on Martin for everything.

Valerie and Ronnie have never stopped being amazing. Gerard was always there: 'Do you need anything? What can I get you?' And Gary of course became more and more important. Even when I was at my lowest, there was no one better to chivvy me along, keep me going, just give me that extra push.

The TT blew away a few cobwebs. It pointed me in the right direction for the rest of my life, starting with the remainder of the season. I decided I'd give Superbikes another blast with a view to a further push in 2009. I also wanted to ride 600s. Unfortunately, I had neither.

Coming back from the TT, I had a real spring in my step but my 600 needed rebuilding and that was going to take a bit of time. Faugheen was coming up and I was desperate to keep my momentum going. But where was I going to get a bike? William was no help. He'd sold his to John Burrows, otherwise I'd have borrowed that.

I think John always knew William might change his mind one day and, although I wasn't my brother, I decided I'd give John a call anyway to see if his offer was still open.

I say, 'All right, John. I don't suppose I could have a lend of that bike over the weekend?'

You could hear his heart sink over the phone. The boy's lost for words. As a rider I'm the diametric opposite in style to William, and John knows that. 'Ah, Michael ...' He's anguishing, I can hear it in his voice. 'I know the way you ride ...'

I'm about to put him out of his misery when he says, 'You know what? I said I would lend it back and if you genuinely need it I will send it to you.'

Come practice he turned up with the bike himself. And

he stayed to watch. He wasn't there to see me – he just wanted to make sure his bike survived. I think he followed the race through his fingers, he was that scared. When we got red flagged he said, 'I've never been so happy in my life to see a race stopped.'

He never lent it again. But fair play to him for honouring his word.

Like I said, people couldn't do enough for us. But there were some problems too big for anyone. My dad handled all the money side of things, paid all the bills, ran all the accounts. The Monday after the funeral I went into the bank on my mum's behalf to get some cash for her, but this geezer in there says, 'I'm sorry, we've closed Mr Dunlop's accounts.'

'But that's my mum's money.'

'Well, it's not in her name.'

'Come on,' I say. 'We've just buried our dad. There's only a couple of grand in the account and my mum needs it.'

'That's your problem, not mine.' He genuinely said that. Actual quote.

I walked to the door and I says, 'Before this is over, my friend, you will know who I am.' I was sick. In my mind I was going to torch that wanker's car. Who says what he did to a customer who's just lost their dad? When I calmed down I vowed that if I ever made any money, his bank wouldn't see a penny of it.

So that was virtually Day 1. Day 2 through to Day 100 didn't get any easier. We didn't just lose Dad's race winnings and his income from the steel side of things. It was a treble whammy, because William and I worked for him, too. That's where our contribution to the family bills used to come from. Now that was gone as well. Uncle Jim was in the same game, so he started to throw me work when he had it, but honestly there wasn't enough to go round. Outside of the TT, race wins were only worth around £350, sometimes less. Unless you won you didn't pick up enough to pay for a set of tyres. If I came home breaking even I'd done all right. I really found that period difficult. I couldn't see a way out. I had no job, no dad and no hopes.

That's when Martin and Maria saved the day. I will never forget it. Martin came to me and says, 'I'll not see you starve but this is all I can do for you right now', and he handed over a cheque for several thousand pounds from his own pocket. He says, 'Michael, that's not for going on bikes, that is for you. I done the same for William. I just want you both to get on your feet.' For me that was the turning point, that man. I knew then there was a light at the end of the tunnel. At the very least, it put the fight back in my belly.

We got through summer on Martin's money but I knew I needed to find some work sharpish. Once again one of my sponsors stepped up. Unfortunately for me it was Gary Ryan.

Gary's business, Street Sweep, did pretty much what it said on the tin. He swept streets. He said, 'There's a job with me any time you need one.'

I really didn't fancy it, but beggars can't be choosers, so I drove to Dublin and he put me in one of his wagons. Lucky I'm thick skinned. As I pulled away in that cart, I floored the bastard – and we hit top speed of 1 mile an hour.

Ah, the shame. I'm the fastest Dunlop in history, it's

official, and a baby can overtake me on its knees. Pyramids were built quicker, I promise you.

At least it was paid work. I'd stay down there a couple of nights, putting in every hour under the sun – and occasionally under the moon too. Gary is a great man but he is a horrible person to work for. He used to ring me every day at 5.30 p.m. and with his whiny southern sing-song accent go, 'How're you doing, lad?' and it did my head in.

He rang me one day and says, 'I just want you to stop there now on the way home and trim that man's yard for half an hour.'

'Gary, it's five-thirty.'

'It'll just take half an hour. I'll give you an extra thirty minutes in your pay.'

'You promise?'

'Guaranteed – an extra half an hour.'

'Deal,' I says.

Two o'clock in the morning, I'm still there. And the bugger knew that. But he knew once he'd got me there I'd finish the job no matter how long it took.

The liberties the man took and he'd laugh when he did it. He worked me like a dog.

Every penny I got from Gary was going to keep the house and everything ticking over, but I was still racing when I could afford the fuel. Some weekends it was touch and go. One day I was coming home from Dublin and there were some roadworks up the street. Typical builders, there's no one on site, so I pulled over, got a tube out of my van and syphoned some diesel out of one of the diggers. Every day for a couple of weeks I did that. I kept my van going for months, although the roadworks seemed to take forever.

I was burning out, I was that busy juggling work and the bikes. Then one day Gary says, 'I think you should be finding something else to do. This work is no good for you. What were you thinking?'

And that's the boss talking.

So then I got into tipping lorries, and from there I began to dip my finger in all sorts of pies until I wound up doing a bit of building. Anything to keep the wolf from the door.

People out there thinking us road racers live like Valentino Rossi, think again. The money in my sport is a fraction of what that side of racing makes. When you aren't winning it's even less. Suddenly the TT wasn't just about winning trophies, it was about winning cash.

I couldn't wait.

The following year, 2009, was a big one for me. Thanks to Gary's funding, I was building up my old R6 in the garage. Then Gary came to me one day and mentioned that one of his lads was using one of his new R6s on the short circuits. It made sense to us both that I should give the lad mine and take on his. We'd give them back at the end of the season.

It was pretty good straight from the box. At Cookstown we had an all-right run, not perfect, but then at Tandragee we beat Keith Amor and Ryan Farquhar on his Kawasaki. Ryan was the boy to watch on those circuits. I also got wins in the 250 and 125 on my Hondas. On the Yamaha I got a seventh in the Junior Open and the 250 came in tenth in the Open. Going to the North West, I was a happy camper, really getting into the groove. I just needed to address the elephant in the room.

Returning for the first time since my dad died could have been an issue but I didn't let it become one. The media as well as friends were going on about it but I put the blinkers on, I would not engage. I was there to ride a motorbike. I'd done my tribute the year before. That's the way I approached it.

On Gary's R6 I got pole for the Supersport race as early as Tuesday, which caught a few boys out. Steve Plater and Keith Amor were two and three. William was sixth. When it came to race day I knew I had the win in me as long as nothing went wrong. I was quick off the line and was dicing for the lead with Plater, Bruce Anstey and John McGuinness. I knew if I got to the final lap in second I'd take it, but suddenly there was a crack and I thought I'd been shot. It was the screen. It had snapped and as a result the bike just lost all drag. It felt like we'd actually lost power it was that bad. I was a bit disheartened coming in third to say the least.

It wasn't all bad news for the Dunlops. William got a personal monkey off his back by winning the 250, the race he'd broken down on last year. He added the 125 for good measure. Dad would have been proud.

I was a bit disappointed about the whole meeting, to be honest with you, but at least ability-wise I felt things were pointing in the right direction. Heading off to the Isle of Man I actually believed we had a chance. And not just on the Yamaha.

In more than a century of racing, the TT has seen a lot of legendary riders and equally legendary marques. At the start of that year I was contacted by some boys running a new Norton team. My dad used to ride a Rotary back in the day, so when they offered me one for the Superbike race, I snatched off their arm. What I didn't appreciate was how many other people would care. Heading into the Isle of Man there were all sorts of journalists and media people wanting a comment. The press thought it was big news: Dunlop rides a Norton. I agree; I just never saw it coming. PR and that are not skills I've spent much time acquiring. It's another world to me.

When I went out for practice on the NRV588 there were snappers everywhere trying to get a picture. People were that buzzed at the sight of a Norton again in those parts. I'd not laid eyes on this bike before the fortnight started. Unfortunately, she looked a beauty but she ran like a beast. I don't think we completed a single practice lap before she gave up on me. There were problems every session. The owners are pulling their hair out so I says, 'Look, if you get her ready for Saturday race day I will ride her, practice or not.'

Sadly, there was too much work to do and we retired the idea of racing the Norton. In it's place Gary found an R1.

Brilliant as it was PR-wise to have the Norton with us, my focus as far as potential victories went was on the Yamaha in the two Supersports. Those are the races I felt had my name on.

First night of practice, no bother – I got into it. Bruce Anstey went quickest, with me close. I went fastest the next night, Bruce the following night, the night afterwards it was me again, and the night after that I broke the lap record. *Boom*. And that is when folk started to realize that I was there.

One boy says, 'We've got another Dunlop on our hands.'

Another one says, 'Aye, he's not a complete wet dog, then.'

I'm sitting there thinking, *You lot are going to have this.* I was that confident. It was like my time at the Manx GP. I'd known then I had the win in me. And I knew it again now. I was already the fastest in the family around the course. The stars were aligning.

Then the next night the engine blew up.

Talk about anti-climax. We got the spare engine in and Gary stitched it all into place. It was that good a job my dad couldn't have done better. Now we were ready to race.

The first event is the Superbike. We got the replacement R1 out, prayed to the mountain gods that the bad luck from practice had vanished – and then broke down. We didn't make it out of the first pit stop. I was more annoyed than disappointed. But I wasn't surprised. Not after the practice week we'd had.

Not a problem, I'm thinking, *we've got the first Supersport next.* I says to Gary, 'This is the one, boy. We're doing this.'

It went to plan. I put the bike on pole and come the race I was that pumped you could have sent Wladimir Klitschko out with me and I would have bossed him. I was ready to go.

I don't remember being more excited at a start. I fly off the line, then *squeak squeak*, and she blew herself up. She was in bits, in ribbons. My God, the mess. She put her crankshaft out through the front of the bike. I was gutted. But, game face on, we had four laps of the Superstock to follow so my luck had to change.

It didn't. Another race, another failure.

Afterwards Gary and I went and sat in the back of the lorry. I was devastated; he was in pieces. He'd paid for everything to give us the best chance. No victory is guaranteed but the Supersport in particular had been as certain as you can get. My pole lap proved that.

'Ah, Gary,' I says, 'where's it going to end? Three starts, three DNFs.'

'I don't know, boy. I don't know.'

I tell you now, if we had had a rope we wouldn't have needed anything to hold it because I'd have been hanging off one end and he off the other, we were that suicidal. We were like two kids whose Christmas has been cancelled. The tears were dripping off our faces when Gary's wife walked in and said, 'What's wrong with you two?'

'The 600 broke.'

Oh, did she kick off. 'Look at you, you couple of wankers, sitting there blubbing like kids over a stupid motorbike. Sort it out or sort yourselves out.'

Chastening words are all very well but we had no engines. Not with us, anyway.

We're sitting there feeling sorry for ourselves and Gary says, 'What about your old bike?'

'That's a completely different spec,' I says. 'And it's in Dublin.'

'Do we have any other option?'

'No,' I answer. 'I don't think we do.'

It was decided. However slim the prospect of it working was, getting my old Yamaha sent over for the second Supersport was our only option.

The bike arrived the next day and we worked like dogs through the night to get her ready to race. I was that stressed during the day I took up smoking – for a day. I was standing with Gary by the car, and when he lit one up his face took on a look of such calmness that I did it, too. It was horrible. But it took my mind off the problem.

Cigarettes will only get you so far. Sticking that 600

on pole calmed me a whole lot more. Still, what did that mean? Four laps, 150 miles. What were the odds that our third engine would get any further than the others? To make matters worse, the track was damp, so the start of the race was put back. I think in later years they stopped running races in these conditions, that's how bad it was. To me it was just another competitor to overcome. And I love competition. By the time we finally lined up to go, the old mojo was back. Maybe it was back too much, in fact, because Gary told me to calm down.

'Look,' he says, 'watch yourself out there. It's not worth pushing in these conditions. We've got plenty more years to get this right.'

I looked that boy right in the eye.

'I promise you I am not doing this again. I'm not coming all this way, putting all this effort in, for no return. This is it, boy. This is the year or not at all. One way or the other, Gary, I'm gonna finish this today.'

And I meant it. Another failure and I was walking away, if not from the sport, then the TT.

Straight out of the box everything felt right. Glen Helen, I'm sliding all over the road but I'm leading. Ballaugh, I'm touching kerbs but I'm leading. Ramsey, I'm leading. Start/finish, I'm leading. First it's by ten seconds. Then it's fifteen seconds. Then it's twenty.

I knew exactly where I was because there was this wee fella holding a board when I exited Greeba. First time round it had 'P1 +4' written on it. I couldn't believe it. They were my stats: I'm in first place with a four-second lead. He's not part of my team or anything; I didn't even know his name. He just took it upon himself to help me out. I think breaking the lap record during practice must have got his attention, or maybe it was my name, because he didn't do it for any other riders. And the thing is, he still does it to this day. I sometimes see him in the pits and he'll give me a clenched fist and say, 'Go on, good luck.' Another boy, Phil, does the same thing in the mountains. Amazing really. They're just guys, like so many others in my career, who just want to help out. And they're all invaluable in their own way. Every success is built up of tiny parts. Like an engine.

Anyway, thanks to this boy with the board, the excitement was building in me as I came round on the last lap. I knew all I had to do was keep it on the road and that would be enough. One slip and Bruce, Steve Plater or Conor Cummins were ready to pounce.

Somehow I hold it together. When I take the chequered flag I've won by thirty seconds, achieving an average speed of 125 mph. The record was 126. *And I did it on my old bike.*

Joey Dunlop: twenty-six TT wins. Robert Dunlop: five TT wins. Now add Michael Dunlop to that list.

Is there a better feeling than winning your first TT? I've never known it if there is. Coming across that line I felt like a man with three dicks in a knocking shop. I didn't know what to do first. There was that much adrenaline, that much excitement, I was struggling to coordinate my arms. My head was gone. This was the feeling I'd wanted for so long and I couldn't grasp it.

Or maybe it was just relief kicking in. I swear, if that bike had broken down, Gary and I would have drowned ourselves on the way home. We would have jumped off the boat. You'd never have heard from either of us again.

I wanted to kiss that bike but what I didn't want to do was a victory lap. I just wanted to hit the pub and drink one for the old man if he was looking down. They even had to drag me up on to the podium.

The way the TT works is that after a race there's a podium presentation where you get the garland around your neck, a kiss on the cheek from a model, the bottle of fizz and then the huge TT trophy for the photos and everything. It's a beautiful thing and it is big. You collect your own private flying lady at an event at the end of the week.

Sometimes podiums can be a fractious place if you've had a coming together with someone but this was as pleased a trio as I can remember. Bruce was second, Conor third. It was Conor's first podium, I think, so he was happy as Larry. Neither of them liked the damp conditions as much as I did. A lot of the Isle of Man is under the trees, so you can't see what's wet and what isn't. You can't even see if it's standing water sometimes. I ride the line I want and deal with what happens when I get there. Other boys are more sensible. It was like racing my dad and William again. I was just prepared to risk more than them. Or, as Bruce puts it, 'You were mental out there.'

People were over the moon for me. I tried to soak up the moment and make the most of all the cheering faces. It wasn't just spectators down there whooping and hollering. There were marshals and stewards joining in as well. In their eyes it wasn't just me on that top step – it was a Dunlop. The most famous name in the sport was back in the spotlight.

And I wanted to stay there.

But first – the party. I don't know how I got away with it but I refused to let that massive trophy out of my sight. In the end the organizers sent a security guard out with us. He was like a gooseberry on a date. I'm sitting on the grass with my drink and my trophy and he's hovering in the background. We got so wrecked I lost count of the toasts we drank to my dad. We even missed the presentation ceremony that evening. They had to drop my little lady round by the lorry.

I broke down again on Friday in the Superbike race, meaning at the end of the week it was four out of five DNFs on the Mountain Course, which was pretty shitty. The only people feeling worse than me were the Norton boys and those fans desperate to see the old lion roar again. A couple of second places in the Lightweight category the next day on the smaller Billown Course went some way to repairing the mood in camp. But as far as I was concerned there was only one number that mattered. And that's the one on the trophy: 'First'.

FOURTEEN

I Ain't Gettin' on No Plane

WHEN YOU ACHIEVE YOUR BOYHOOD DREAM there's only one option after that: you have to walk away, retire. Live happily ever after.

Well, you do if you're Nico Rosberg. He won the 2016 Formula 1 World Championship. Then he quit. Why'd he do that? Because he says it's been his dream since he was nine years old to win that title like his dad did and now he's done it. He never dreamed of winning two or three or seven like Michael Schumacher. He had one target, he achieved it, time to move on. Clean break.

Did it cross my mind to retire when I won my maiden TT title? Did it hell. Rosberg's old man set the bar pretty low by only winning the one title. Mine got five. Uncle Joey got twenty-six. Even in 2009 I'm thinking, *I'm not leaving this sport until I am worthy of being spoken of in the same breath as those two*. I was only twenty years old. I had a lifetime to catch those boys up.

Winning's addictive. It's like speed. The faster you go, the faster you want to go. The more you win, the more you want to win. I had a right old party when I got home from the Isle of Man, but even as we were unpacking I was thinking of the following year. I wanted another trophy. I didn't want my little winged angel getting lonely, now.

In the meantime I'd just have to feed my addiction elsewhere.

You wouldn't know it from the noise I was making about that first TT win, but I wasn't the only Dunlop on the island that year. William was over as well and not to help me. After his year off he came back and quietly went around doing what he does, getting a solid ninth, an eleventh and a twelfth in all the races I was busting out of. That's us all over, I think. I will fly or burn. William is so smooth; he never lets you down.

Our other brother is something else entirely.

Daniel is the one that nobody knows about. He's a phantom, a figure of the imagination some people say. Nobody outside the family knows who he is. He is just Daniel.

I don't want to make him sound more interesting than he is, because that's not what brothers do. But after the TT, I was buzzing and he was showing no interest. The next month I'm loading the Transit ready to go to a new track in Armoy, about eight miles north-east of Ballymoney. It's about 7.30 in the morning.

'I'm going with you,' Daniel says.

'You what?'

'I'm going with you. To Armoy.'

'Er, okay, if you want. But you won't last two minutes.'

Because Daniel had – and still has – no interest in bikes. It was only because our cousin Adam was down that he was even going near the circuit.

'Shut up and get in the van,' he says.

Ten minutes later we're approaching the circuit and we hit a bit of traffic near the course. Right on the left-hand turn into the start/finish there's a barn that's turned into a pub for the event. As soon as he sees it Daniel's got the door open and he's jumping out.

'See you later, dickhead,' he says.

Blimey, I'm thinking, *he's really going to watch motorbike racing.* I never saw that coming.

Armoy is a nice little meeting. I parked up, got ready and went about my day. I got a win on my Honda 125, beating Nigel Moore, Wayne Kennedy and Cousin Sam. In the Supersport I came third behind William and Ryan Farquhar's Kawasaki. Ryan got me again in the Open on the same bike, this time Guy Martin separating us. I finally got another win in the 250, leading William, Guy and Davy Morgan ahead of Ryan, so not a bad day's work, by any means.

Everyone's heading for the barn pub afterwards and, as I walk in, spectators are slapping me on the back, congratulating me, the usual business when you've had a bit of success. I head to the bar to get the boys a round and there's Daniel on a stool next to our cousin.

'All right, dickhead?' he says.

'Aye,' I says. 'How're you doing, Adam?'

'Grand.'

'How'd you go today?' my brother asks.

I says, 'What do you mean, how'd you go today?'

He says, 'How did you get on?'

I says, 'I won a couple.'

'Ah, very good.' And he goes back to his drink.

I'm not having that. I says, 'How come everyone else in this place knows how I got on except you? Tell me you haven't been on that stool all day.'

'Where else am I going to go?'

'The track is just there. You could have stuck your head out once. I went past the door a dozen times. You could've touched me.'

'Why would I want to watch that crap?'

He's a rare one. Not a tiny bit of interest in motorbikes at all. He didn't even ask how William got on. It wasn't personal. He couldn't give two hoots.

I had various wins and near misses the rest of the season. The Ulster Grand Prix is always a good one with the big bikes there. I got a third in the Supersport after some wheel-to-wheel stuff with Ian Hutchinson and Ian Lougher. Ryan took first place. But I could only manage a seventh on my R1 in the Superbike. Guy Martin was untouchable in that one.

He's a funny lad, is Guy. He started getting a wee bit of TV fame in 2009. Some cameras followed him around the TT and he'd been a natural on the screen, fair play to him. He'd go on to become a household name for his programmes about boats and speed and stuff. But here's the thing. You mention the TT to non-racing fans and they think of Guy Martin. He's become the face of it because he's the one on TV all the time and people know of his association with the bikes. But how many TT trophies has he won?

Lots of people have one or two and you never hear of them. The big hitters like Mike Hailwood, with fourteen, or the boys with eight, nine or ten – you'd know their names. But lower down, there are people who you never hear of who've won four or five TT races – which is a real achievement, believe you me – yet you *do* hear of Guy Martin, who's won precisely none.

For someone who's not a particularly successful TT racer – who is good without being great – he seems to have done very well as a TT racer, if you know what I mean. His fame from elsewhere means people assume he's had more success than he's actually had.

Don't get me wrong, he's a decent racer. He's beaten me enough times and he's paid his dues. There've been enough bones broken in his body to settle that score. And before he became Mr Speed you could have a real good conversation with Guy, one to one, no bother. He's into his cars, his engines, that sort of thing – basically the sort of crap I like to talk about. V8s and V12s, we chew the fat on all that and the hours fly by. I have a real good time with him. We're a couple of men, we're equals, we've both been through the wringer. But as soon as there's a sniff of an audience he changes. That's why he's a natural for the screen, I suppose. He starts pulling facts and stories out of his arse and playing to the gallery. Every person listening magnifies his bravado to the power of fifteen. He's a nightmare for that at press conferences. Guy's made a few bob, though. I'll give him that. So I guess it works.

The downside to the money is the fame. Sometimes you look at Guy and think, *That man is tortured.* He can't even have a piss in peace. People think they know him and want a piece of him. In 2009 I already knew a bit about that myself.

The problem with sticking your head above the parapet is that people start to take an interest. Winning the TT a year after doing what I'd done following my dad's death got me a bit of press outside of Ballymoney. Wherever I went I started to get strangers calling out. It's nice, I like it, because most of them are friendly. But there's always a few who are wankers and they ruin it for everyone else. I had a man at one of the smaller races shake my hand, then tell me I was a shit rider because I put other people in danger. I think he called me a cheat.

That leaves a sour taste, and the very next time a lad tried to stop me I carried on walking. I expect, now, he thinks I'm an arsehole for that.

The internet warriors are the shit stirrers. But I can ignore them very easily. The ones who get in my face are harder to walk away from. I went into a pub shortly after the TT and there's a crowd of lads, maybe thirty of them, all having a laugh. One of them recognizes me, so I'm bought a pint and people are talking about the racing and the craic. But I know, from experience, that in a crowd that size, especially when alcohol has been taken, there will be at least one wanker who resents me somehow, who won't be satisfied until he's told me how shit he thinks I am.

And I was right.

He comes up and says, 'You're only famous because of your name.'

Here's the thing. Even if he truly believes that and even if he's right, where's the boy's mother to tell him not to be rude to strangers? Would you go into a butcher's shop and slag him off for his family name? Pick a fight with a lollypop lady, would you? You probably see her every day, more often than you see me. Why don't you tell her what you think of her?

My problem is I find it hard to walk away. That boy in the pub just wanted to look big in front of his mates. Believe you me, he didn't when I'd finished with him. But other blokes come over with their fists clenched, like they want to snap your head off. That is not a good thing to do to me. My fuse is like a Black Cat Banger. You only have to strike the matchbox and I go up. There is no warning. I will smash anyone before they can smash me. And I have done. I've probably lost a few genuine supporters in the process. But I'm not in racing to put up with shit like that, just like I'm not here to kiss arses.

There's no knowing what kind of shape I'm going to be in in ten years' time, but I have to be able to look back on my career and say I enjoyed it. And I won't if I have to go around being fake to idiots. I know people who raced motorbikes who get genuinely upset when they find someone who doesn't like them. They want everyone to love them, so they put up with all kinds of shit. I believe you have to be happy with the decisions you've made in your life. If, hopefully, I do get out of this business scot-free, I need to be able to stand up for the choices I made. And I believe I can.

Although on the track that's a wee bit harder.

There were certainly some questionable choices at Killalane. It's a nice little meeting and you get plenty of action. Farquhar pipped me in the 600 and again in the Open race, which got my mettle up. In the 125 we scored a Dunlop hat trick, but again I was second, this time to William, with Sam behind. In the Grand Final I'm thinking, *Not this time, Ryan*, and for one glorious lap I'm pulling away from him like he's got BO. It's a beautiful sunny day, there's not a drop of moisture on the track. There's no reason why I won't go on to victory.

Then I go too wide, clip the grass and I'm flying.

If I'd taken Farquhar with me it would have been me and William all over again.

I have to say, I love riding. Anything and anywhere. The shorter the race, though, the less I get from it. I still enjoy these on their own terms, but my life is about the TT. That needs different skills.

I was determined to take another step forward the next year. Another win, maybe two, that would do me nicely, get me established among the players. What I really didn't want was the embarrassment of only completing a couple of laps out of a possible twenty-odd. It all depends on the equipment. So that year, 2009, I started combing around for the tools I needed.

Gareth Robinson, of Robinson Concretes, had a real good Honda Fireblade, a great Superbike. It had all the fancy stuff. I wasn't riding anything in that sort of line. Couldn't afford it. This is a 50k bike if it's a penny, all paid for out of his own pocket. A Superbike that came with its own mechanic.

We went to Skerries to give it a run-out. It was a bit of a handful to be honest. We struggled – the chassis gave me trouble. Then we went back to the Isle of Man, to the Southern 100. All the big boys were there and I really felt we had a chance. When I got going I knew we did. The only thing that could beat me that day was me.

Which duly happened.

I got done by my own stupidity, that's the long and short of it. I was hyperactive being at the front, surrounded by boys who knew what they were doing on those kind of machines, boys like Guy, Ryan and Conor. This was his year. To have him behind you, that's a win in itself. I was starting up front, so I say, *I'm getting stuck in here*, and I did. For most of the race it worked. We had the bike running just so, no problems on that score, and I tore through the lap record. I was so bent on making my mark that I ran too deep in one corner, which took me too deep into the next one, and *bang*, it's all over. I didn't fall but I might as well have done, because those boys are past you in a heartbeat. I was that eager at leading that I missed out on winning. I wanted to get to the front so much that I missed out on taking the race. A salutary lesson, you'd have to say.

It was no surprise to anyone when I announced that I'd be riding for Gareth in 2010. That was the big news: that I'd be riding the Fireblade 1000cc in the Superbikes. But I had a full plan for the year. I'd formed a relationship with a boy called John Brown at Hunts Motorcycles and we did a deal that I would get a Honda Fireblade off him and build it up for the Superstocks. Gary weighed in with a couple of R6s for the Supersports. For the smaller races, as and when, a boy called Derek Wray from D&GW Racing had my two-stroke needs covered. It was the full complement, and I was equipped for anything. What happened in May and June that year, however, would determine whether we'd done enough. I couldn't wait to find out. But first I had a bit of personal business to sort out.

When my uncle died, the council of Ballymoney erected a memorial garden in his honour. It was a lovely mark of respect to the man who'd done so much for the town. When my dad went, there was a movement to get the same done for him. For some reason, the council dragged their heels, so it was actually donations from the community, with the council chipping in, that got a memorial to Robert going.

On 8 May 2010 we gathered in a little square oasis next to Joey's garden. It was packed, with hundreds more people gathered along the road craning to get a peep. Mum, me, my brothers and my gran were centre stage – or as much as you can be when there's a sheet covering a large object. After a few words the cover was removed and there was my dad, the 'Mighty Micro', captured in stone. It's a decent likeness, I have to say. I thought the whole day was incredible. To see all those people turn out to celebrate my old man gave me goosebumps. And knowing they'd dug into their own pockets to help pay for it was mind-blowing. I didn't know most of them from Adam but they'd done more for me than some people I'd call friends.

It was a perfect day in many ways but there were one or two dissenting voices. The loudest of them was my gran's. She couldn't fathom why her boys weren't in the same space. From the road you had my dad's tribute on the right and Joey's on the left, behind a high hedge. She got so taken by the idea she wrote a letter to the council, which was printed in the paper.

'Why?' she kept asking. 'Why can't my boys be together?'

The thing is, not all of the family agreed with her.

There are two sides to every story. Where my gran and plenty of the rest of us wanted the Dunlop boys to be together, other members of the family were only concerned about Joey. That's not a problem. In their minds, it would have seemed sacrilegious to alter Joey's memorial from how it was originally intended. It would be an insult to his memory, they felt, if contractors were trampling all over that sacred ground while mourners were trying to pay their respects.

You have to see both sides. What I can say is the row tore a hole in the community to some extent and overshadowed the beautiful unveiling ceremony. It wasn't the best preparation, either, for what I had planned a few weeks later.

The petty squabbles back home were forgotten the moment we arrived in Douglas. This is what my whole last twelve months had been gearing up towards. Now it was crunch time.

Unlike the previous year, we got off to a flyer at the 2010 TT. In the first Superbike race I came second – the highest I'd ever been on a bike that big. It wasn't quite a win, but I did get a 130-mile-an-hour lap in. That was all the rage at the time. 'Can you do a lap that fast?' We were peaking, and

I was dribbling at the prospect of the rest of the week. Aye, being the first of the losers is frustrating, no question, but I felt we were on an upwards curve. As long as the next race earned me a place better, all would be fine.

The 600 was going well, the Stock was going well, everything was going well – so well that I was disappointed when I only finished third in the first 600 race. It was my own fault. There was a wee issue and I couldn't get over what it might be doing to the bike. It was making something of nothing but when your life is in the bike's hands – and my dad is the perfect example of that – mechanical aberrations play on your mind. Afterwards we stripped it down to get it ready for the next race and identified the problem. Annoyingly it was nothing major. I'd taken my foot off the gas for nothing.

I knew I had to make amends in the Superstock, and it started well. I was leading in the first lap, definitely up the front, I was having a go. Then, second lap, she blew a tyre. That is a kick in the face. I knew it was going off, I could feel it, and this time it wasn't my imagination. There's nothing you can do to stop it, but at least you don't get thrown, and I came in eighth.

Wednesday: the second 600 race. I was nailed-on favourite for this one. In my own head, anyway. Nothing I saw in practice told me that I would not be ending the day with my second flying lady. I could almost taste the beer of celebration as we lined up.

There was nothing wrong with the bike and I ran well. But it seems there's always a new problem waiting to find us. This time it was the yellow flags. If you see one, you have to slow down and be prepared to stop. I did that; I respected the rules and I believe it cost me the win. I lost a lot of time because some people weren't backing off for the flags as much as others. That's ridiculous and dangerous and selfish. When marshals flag you because of an accident, they need the respect. It's proper clear. If marshals don't think we obey the flags, they won't be in a hurry to get over to help in an accident in case they get hit.

I came home second to Ian Hutchinson. The team was that gutted that someone actually put in a protest. It wasn't me; I know you can't change history. There was a lot of huffing and puffing, and the world and its mother gave a statement all saying they'd backed off and it was outrageous that some folk hadn't. I believe one rider was fined, although the name was never released. I know who it should have been but, as with a lot of these things, it was swept under the carpet.

It's sickening, it really is. I broke the record on the last lap and what have I got to show for it? There's no trophy for that. All it proves is that I was fast enough to win the race, but to cut a long story short, I didn't. My press conference after that race showed exactly how happy I was.

So now it was all on the Fireblade in the Senior TT. I'd right had enough by then. With two second places, which I considered should have been wins, I was determined to ride the wheels off Gareth's machine. It wasn't to be. We broke the crank and so ended the meeting in the most disappointing way possible. Big smashes for Guy Martin and Conor Cummins put the loss into perspective, but it still hurt.

A lot of boys would be happy with second, second, third and eighth. I couldn't find it in me to be one of them. I wanted trophies, not excuses. Hutch was sitting there like the cat that got the cream, with five of the things. I wanted that. I believed I was capable of it. I believed it should have happened that year.

I was scheduled to ride the Superbike again at the Bush Irish National but, what with one thing and another,

I didn't feel we were ready. We made it out to Skerries, though, and took a third behind Ryan and Keith Amor. Not what I wanted after the disappointment of the TT but at least it didn't break down.

Going back to the Billown Circuit for the Southern 100 I knew we had to start converting near misses into hits. And big hits, too. In the first race we did it. Ian Lougher was the only boy who came anywhere near me. Ryan, on an identical bike, was more than half a minute back in third. I got a couple of other wins, as did William, then came the big one. The main event: Race 10.

This is the one everyone cares about here, like the Senior Superbike race at the TT, which is why I was so mad keen to get it. I had a bad start, but caught the leader – it was Ryan, surprise, surprise – inside a couple of laps. If he'd been in any sort of form, that shouldn't have happened so quickly. But I was burning through those laps. I had him in my pocket, of that I was sure. I'm sitting behind and I'm literally wondering not if, but when, I'll take the lead and grab the title.

Cocky? A bit, aye. But I'm twenty-one years old. I think it's part of the job description.

Anyway, I went into a right-hander in second gear and she locked the back gear. I put the clutch in and she spat me over the handlebars and towards the wall lining the road. I was doing about 130 mph when I took off. There were bales of hay against the walls and somehow I landed with my head between two of them. My helmet crashed into the wall but the force of my shoulders hitting the hay bounced me back on to the road – back into the path of my own bike, which gave me a nice wallop.

It's two seconds, if that. One moment you're here, the next you're over there. Or over there. You're a spectator of your own demise. It's too fast to do anything about it, but it's slow enough that you know that it's not over. You're in the hands of the gods. They'll decide when it ends.

When you have a fall like that, it takes a while to come round. If you're lucky. I opened my eyes and stared up till I recognized I was looking at the sky and not the gates of St Peter. There's a little roll call you go through. I counted my eyes, I counted my ears, my arms, my legs, my brain. My whole body was in excruciating pain but I know from experience that's good. It's when you can't feel something that you have to worry.

As I lay there, I remembered seeing my dad in a similar position. I wondered if some fella would come along and think that I was on my way out as well. I had no idea how serious it was but I could feel it wasn't good.

Suddenly I was aware of a helicopter overhead. There's not much in this life that I'm afraid of but those things are top of the list. I'm an engineer; I know exactly how temperamental machines can be. And those machines are not even natural to start with.

As it landed nearby, I remember thinking, *I'm not surviving this crash to be killed on one of those death traps.* In my head I was doing the full B. A. Baracus: 'I ain't gettin' on no plane.'

When you're ill, when you're desperately in need of medical attention, you don't have much to bargain with. But I made it clear to the air medic that, as grateful as I was for help, the only way I would be leaving the circuit was on board something with wheels. Eventually he agreed and an ambulance – one without rotors – took me to hospital, where they said I'd broken ribs and the bottom of my back. There's not much you can do, plaster-wise, about any of that, so as soon as the white coats finished yacking I signed myself out. Nothing good ever happens in a hospital. Not in my experience, anyway.

At least I was in better shape than the bike. I felt like I was in bits; that Honda really was. Somebody carried the front forks, somebody carried the frame, somebody carried the exhaust pipe. It was a mess.

I was dreading seeing Gareth. That was fifty grand of his own money down the toilet – there's no insurance on these things, not for what they get used for. In fairness to him, he was as good as anything about it. I don't know how else you can react if you've given a bike to someone who rides at 200 miles an hour. But I did feel bad. Inside and out.

I don't know if it was the injuries but the rest of the season kind of fizzled out. None of my results at the Ulster Grand Prix were of the calibre I care to remember. But at least the circuit never insulted me. Unlike the Mid Antrim 150.

William and I have supported the small circuits since the early days, when you're just another entry fee for an event. After you achieve a certain level of success you become more of a draw, and the organizers ask you to do press conferences and the like to drum up interest. If I have the time I'm always happy to do whatever's needed. I even put the hay bales out one year. Without the little races there are no big ones. That's my view. You have to support your industry.

So, 2010 I send off my application to the Mid Antrim. William does the same. I'm looking forward to it, actually. It's only two miles up the road – I get to sleep in my own bed at night. They rang me looking for an entry fee and I said, 'No problem. How much are you looking for?'

They said X amount. Not scandalous money by any means. Maybe 150 quid.

I says, 'No problem. I will sort it out today.'

Then I heard a whisper that Ryan was getting free entry. Now that put a different perspective on matters.

I am always straight as an arrow. I call it as I see it. And what I saw here is, if everybody else pays, I pay. No problem. I've won at virtually every circuit there is by this stage. William's the same – we were winning internationals. We were two big names if you want to look at it that way.

Part of me was thinking, *It's fine, it's only £150, just support your local race.*

But the other part was going, *What's Farquhar got that you haven't?* – and on this occasion that part of me was speaking louder.

I rang them and said, 'You're not charging Ryan but you want to charge me and William? Two local lads as well. That is not going to work for me. Everybody pays entry, *I* pay entry. He gets free entry, *we* get free entry. It's very simple. It's got nothing to do with money; it's just pride and principle.'

The boy says, 'Ryan isn't getting free entry.'

'Well, then we have a problem, because I know he is.'

So the boy says, 'Don't bother coming then.'

'Okay, that's fine by me.'

I rang William and told him the score. I said, 'I'm not going, what's your feeling?'

He says, 'I'm with you.'

So we didn't go and we have never been there since.

They ring every year. They plead and they beg. The club fell apart three or four years after that and all the people there started dropping each other in it. Obviously the truth came out: yes, Ryan Farquhar was getting free entry.

My race year was over but there was a wee glimmer of happiness back home. In November the Ballymoney Borough Council voted to join my dad's memorial garden with that of Uncle Joey.

My gran did a jig she was that happy. Linda promptly removed various items of Joey's from the Ballymoney museum in protest. I didn't want to get involved but I will say the council did a sterling job. They cut a hole in the hedge and constructed a TT winners' wreath out of metal to form an archway linking the brothers. It's clever actually, beautiful even. And it was a constant reminder every day I drove past it that I had unfinished business with those wreaths myself.

Next year, I swore, *I'm not coming back empty-handed.*

FIFTEEN

We Need to Make This Right

AH, CHANGE THE BLOODY RECORD, MAN.

Coming into 2011 I was plotting with Gary how we were going to mount a proper assault on the TT and I realized I'd heard the words somewhere before. From me. And him. Last year and a year earlier.

'We can't keep going in circles just doing the same old things,' I told him. 'We have to make some changes.'

What we were able to alter was limited. We were basically a two-man outfit. I drove and built up the engines the best I could. Gary did logistics for the entire operation, supplied the 600s and was the entertainment on race weekends for everyone who gave their time to help us out in the pits. At least that, we decided, was an area we could look at. The team I'd run for in 2010, Robinsons, was going to fold, so a couple of the lads I'd worked with, Neal Eakin and Tommy O'Kane, agreed to join us. Tommy was your boy in the pits, on wheels, tyres and tyre warmers. Neal was more on the mechanical side, so he'd help with the engines.

The thing that would help me most was if someone else built up the bikes so I could concentrate on riding them. The obvious avenue was to get a factory deal, as with all the big boys out there. McGuinness is 'Mr Honda'. All he has to worry about is pointing the bike in the right direction. Honda take care of the rest.

I'm not sure I had the kind of reputation that would sit well in the corporate world. Being known as a bit of a hothead off the track and a wild dog on it kept me just enough under the radar, I would say, to be left alone. That suited me. Even at twenty-one years of age – and before that – I considered myself my own man. The only fella who could tell me what to do died in 2008. I wasn't necessarily looking to give my autonomy away that lightly. Imagine if I couldn't say what needed to be said at a press conference one day in case it annoyed some boys in Tokyo?

'No,' I says to Gary, 'rightly or wrongly we need to concentrate on making Michael Dunlop Racing as strong as we can without giving anything up.'

The big change for us was bringing in Kawasaki. We didn't get a deal with the factory or anything – we weren't in that league, nor did we want to be tied to corporate responsibility. But we did the next best thing.

Paul Bird over in Penrith was building a 22-carat reputation on delivering high-end Kawasakis to boys in all different formulas. Gary got us over there for a chat at the start of the year and I was mighty impressed looking at the ZX10R that Tom Sykes rode in the World Superbikes. Birdy had also done the bikes for Chris Vermeulen, Joan Lascorz and Stuart Easton over in the BSB championship. We struck a deal whereby Gary bought a bike and Birdy would run it for us in the North West, the Ulster GP and, of course, my beloved TT. We are talking a full-bells-and-whistles machine. Brembo brakes, Paul's bespoke PBM swing-arm, K Tech suspension and a WSB quality engine – you name it, if it was on Easton's bike we had it.

For consistency, Gary got us another ZX10R to be run in the Superstock, but I'd be looking after that one myself, with help from Nick Morgan and Jeb Cobbold.

On paper then, we were raring to go in the big leagues. I couldn't get through the early meetings quickly enough. We did all right on the smaller bikes, just finding our feet and getting the odd win. My focus was on May, though, and the North West. If it went to plan this would see us put down a real marker for the TT.

We weren't the only boys making changes. The NW itself had streamlined its operation, getting rid of the 125 category, which in my eyes they would never have dared do if my dad were still competing in it. They extended the race lengths for the five big bike races they had left, though, which I did support. The more miles the better as far as I'm concerned. I'm there anyway; I might as well ride.

The omens were good – for me personally if not for the meeting. I put the Superbike on pole but come the race I couldn't get it to perform. Alastair Seeley got the win on his Suzuki. I came fourth.

We should have had four more bites at the cherry but everything that could go wrong did go wrong. The weather was a bastard, so that claimed a lot of races. Then some idiot phoned in a bomb scare, which finished off the rest.

That was a new one on me. I'm not a superstitious person by nature but the number of crazy mechanical issues I'd been collecting over the years was beginning to make me feel like I'd run over a cat at some track. I was just relieved the bomb scare only screwed over my team.

All in all, we arrived on the Isle of Man knowing about as much about the ZX as we'd done in January.

I'm a fast learner, though. The first Superbike race, we did okay. According to my pal with the board, I was holding steady in fifth when I came into the pits, but everything there took a bit too long. The next time I saw my board I was well down. *We've got a job on here.* For the next four laps I threw that Kawasaki around like a Rottweiler with a ragdoll. Lap after lap we clawed back a bit more and a bit more and a bit more until I crossed the line ... in fifth. Exactly where I'd been coming into the pits. It was an exhilarating ride, I'll admit; just a bit of a kicker to finish where you started.

I had higher hopes for the first Supersport. The R6s Gary had given us were top notch, and in practice I was playing them like a fiddle at a wedding. Bang, off we go, and for a lap it could not be more obvious that the win is ours. I'm already thinking of my new little trophy to keep the other one company back home when cough, cough, splutter, splutter – and it's the same old story.

Back in the pits I'm distraught, I really am. *Who does a boy have to sleep with to get a win round here?*

I'm putting it out there. I could be an obnoxious brat, like lots of twenty-two-year-olds, but I had talent to spare, I firmly believed that, and there was a lot of evidence to back that up. I was competing in my fifth TT and, by my calculations, I should already have had five or six wins, not just the one. It was pissing me off. It made me wonder how the hell Joey ever got into double figures, let alone to twenty-six. At this rate I'd be 103 before I got anywhere near him. In fact, sitting there with just one victory in twenty-five-odd attempts, you think, *How the hell did Dad win five?*

Race 3 was the Superstock. Time for my version of the Kawasaki to show its teeth. My best big bike result to date was silver medal and I was desperate to go one better. I got off well but Guy Martin, rebuilt after his accident, and John McGuinness were the boys. They were older and wiser and more experienced in the big categories, and it showed. They both pulled away. But that ZX, let me tell you, was humming. She could have carried a tune in a choir and I was not going to let that go to waste. I'm pushing and pushing and by the end of lap two I've done enough to scrape ahead. But Guy is a bloody pain. Every time I see the boards, I'm barely clinging on. His TAS Suzuki is there or thereabouts every inch of the way. It's only on the final lap I begin to break him. When I cross the line I know I've been in a battle.

Afterwards I wondered whether my little pep talk with myself had played any part or whether it was just one of those things. It wasn't the first race by a long chalk in which I'd had the tools to pull off the win, but shamefully it was only the second time I'd managed to convert potential. The fact I'd done it on a bike I'd put together myself got the old chest puffing out a bit. That I'd done it in the dry was also a big thing. My first win had been in the damp. For my money, conditions like that separate the wheat from the chaff. Others don't see it like that. Wet conditions equals a lottery. If you win you're just lucky, not necessarily the best. So to stick two fingers up to the wankers who decried my achievement gave me a Ready-Brek glow.

But most satisfying of all? I'd broken my duck on the big

bikes at the most demanding course in the world. Now I really was a Dunlop.

Gary's Street Sweep branding was all over the red and green Superstock, which I was pleased about. I hoped its association with the R6 would bring us better luck in the second Supersport but in fact history repeated itself. I was leading again but ended the day another DNF in my ledger. You try not to get up yourself, you try to remember how much one win would mean to 99 per cent of people. Yet all that's going through my head is, *Should have been three wins this week, not one.*

In the final race it was time for Birdy's version of the ZX to see if it could match mine. The racer in me hoped it would. The engineer was maybe a wee bit more on the fence, at least till we got underway. I got a sixth, so another solid result, and it was the fastest Kawasaki out there, but I was never really in this one.

Coming home an owner of multiple TT trophies is a good feeling. You feel you belong to the club a wee bit more. Like your membership has been upgraded from 'admission only' to 'platinum card'. But I knew I could do more. I'd won on the Supersport and now the Superstock. To gain access to the inner circle I needed that Superbike victory and I needed it badly.

The rest of the year the big bike started to come into its own. I went to the Southern 100 and, I have to say, if I'd got the same results at the TT I could have died a happy man. My Kawasaki came home first in Race 1, ahead of Guy

Martin's Suzuki – again. In third and fourth place were two bikes from the Wilson Craig Honda outfit, relevant to me because one of them (the one in third) had William on it. He'd decided to go with an established team rather than shout into the wind on his own like me, and it was paying off. The resources he had were incredible. A real network of support. The only downside is having to share it with a teammate, in his case the Aussie Cameron Donald. I see bikes as an individual sport. I want the focus of my team to be on me. *How else am I going to win?*

Guy got me back in the Seniors race but it was my turn again on the 600s. William split us. The one we all wanted, though, was Race 10: the Championship. I'd never done it before. If I was ever going to, that Kawasaki was the beast it was going to be on. All I had to do was beat Guy Martin.

Some meetings you go to and it's higgledy-piggledy: this fella's winning one race, this fella's grabbing the next. There's no story, no narrative for the spectators. Other times, like here, there're only two players in town: me and Guy. He was a real thorn in my side. I was getting sick of the sight of him, either in my mirrors or in my face. Whatever I did he was there. No wonder his sponsor was Relentless.

One of us would win the Championship race. There was no question about that. And, as it turned out, it was me by a 'massive' four seconds. In a nine-lap race, that's close. It topped a meeting that will stay long in the memory because, not only did I run well, but there were also no stupid mechanical failures like I kept getting at the TT. It was so refreshing to attend and win a meeting with no controversy. Unfortunately, that luck was soon to run out.

Straight after the Southern we headed out to Kells. Fresh from winning around the Billown circuit on Gary's R6 I was confident of doing it again up the road. On paper it looked like William had other ideas. The behind-the-scenes story is a wee bit more juicy.

It was wet, which I was fine with. We go off and, early on, it settles into two races, with me, William and his teammate Cameron Donald in one bunch, and the rest further back. William was riding really well that season and I think Cameron's nose was getting a bit more out of joint with every meeting. There were rumours of friction in the team, but I can't possibly reveal my sources.

I've never got the teammate logic. Everyone for himself, in my book. But blood is thicker than a contract. I was comfortable in third, waiting for the moment to take the win. It was only a matter of time, no fear about that. Suddenly I see Cameron make a move on William, which I felt was a stunt straight out of my book.

In other words, it wasn't very nice.

We're all racers together but I got a bit angry over that. I'm thinking, *That's my brother, you prick. I'm going to sort you out.*

I felt I had the capacity in the bike, so I move up and do exactly the same move on Cameron that he'd done on William. *How'd you like that, you dickhead?*

I'm ready to let it go but later he passes me again and swipes across my front wheel. I knew if I carried on schooling him I'd be letting William walk away with the win, but sometimes you have to do what's right.

And sometimes what's right is pushing a bastard right up against the hedge as we're going at 150 miles an hour.

Was it dangerous driving? It's less dangerous than crashing, which is what he nearly caused both William and me to do. Did I make it clear that if he pulled another trick like that he and I were going to have problems? Yes, I think I did.

With two idiots playing chicken behind him, William took the win a fag paper's breadth ahead of me. Cameron was back five or so seconds.

After the race I'm sitting on my bike in the paddock, doing a wee debrief with the boys, and the next thing Cameron's there and he rides into the back of me. My bike goes over, I'm nearly underneath it, but what really sticks in the memory is that manager of mine, Gary, leaping up to stop Cameron's bike from toppling over.

I says, 'Gary, what the hell are you doing? That's your bike he's just knocked over.'

Knocking me in the back? That's a coward's move in my playbook. And keeping his helmet on when he did it just underlined it. But if he hadn't been wearing it, his ears would be in different places by now because I leapt on that boy and I was smashing his helmet with my fists. One, two, three, four – five massive punches. I got through the visor. One more go and I'd have found his nose even if it meant cutting my own hand. But then his mechanics were suddenly on top of me and I was hitting out at them until my own boys dragged me off.

It's not in my nature to rat somebody out, even if they have tried to run me over and nearly broken an expensive bike. Other people aren't so principled. Before you know it, the girl who ran Kells had been told all about it and was ringing the police – to get *me* arrested. I was the victim, I have witnesses. But they made up some stories and she believed them. I don't think she liked me for some reason and I believe she actively tried to get me banned. The next day I was nice as you like to everyone. They hated that. They don't know how to respond.

I didn't think much more about it until just before the

Ulster Grand Prix shortly afterwards. I heard from a reliable source that Cameron Donald's boss, Wilson Craig, would be arriving all lawyered up with the intention of getting me thrown out for what I'd done, allegedly, to his boy at Kells.

That posed me with a problem but I knew a boy who knew some boys who happened to be two of the biggest barristers in the country. I explained my situation, outlined my lack of financial clout and asked if there was anything they could suggest.

'Forget the money, Michael,' one of them says, 'we're coming over to Ulster for the craic.'

So there we are: Wilson Craig lands with two solicitors, as rumoured, and I pitched up with two lawyers. Wilson's none the wiser but as soon as his lads see mine, it's over. Those solicitors recognize my boys as two of the most shit-hot legal brains in the country and they decide to go for an honourable retreat. Wilson disappears like he's never seen us and that's the end of the matter. I can't say it was plain sailing with Cameron after that, but life's too short to care what other people think.

William could have been in a tricky position but he enjoyed the craic as well. He saw me landing blows at Kells and decided that, rather than help either of us, he'd work it up into an after-dinner story. Typical. There have been many nights over the years when I've been out with William and he's having a drink, having a laugh. But on more than one occasion he winds some boy up and before you know it there are punches to be thrown. But the second they are, he's gone and muggins here is the one left swinging. William's definitely the thinker in the family. Me, I act first and try to dig myself out of it later. In life and on the track.

Lawyers aside, the Ulster was a mixed bag for me. In the two 600 races it was just me against William, that's what it felt like. From about halfway on in each of them it was like he and I were glued at the spokes. We were dicing and splicing the whole way round, wheel to wheel, brother versus brother. Each could have gone either way but I passed him both times on the final lap. I'll never forget it. That's how close racing should be done.

My trusty Superstock also did the business for me, but once again it was the Superbike that, I felt, let the show down with its reliability. Come the end of the year one thing was clear. Failure was not an option.

After a lot of head scratching and heart searching we decided that, for 2012, we'd go our own route again and try to build our own Superbike. Gary thought we'd be best served returning to Honda stock, so with John Hunt's help we got a Fireblade road bike for me to build up.

It looked good on paper but in the garage it was a different story. We were too late getting going, I think. I'd never built a Superbike before and each hurdle that I'd step over these days was a big obstacle back then. The worst thing is that Gary and I stopped seeing eye to eye on how to solve them. It cut me that we were turning on each other when the enemy was out there.

It was a good bike. Fair play to John Hunt on that score. He gave me all the help I could want. But that last leap in performance was just out of reach for too long. By the time the TT came round we just weren't where we needed to be. When you're an independent, running three bikes is hard enough anyway, but when one of them isn't pulling its weight things get really difficult.

I get asked a lot about being a privateer in such a commercial business. It suits me now, it suited me then. I like being the boss. If I need something, I get it; if I need someone, I get them. Succeeding on your own is harder than succeeding in a factory outfit, but the rewards are greater. You might not get the trophies you deserve but you can't tell me it's not more satisfying winning on a bike you've built yourself. At the start of 2012 I believed that more than ever. As June came round I wasn't so sure.

I knew in practice that I hadn't had enough time on the Honda to get it to where it needed to be. After a lot of anguishing we made the decision to start the first Superbike race on our own Kawasaki. Under the circumstances, tenth place is half-decent. In the first Supersport I genuinely thought I was on for my third win. I was riding well enough and the bike had been hard as nails for so long, but a rare failure put us out. Gary was more gutted than me.

Neal had got my Kawasaki purring like a pussycat in time for the Superstock and I managed to get on the podium behind John McGuinness. There's no shame in following that man across the line but, three races in, the realization that I could be going home empty-handed yet again was beginning to weigh heavily on my shoulders. Knowing that the other Supersport was next and that the R6 had already let us down once didn't exactly fill me with hope.

But what do I know? I took the flag as the quickest racer out there and went back to Martin's house the proud owner of my third flying angel.

Sometimes you only need a bit of luck to get you going, and I thought that win would see me right in the Senior Superbike race, but bad weather saw it called off. A fifteenth in the reintroduced lightweight category rounded off an up-and-down week.

Our van on the way home was like Groundhog Day on wheels. On the one hand you're celebrating a win. On the other hand, you're frustrated there was only one. It's a story we'd heard again and again. Frankly I was sick of it.

'Boys,' I said, 'we can't go on with one win here, one win there. We're better than that. We've got to make this right.'

A possible opportunity for how we were going to put things straight had come up, but I didn't tell the boys. Not immediately. I didn't even think about it properly myself.

Once again the Southern 100 was better to me than the TT had been. Our Fireblade finally got a win. Two, in fact, leading up to the big one. Once again Guy Martin was there trying his best to ruin both. He kicked me by a couple seconds in qualifying and, on the day, both could have gone his way. Gary's Yamaha did the business again in the 600 races. By the time Race 10 came around, we couldn't move for trophies. But there's always room for one more and at the Southern 100 that one has to be the Championship trophy. Guy was once again the only thing between me and victory, and I just managed to get by him to make it a full house. I also set the fastest lap and new course record. All in all, not a bad end to the week and hopefully the kind of form I could take to Ulster.

Arriving without lawyers was a bit of a comedown from the previous year but I guess I decided to provide the drama myself. My Honda, in its black McAdoo/Hunts livery, was up to the task. The weak link was between my ears.

After our clashes around Castletown, I knew I had the measure of Guy Martin and his Suzuki that year. It didn't matter to me if it was a factory bike or not. We'd finally got the Fireblade singing and she was hitting all the right notes. The first Superbike race, in my eyes, was a mere formality.

Guy was buzzing like a blue-arsed fly. He did a bit of a move on me at Jordan's Cross. He pulled over in front of my front tyre. I don't know if he was just trying to rub my shoulders or what, but I said, *Right, you're for it now. I'm going to show you what it feels like.*

I don't take it personally. Not unless my brother's involved. I just think, *Okay, that's the level we're working at, is it?* I give as good as I get. I can race clean or I can go over the top and take everybody out. Sometimes somewhere in the middle. This was one of those times. For now.

I did virtually the same move back on him, but Guy's tough. He just passed me again. Every time I passed him he had a go at me, and got me back. He passed me, I passed him, he passed me, I passed him. We got into such a rhythm that I could predict exactly what he was going to do. The problem came when he made a mistake.

Normally his line into the hairpin was clinical. It never deviated. So as it's coming up again, I'm thinking, *You're for it here.* I know where I'm going because I know where he's going. Except he doesn't. For the first time in the race he gets out of shape and goes wide, and suddenly the move I have in my head isn't going to work because he's not there.

Normally, a boy's error is the time you pounce. But I'm all over the place anticipating the wrong thing. The racer's instinct in me said he needed to be punished for his mistake but another voice was saying, *There will be other chances. Other races.*

Which one do I listen to?

No decision. I pull alongside Guy to go round the inside but there's not enough time to brake and the front just goes. *Bang.* Goodnight Vienna.

We dragged the bits back to the lorry. You could see the handlebars and footpegs were write-offs for a start. Neal would strip her down and see what else needed fixing before the next race.

I was annoyed with myself. I thought I'd outgrown the petulance that had marred my earlier years. But no, some things never change. I had a point to prove though, to the boys and Guy. In the next Superbike I played the percentages and took the win. In the Superstock my Kawasaki did the business.

Ulster showed me I still had the capacity to mess things up for myself without anyone's help. The only thing worse than doing it there would have been if I'd done it at the TT. Looking back, my record of poor decisions on the island was a bit too long for my liking. Like I'd said to the boys coming back in June, I needed to stop messing around and get consistent wins. Single victories here and there weren't going to cut it any more.

I knew it was time to make some changes, and big ones. And I knew by then what those changes needed to be. The question I asked myself was: *Do you have the balls to do it?*

SIXTEEN

Big Man and the Bear

WITH SO MUCH HAPPENING ON THE CIRCUITS it was hard to get my head around to sorting my home life. Things in Ballymoney since my dad had gone had been shite and had only got worse. A lot of dice rolled at once and none of them were sixes. Being older, Daniel and William had moved out of the house when they found girlfriends. Daniel joined the army soon enough. While I'm fannying around on the Isle of Man he's on the frontline in Afghanistan. They had their own lives, basically. Mum and I love each other but we're too alike to be alone in close proximity for any degree of time. I can be stupid and say things without thinking, and so can she. Some days it was fireworks for breakfast, lunch and tea.

Ultimately, we were both scraping away in the same direction to keep the bailiff from the door. After Dad went, a whole load of crap came out about his financial situation. He'd built the house from his 1994 accident's payout, but then a so-called friend had persuaded him to make some investments and he'd mortgaged the house to do it. After his death, we spent years in legals trying to get to the bottom of it. The long and short of it is that Dad's money disappeared in dodgy deals quicker than you can turn a TV off. Unless you had a jerry can of petrol and a lighter, you would not see money disappear as fast. It was a con, start to finish.

Knowing how close we were to defaulting on the mortgage every month, especially added to the fuss over Dad's memorial, was tough, and Mum took ill. Lawyers looking into the finances stretched their bills across years, not weeks. I knew I needed to sort things out, once and for all. In the back of my mind I had a plan. It was risky, for everyone involved, but needs must.

Honda approached me at the end of 2012. Not a Honda dealer, not a mechanic, not a boy with a Fireblade in his yard. The actual factory team that my Uncle Joey had driven to greatness with. Obviously there's a lot of history between my family and that marque. But working with a factory team? After all the effort I'd made to stand on my own two feet? Would it look like I was giving in if I agreed?

We went backwards and forwards, to and fro, and eventually I decided to look at it like this: the thing that had let me down at the TT more than anything was reliability. If you can't bet on a factory Honda, what can you bet on?

Like a lot of owners, they only wanted to do the big

internationals with me, which was fine, because I had my own 2012 bike for the rest and I'd have some freedom to be my own boss for most of the year.

We built a team up between us. I kept my own boys; that was important to me. The fellas from Robinsons were already part of the furniture and Martin had done my fuel since day dot, so that wasn't going to change. Honda supplied their lads, Adrian Gorse and Graham Parker. They travelled everywhere with the bike. They brought it to me, spick and span, ready to go. Any hiccups and they had a whole factory to fall back on.

Machine-wise we had our Honda 600 Stock, our house Superbike, supplied by Hunts, the Superbike from Honda, plus the various 600s. Despite my reservations, I felt good about it. When I went to the North West and won in what, I think, was the only wet race they've ever done, I was actually a bit sad it was on the Supersport and not the big bike. I was even more gutted after I qualified in pole on the Honda Legends TT, then was forced to twiddle my thumbs and wonder what might have been when, frustratingly, the actual race was cancelled due to bad weather.

The North West wasn't the first time I'd ridden the Honda. In March I'd gone out to Miraval in France and Albacete in Spain to test-drive the wheels off it. I could tell right away that it was going to take some beating. If both Honda and I played to our strengths, I could see a very golden future in the short term. While I was over there I also tested Honda's EWC bike. It made sense, considering I'd agreed to become the reserve rider for their endurance season that year, which dovetailed the road races. Places like Suzuka in Japan were being mentioned as race-day destinations. I thought, *I could have a bit of that, no bother.*

Everything before the TT is the dress rehearsal. That goes as much for the North West as it does for test-driving around the Med. I began to appreciate that better with every year that passed. And this year I was looking forward to the main event more than ever.

The biggest change at the Isle of Man, for me, was having teammates. John McGuinness is seventeen years older than me. I was seven when he did his first TT. The man's a legend around the circuit, second only to Uncle Joey in terms of number of wins. You'd have to say, he's got every chance of overtaking Joey if he sticks with Honda, and he'd deserve it. But it was a rare experience for me having someone sort of on your side but sort of your closest rival as well. I'm not saying it was hard, but the man is 'Mr Honda'. He knows everyone, he's like the king of the team. I felt on the back foot from the start, like I needed to work twice as hard to be judged equal. Michael Rutter was there as well. They both ran at the North West until rain stopped play.

In theory we all had the same bike, but we had our own mechanics, so there were probably different bits and pieces. I worked with John but not overly. I had my own team for more races than not, so I'd be over at Honda when I needed to be, then back with my boys the rest of the time. It's quite mercenary when you think about it. Go over, get the job done, go home.

If I'd never jumped on the bike before, I'd have expected a few gremlins. But after days of testing in the sunshine I knew every inch of it. Yet it decided not to work now. Why? Practice on the Superbike was tricky – it was nothing like I remembered. There was this wrong or that wrong. The boys got it patched up each time but it was frustrating, especially when your teammates were bombing around at full capacity.

By the end of the week we finally started to perform. I was fastest in practice, nudging 131 mph the second day, so come race day I was anticipating a procession clinging on to my coat-tails. It's been a while since I said it but I really was the boy to beat.

On paper, at least. When we were getting ready to actually race, Honda blindsided me. All that stuff about us having identical equipment might have been true. But to commemorate one of Joey's anniversaries they'd decided to kit out one of their riders in his livery, from chassis up to helmet, gloves and leathers, you name it. What struck more than one person as a little bit odd is that I wasn't the rider they asked.

Gary is never one to hold back. 'They've got a fucking Dunlop here,' he says; 'did they forget?'

It's weird, yeah. I don't know what else to say. John was a teammate, so that's his connection. But I'd have felt maybe a wee bit fraudulent if I'd been asked to dress up like the McGuinness family and John hadn't.

I had to believe there was nothing sinister in it. Just one of those PR things that didn't get thought through properly, and of course John was never going to say no. He's a big fan of my uncle; of course he wants to honour him. But it was disconcerting, more than anything, seeing this Tribute Act to the King of the Mountain – my uncle – lining up alongside me to start the first Superbike of the week.

I had one goal that week and that was to break my duck on the Superbike. I'd won on Supersports and Superstocks. To be considered the complete rider, or anything like it, you need to cover the spectrum.

Just before I pulled my visor down I say to Gary and the others, 'Right, boys, it's time I shone here today.'

And, to cut a long story short, I did.

There's hardly any story. I went away at number 6 and I never looked back. I was in such harmony with the bike that everything I thought, it did. Without wishing to sound too wanky, I wasn't just riding it, I was part of it. By the end of lap 1, according to my mate with the board, I was three seconds up on Guy. The pit stops went precisely to plan; there really was no drama. Even when I broke the 131 mph mark, I never felt I was on the edge at any time.

By the time I took the flag and found the middle step on the podium I had to put things into perspective. I'd won four now, and I'd completed the set. I deserved to be considered in the same frame as McGuinness standing next to me, but also, more importantly, as the man he was impersonating.

My God, it felt good.

I'd had a fair number of race meetings, though, where the end of the week fizzled out. I had no reason to believe this one would be the same, but it remained a possibility if I didn't wring similar performances from my other bikes.

For the Supersport I had put a new team in place in an attempt to recreate what the Honda boys were doing with their bike. Simon Buckmaster was my guy, and he brought with him two boys he trusted: fellas called Stan and Mark – although they were known solely as Big Man and the Bear. They all knew their stuff. We already had a great bike supplied by John Brown of Hunts, but what they prepared was class: it never missed a beat. Despite some serious opposition from Bruce Anstey and, I'm pleased to say, William, it was no surprise to me when I won my second trophy of the week and my third in that class. I also broke the lap record that I'd set the previous year.

Now, this is more like it.

My third race was the one that gave me the biggest worries. My Stock bike was not, in fairness, the one you'd choose power-wise. I was the only Blade rider in practice to get anything like a tune from one. Gary Johnson had a ZX10R Kawasaki, which I knew all about, and, to be perfectly honest, I'd rather have been straddling that than the shop Honda. On lap 1 Gary led. On lap 2 Gary led. On lap 3 Gary led. As we started up the mountain for the final time I was still a fraction behind. But by the time we came back down, I'd done enough. The Fireblade hadn't let me down and I picked up a third winged lady – and another lap record to boot.

When everything's falling for you it's tempting to wonder when it'll end. Or when you're going to wake up, more like. Going into race 4 I was confident, of course. My 600 hadn't let me down yet and I was the record holder in that class. But Thursday is different to Tuesday. You never really know what goes on with bikes when they're left alone, but sometimes they definitely change. I'd only get a true picture of whether my Supersport had changed for the better when we started the warm-up.

Once again, wily Bruce Anstey was the man to beat. We traded lap after lap, nicking fractions of a second off each other as we went. When I crossed the line I literally had no idea whether I'd done it or not. We'd been that close. I was reminded of my Manx debut at that very circuit, and not being sure of my position until I was waved over to park behind a sign with my placing. Back then I'd had an inkling. This time, not so much. It was genuinely 50/50.

Only when a marshal finally directed me to the board marked 'First' could I finally relax. I'd won by barely two seconds – and I'd broken my own lap record.

The final race of the week, the Senior TT, was a tricky one. The weather was turning and as comfortable as I am in wet conditions, I knew if it got too bad the race would be cancelled and there would go my shot at history. Luckily we got away but it was flagged off after I'd been leading. There had been an accident on Bray Hill involving Jonathan Howarth. When we restarted I again rode well and had it all to play for until a slower-than-usual pit stop allowed John McGuinness to jump me.

Normally I'd be happy – well, happyish – with a second place in the Senior TT. But after four firsts, that second stuck out like a wobbly tooth. *I suppose I'll get over it …*

Say what you like about Honda, they give their boys the tools to do a job when it counts. There were one or two teething troubles at Ulster but I'd trade every single little race for a win on the Isle of Man. The truth is, by June, July, I'm already plotting my 2014 campaign. Me and Honda are the team, we're the Batman and Robin, the Mario and Luigi, we're going places. *This is just the beginning.*

But then I remembered my principles.

I'm not at liberty to discuss in great detail what happened, but essentially John McGuinness was being paid a shitload more money than me. I got my race money from the wins plus a wee salary and small bonuses, whereas his retainer was massive, I believe. In 2013 that hadn't been a problem. I'd gone into the deal with my eyes open. But after the year I'd had, especially compared to John, I felt I was due some parity. It was like my argument with the Antrim 150 all over again. I couldn't countenance being in a team in which I was treated like a poor relation. Poor relation I might have been to Joey, but not to John, no offence. I wasn't asking for the same as him – he'd been there forever – just a nudge towards it.

It's a hard gig when you have principles. Honda had given me the tools to have the kind of TT that I'd dreamed of. The level of success that I thought I deserved. Yes, we'd fallen short in the Senior but, based on everything I knew about the team, there'd be an even better chance of winning the following year. Not surprisingly, that voice of reason I often heard when I was racing, the one that advised not doing anything reckless, was piping up large.

'Don't throw it away, boy. It's only money. This team is where you belong. Do you want TT wins or don't you?'

Of course I did. That's why I raced. For the last few years that's the *only* reason I'd raced.

The other voice, the one that always says, *Go for it if you want to win*, was loud as well.

'Who do Honda think they are? They won't find a better rider than you.'

I'm not a madman, but two conflicting, equally logical ideas will drive you crazy eventually. I knew the risks: I knew full well I might not get a Superbike as reliable or fast as Honda's ever again. I also suspected they knew that, too. As Gary said, 'They know you're not going to throw it away. They know they're the best team for you.'

Which is why I came to the decision I did. There was no other choice.

Shortly after the season ended, your man from Honda announced to the world I wouldn't be racing for them again. He said he was sorry and that they'd offered me two or three deals and I'd rejected them. It's true, I did.

But what he didn't say – and what nobody knew at that time – is that it wasn't just my relationship with Honda that was over. It was my relationship with the sport.

At the end of 2013 I decided to hang up my helmet – for good.

SEVENTEEN

A Man's World

MY WALKING AWAY FROM THE ROADS was nothing to do with money and everything to do with money. Aye, I was pissed off at Honda but I realized they were the tip of the iceberg. The things on my mind would sink the *Titanic*.

The problem, I have to admit now, is that I never dealt with things as they crept up on me. Maybe if I'd told Honda what I needed more money for, they'd have struck a deal better suited to my needs. Because I wasn't after big bucks to spend on booze and birds. I just wanted to keep a roof over my ma's head.

In 2013 our time ran out. The bailiff knocked on the door and said the banks had claimed back the house. It was a shitter. Mum was alone when they came. I'd have lamped them if I'd been there, even if they were just doing their jobs. You don't terrorize someone like that. We had to pack our bags and get out. As simple as that. We both found little places that weren't what you'd call 'home'.

I let the problems build up, I know I did. When I was

racing I was doing so well that the real world didn't touch me. I ignored the shit going on with the house, with Dad's estate, his memorial, everything. It was denial, plain and simple. The debt collector was ringing every day but while I was on track he couldn't touch me. He couldn't get into my helmet. There was no phone in there. But at the end of the year, when I took the helmet off, it felt like the floodgates had opened – as though I'd been Moses parting the Red Sea but now it was all about to come crashing down.

And there wasn't a thing I could do.

I was lost to the point that I didn't know where it would end. There were all these things going on and I was just being worn down from every side. It starts gradually and then builds up. When so much stuff is punching you at once, it's very hard to see anything positive between the blows. When the Honda thing fell through, I couldn't actually be bothered fighting any more. I couldn't see any light at the end of the tunnel.

I didn't realize it but racing was my crutch. My enabler, I think you'd call it. I had reached such heights in 2013 that below was a long way down. And I fell all the way without a parachute.

I never spoke to anyone about what I was going through. I'm a man in a man's world. The only person I could discuss things with, apart from my dogs, was myself. I've never told a soul about any of this before now. I'll be interested to see how it goes down. I can't be the only man who's felt everything slip away yet not care enough to stop it; the only boy who's felt like he was in the eye of a hurricane and just wanted to curl up and hide.

As soon as the Honda news got out, my phone started ringing 24/7 with offers of bikes for 2014. Because I'd never told anyone I was retiring I had to go through the motions, putting people off. I began to pick up less and less. One day I stopped answering the phone altogether. I couldn't be bothered to lie anymore. Whatever they had to say, I wasn't interested.

At some point the media must have started speculating on my future, because then journalists started ringing and emailing and texting. Social media went a bit overboard with predictions and theories. I sort of acknowledged them without taking them on. It was like I was reading about someone else. I was finished with bikes. They'd find out in my own good time.

At the start of 2014 things were bleak. I'd sold my bikes or locked them away. The banks were putting Mum's old house up for auction. There was nothing on the horizon worth looking at. I just wasn't interested.

Still the phone kept ringing, though. I'd ignore the calls, then look at numbers. I noticed one number kept calling. For days on end it kept ringing. Eventually I picked up.

'Michael?' said a surprised voice.

'Aye.'

'It's Stuart Hicken from Hawk Racing.'

'Oh, aye. You used to work with my dad.'

He was with Dad during the accident in 1994.

'Listen, Michael, are you riding a motorbike this year?'

'No.'

'Why not?'

'I can't be bothered, with everything going on.'

That was the truth.

'Will you meet me if I come to Ireland?'

He was in England.

'Stuart, I don't mean to be disrespectful, but no, I wouldn't be up for that.'

'All right,' he says, 'I will ring you back in a week.'

Seven days later, 'Will you meet me now?'

'No, Stuart.'

'Okay, I'll ring you tomorrow.'

And so it went on.

'Will you meet me now?'

'No, Stuart.'

'I'll call you again.'

So he keeps calling, and I sometimes answer but mainly I don't. He's persistent, though. He keeps asking to meet me. Eventually I just agree. It's been months since I've said the word 'yes', but I say, 'Okay. If it gets you off my line.'

He flies to Belfast but he's not alone. With him is a boy from BMW.

He says, 'Michael, we've got a bike nobody is willing to ride. It's an unproven package, but we think you're the man. It is seventy-five years since BMW has been to the TT. Will you ride her?'

Ah, God, not this again.

'Stuart, no. *No.* I'm sorry.'

I fully expect him to say, 'I'll call you tomorrow', but he doesn't. He gets devious.

'I worked with your dad, you know,' he says. 'He was a great man. If he could have ridden this bike ...'

'Stuart, no. No. You're not guilt-tripping me. I'm going home.'

I'm in the door no more than two minutes and my mobile rings. At least I can put a face to the man monopolizing my phone lines now.

'Are you going to ride this bike for us or not?'

I hung up.

I don't know if it was leaving the sofa that did it, or what, but I found myself thinking about BMWs, of all things. The season was about to start. The North West was around the corner, which meant the TT wasn't far behind. I hadn't thought about bikes for months but just the image of those two little letters sent a little spark of memory into my brain. I might even have smiled. If so, that was also a first for a long while. There was no great transformation. I just began to think of something other than my cloud.

The following day the phone rings again. To his eternal credit Stuart never once sounded jaded, as well he might have done after so many attempts.

'Are you going to ride for us?'

I hear myself say, 'I might have a run on her, aye.'

For once the man is silent.

'Well, you're too late,' he says, 'but we'll have it ready for the North West.'

'Hey, I only said I'd ride it. I don't want to actually race the thing.'

'Don't you worry, you'll be grand.'

And that is how I got back into bikes. It all snowballed from there. Other things were beginning to sort themselves out as well. Our old house hadn't yet sold at auction and I wanted it to remain like that until I could get some cash together to make my own bid. Some acquaintances of mine offered to run interference. Both were exactly the types who could turn up at an auction house and make sure no one bid on a certain property. Just from their appearance when they walked in, people knew who they were, or the type of person they were. You knew not to bother going against them. If someone had done so, the whole event would have been sabotaged, so nobody would have bought the house. If any prospective buyers made it as far as the actual property, we made their visit hell, no problem.

Eventually the bank lost patience with the lack of bids and I was able to get the house myself.

My dad's legacy, the house that Robert built, was staying in the family.

It was an emotional time. Apart from the bikes, that house was our connection with our dad. Over the course of a few weeks I felt a bit of light beginning to shine in my head again. The light at the end of the tunnel, I suppose. And I can trace it all back to Stuart pestering and pestering me. He got me angry, he got me irritated and eventually he got me interested. And that's all I needed, to be interested in something again.

Who knew cold callers could do such good? But he saved me. Certainly my career. He doesn't know it, but he did.

Mum was happy to have the house back in the family on principle – *that word again* – but she didn't want to live there any more. It was too big and there were too many memories of Dad, so we found her a nice, smaller, place she could rent and make her own. As for me, I took a slice of the old grounds and decided I'd follow in my dad's footsteps and build my own home. I rented out the main house to pay for it.

It would take a couple of years but I loved getting out there, personally taking every job as far as I could then getting the experts in to finish it off. The skills I learned. I can't think of anything more satisfying. When it was finally ready to move into, the first thing I did was put my

TT trophies in pride of place on the wide mantelpiece, all seven of them. They looked the business, but there was space for plenty more.

Could I achieve it without Honda? Had I been stupid to walk away from the best Superbike I'd ever ridden? Was it too late to go grovelling back to them?

Doubts will do for you in the end. Sometimes you just have to trust yourself to do what's right. *I'm finished with Honda. I'll either make a go of it with Stuart or I won't. If I don't, I'll find someone else.*

I went to Cookstown, as per tradition, to test the water, see if I really did have what it takes to keep going. We did enough to make me think, 'Yes.' When the North West came round I was looking forward to seeing what the Hawk/Motorrad BMW could do on a larger track. Stuart was bouncing around like he'd a pogo stick up his arse, he was that excited. The BMW boys just looked quietly confident.

The bike was fast, no question, but the way the power was distributed was not pleasant. It had potential, I could see that in practice, but in its first race I spent a lot of time fighting the spin. I was struggling, to be frank, but the whole business of retiring, then being persuaded to come back for this bike, started playing on my mind. Maybe I was regretting not being on the Legends TT. Anyway, I'm not thinking straight. How else do you explain nearly chucking it all away just to make a point to your brother?

William was riding a Tyco/Suzuki, the same as Guy, and

he was riding it well. It was wet and I was struggling. Me and the bike were like dance partners that had never met. We're both trying to lead. I got a terrible start and after that it was about trying to stay facing the right way as much as reel in the boys ahead of me. As we went on and with a few miles under my belt, I got a bit of a feel for the BMW and, before long, it was just William ahead of me. Going into Metropole on the last lap I thought, *Coming, ready or not ...* and I got myself past him and into the lead. In my head this was it, game over. The big homecoming, the grand two-finger salute to Honda and all my doubters who said I was nothing without them.

Nobody told William that. We're that close the rest of the lap the crowds are going nuts. Along the Coast Road we're in formation like the Red Arrows. I still think I've got it in my pocket when we get up the top to the chicane and he goes past.

It doesn't matter. We're on Juniper Hill and I spy a chance. A small one. There's a wee gap up the inside so I go for it.

And William slams the door.

Now, I've done that move to enough people, but not my brother. By the time we finished my blood was boiling and when I saw him in *parc fermé* I let my frustrations out.

'I would never have done that to you,' I say.

I instantly regretted it. In my own mind I've made this grand gesture to come back to racing, I'm expecting red-carpet performances from myself, I want to make a statement to the world that I don't need Honda, and it hasn't worked out like that. William's won and he thoroughly deserved his first international success, but it wasn't part of the script. Not my script. It's hard to explain. The cameras were all on him, not me. But the second the words left my lips I knew I was out of order. Obviously when he came across me he'd had no idea I was there. I know that now. I knew it then. But I still said what I said.

Genuinely, deep down, I was happy for him, I still am; he earned it. I was just cross with myself, I was looking for someone to blame for my failure and I took it out on him. But I never told William that. His drawbridge went up. He saw a side of me he didn't like, a side he didn't know, maybe didn't trust, and that ruined the rest of the meeting between us.

I wish I could take it back. He's my brother and I'd do anything for him. But actually it was a long, long time after that before we got ourselves back on track. Thankfully everything is fine now but it goes to show how one stupid remark can cause damage and pain.

I managed to get my head together and somehow salvaged the rest of the meeting.

I got the Superstock win; then, into the last Superbike race, it was dry and I was on a mission. I remember saying to the boys, 'I'm doing this.' The start was another poor one and Josh Brookes and Alastair Seeley were doing the business up front, but I got my head down and broke the lap record twice in the process. I was possessed. When I came up behind Josh at Mather's he ran wide on the grass but it was Alastair I wanted to stop. He was the only one who's ever come close to my dad's record of victories at the North West. Protecting the family name after the mess I'd made earlier seemed right.

I'd now won in the wet and in the dry, and after Honda, Kawasaki and Yamaha I could add BMW to the list of bikes I'd won international road races on.

But how would she do in the TT?

Clearly the bike wasn't ready for the TT, but I was. It was good to be back where I'd stamped my name the year before, even if the BMW wasn't behaving. Stuart's son, Steve, was in charge of the team. After practice he knew the wringer the bike had put me through. She was a dog, no mistake.

He says, 'I'm not going to force you to ride that thing. It's up to you.'

I'm that hyped about my own abilities, I felt I could have got a result out of my old tractor.

'Shut up, Steve. It's time we do this. Forget the bike, let's see what I am made of.'

We made changes, we switched tyre brands, we did everything we could, but eventually it was just me and her on the track in the Superbike. I got on the road and she tied me in knots. The blisters were busting on my hand, I was just wrestling with her so much. She worked so hard she blew the shock at the back. But oh my, the power. There was 215 HP in that baby and she let me have all of it. After one lap we had a lead of nine seconds from Guy and a new lap record speed of 131.730 mph. We went quicker in lap 2 and by the time I crossed the line there was that much air between me and the next fella it was like a victory lap, not that it felt like it. I was knackered.

Steve was ecstatic. He was happier than I was. We had to walk around *parc fermé* looking for his head. Stuart had run teams for years but Steve had never won a TT.

And then there was BMW. Those boys were like kids at Christmas. Seventy-five years after leaving the TT they'd returned in style. In fact, Steve said that all the head honchos from the company would be flying in for the second Superbike on Friday. 'So no pressure, then.'

Whatever happened at the end of the week, that first win vindicated, if you like, my decision to part from Honda. In my head it was their call. I also thought I would have won that day whatever bike I'd been riding. As the boys were saying, 'It's their loss.'

We got a third and a first in the Supersport – I think the only solo win on a Honda that year – and another first in the Superstock, making it my third win in that category with my third different manufacturer – Kawasaki, Honda and now BMW. Then came the one that mattered. All the German big dogs were in the paddock, many more soaking up the press interest in the marque's incredible comeback. On paper they thought they'd given me an angel to ride. Steve knew the truth.

Before the race he says, 'I don't know what to say to you, Mick. We've tried everything to make it better but you know it's short. I'm sorry, you're going to have to ride round our problems.'

The boy's stressing and he genuinely has done as much as anyone could have done to get things sorted.

I says, 'That's no bother. We'll be fine.'

Famous last words but they were true. Sort of. I got the win. I blew everyone away but it wasn't pretty and it wasn't pain-free. When I took my gloves off, blood was pouring out of my hands. My shoulder was knackered. I felt like I'd been chucked out of a window and run over, then chucked out the window again. But we'd done it. Another win, another TT, another lady for my mantelpiece.

In fact, another four.

As we were leaving the Isle of Man, it had to be Gary.

'Honda who?'

It took me a while to recover physically. I was lucky I had the strength to make the bike work in the first place. A weaker man would have been thrown off. There were places where she was a bucking bronco, there's no other way of describing it.

In a way, that bike, for all her problems, suited me. I like to tame a bike. When I race, I put the motorbike where I want it to be rather than let it put me where it needs to be. I'm probably one of the very few who do that, if not the only one. You watch me race that BMW and it looks like we're in a punch-up.

William's the opposite of me. He's smooth, he likes to move with the bike. I like to move against it. He's tall and lanky. He's lighter so he can go faster, and thinner so he can tuck in. It's swings and roundabouts. He can get things out of some bikes that I can't and vice versa.

I could not ride any other way and maybe he couldn't either. What we both are is natural talents.

My build and my weight always look like more of an issue than they are. I get the odd bit of criticism. But it suits me fine.

Fitness-wise, I could not run down the end of the lane. There's a reason why they built the car; it's to save you walking. Some of these boys I race against can run for ten miles, a hundred miles. I can't, I'm not fit enough to run a bath. But I am fit enough to ride a motorbike the way I like to.

There are a lot of the top lads who need to go to the gym to get in the saddle. For me that is not a natural racer. I don't need to go to the gym to race a motorbike; William doesn't need to go to the gym, my dad never needed to. We get on the motorbike and we race it. Don't get me wrong, there are a lot of talented, athletic guys riding out there, but they're paying a price. And that price is a bloody expensive gym membership and no life.

You can probably tell, because I have a gut, that I'm not in the gym very often. I like my food and I like a beer. On the rare occasions I do go it's just to stop myself from getting obese. Basically, I'm just tight. I don't want to have to buy new jeans.

The rest of the year took the same format as the previous ones. Nipping here and there doing road races, winning road races, breaking records, having fun. I was still only twenty-five, but with eleven TT trophies on my shelf I felt like an elder statesman. There was a definite target on my back at some of the races. I was the boy to beat.

I started riding elsewhere for the craic, in different formats and countries even. The previous year I'd gone over to Scarborough and won the Gold Cup, the first Dunlop to do so. This September I decided to be a bit more exotic and went over to Frohburg in Germany for a race named after my uncle because he won it so many times. My dad won there as well.

Rico Penzkofer, owner and team manager of Penz 13.com, was the lad behind it. He said he'd sponsor me for the event and since he was using BMWs, I took that as a sign. The first time out we struggled a little: we broke down in one race, and in another we fell apart. But the big race, the one I wanted – The Joey Dunlop – I broke the lap record and won the thing. We celebrated with beer and sausages, which is no bad thing.

I really enjoyed it. And being among happy Germans again seemed like an omen for the future. By the end of the season I was buzzing for the next year and looking forward to taming that BMW once and for all. There would be no walking away this time. Not by me.

But then I learned that Stuart had lost the contract with BMW. He took it a wee bit personally and so did I, on his behalf. After the success we gave them on their seventy-fifth anniversary, I thought it was low. At the same time, Stuart began to have a few health problems. From being on the crest of a wave I was suddenly in the shit. Out of solidarity with Stuart I didn't want to go with BMW to their new team, but I couldn't afford to keep riding for him and hope he got a decent bike as a replacement. I would not be a pleasant person to work with if things didn't go well, and he had enough problems with his health.

Since adding to my TT collection was my only motivation, I decided that, for the third season running, I'd be out with a factory team.

What could go wrong?

EIGHTEEN

Go Faster

THE YEAR OF 2015. THE YEAR I went 133 mph around the Mountain Course. At least, I should have done. Everything that could go wrong did go wrong. For starters, I wasn't even racing on the bike I'd turned up with.

BMW didn't want Stuart and so I didn't want them, but another manufacturer appealed. Yamaha, run by Milwaukee Yamaha, came in with the promise of good things. I'd had a lot of success on their bikes when I was managing my own outfit. It seemed like a good partnership and appeared to offer the best possibility of me winning again.

But controversy has a way of finding me. The North West is always the litmus test for where you are and I knew we were in the shit. Yamaha were a factory team, or near enough, and they should have had the resources to get things fixed. They made the right noises.

'We'll change that; we'll do this; we'll add that. You won't recognize her.'

Come the TT I was expecting some serious improvements but if they'd done them, they hadn't worked. First practice, second practice, it was shocking. I can cope when I think we're all pulling the same way. If we're in a sinking ship and the captain's helping bail us out, I'm there with him. But I didn't feel that I was being supported. Things I asked to be sorted just weren't.

I've done a lot of hot-headed things in my short career and in my life. I've done things people have criticized me for or said, 'He's brave.' I can honestly say I only do what I think is right. I won't say 'yes' if I mean 'no.' Which is why, at the end of practice, I had to tell Yamaha, 'I can't do this. I'm walking away.'

I can't go into details for legal reasons, but to put it in perspective: the TT was the be-all and end-all of my life. It still is. It's why I do what I do. So to resign from a team without a replacement I had to be mad or angry.

The media couldn't get their heads round it. For me it was simple: I wasn't going to win with that team. I wasn't sure by the end that I even wanted to. So I went.

I still had two bikes to run, but if there was a sniff at the big one I thought it was worth exploring possibilities. It was Thursday morning when I rang Steve Hicken, Stuart's son. Obviously he'd heard.

'Steve,' I says. 'I need a bike. Anything you got. I just want to ride in this race.'

'Leave it with me. I will find you something.'

I missed Thursday practice and then on Friday Steve arrived from Mallory Park in a van carrying – a BMW. And she wasn't half bad. By no means the finished article, but when I started the first Superbike on the Buildbase BMW I thought, *We might actually have a chance.*

I wasn't wrong. We were flying. By the final lap I got into third and I honestly felt we were capable of greatness.

There was 132+ mph in us that day, I could feel it. I had seventeen more miles in which to do it.

But I never did. Because I never finished.

I'm a few bends from the end, driving in clean air and almost tasting a new record average speed. I'm coming into the right-hander at Nook and it's blind. I'm a mile from home, all is good, and the last thing I expect to see is a bike flying across the road.

I'd been catching Scott Wilson, a backmarker. Out of sight he'd fallen and gone through a hedge. He'd stayed still but his bike hadn't. By the time I came tearing round the corner, it was bouncing back into the middle of the street. And right into me.

It all happened that fast. I'm grateful to still be here. I was down, I was off, I was sliding at 100 mph on my arse. When I finally stopped spinning and rolling, and I'd done the count-up of limbs, my first thought was, *Shit, that was going to be a 133*. That's all that I could think of. After nearly six whole laps, I just wished it had happened on the first mile, not the last.

I could see Scott where he'd landed. I don't think he knew what day of the week it was, but he was okay. To this day we've never spoken about it. Maybe he didn't realize I lost twelve grand in prize money. Maybe he didn't know that I was on for the lap record. Maybe he just felt thankful to be alive.

What he definitely didn't know was that his accident cost me a broken wrist, a damaged leg and a wrecked shoulder. He didn't know because I didn't tell anyone. I couldn't afford to. If the stewards found out how bad I was they wouldn't let me race.

But maybe I should have come clean. It would have made the results over the next few days more palatable. I came second in the Superstock; though I know in my heart there was a win there, with my grip at 50 per cent and everything screaming, I couldn't do enough. The last Superbike was even harder. I hurt enough going in a straight line. Dragging the BMW around lines it didn't want to find caused us both distress. Fifth was the best I was ever going to do. Add to that a cockup in the pits and two more DNFs – plus another one in the Lightweight at the Billown circuit – and it was not the mighty fortnight I had hoped for. But it was a damn sight better than it looked like being one week earlier.

Steve Hicken really came through for me at the TT that year, probably even more than he'd done the year before. When I started thinking about my options for 2016 I pretty much started with his name on a piece of paper. I'm not lying when I say that some very big names, with big money behind them, were on the phone. But without wanting to sound patronizing, I honestly felt Steve deserved a year – and a TT – of my services. The boy had dug me out of a hole, so I wanted to repay the favour. Don't misunderstand me, he'd have to give me a bloody good bike, but as long as we were competitive that would do for me.

I gave him a ring and said, 'Come on, Steve, let's build a Superbike to blow them away.'

We spent a bit of time on getting it right. After our success with BMW we decided to stick with their basic package. It wasn't a time for egos. Anyone can buy a road bike; it's what you do to it that is important. I think Steve spent about twelve grand in the showroom, then about five times that transforming it. Stuart, his dad, was back in rude health, so he built the motor. That's his job. By the time the boys were done, I was pretty pleased with what we had.

As far as I was concerned, we had a BMW to challenge anyone. But factory boys will always have that extra bit of advantage. If I had an idea I'd phone Steve and he'd mull it over with his dad. If you're on a factory bike they've got five hundred people coming up with ideas and a thousand mulling them over. The odds are with them. It doesn't guarantee you wins but it does stack the deck in your favour.

For the sponsor, that's part of the craic. Yes, it's an expensive business, but if you can beat a factory outfit with the same basic package you are in clover.

Since leaving Stuart, BMW were supporting Tyco, who'd been tearing up trees with Guy and William on the Suzukis a couple of years earlier. For 2016 William was being replaced by Ian Hutchinson. He's another one older than me – everyone who's done anything in this sport is. Whenever I look at his achievements I have a little reminder to myself, 'He's ten years older. How many TTs did he have at your age?'

Even so, a German precision-engineering factory line-up of Hutchinson and Martin versus our little privateer team consisting of a fat driver and two old boys in the Midlands – we were going to have to go some.

Come the North West I went out on the Superbike in the first race and I just smashed it: I won it by eight seconds.

I'd like to add some drama to it but that's basically what happened. All the boys were there: Ian Hutchinson, John McGuinness, Bruce Anstey, Ryan Farquharson, William, Conor Cummins, Michael Rutter, Peter Hickman, James Hillier, but I came out, grabbed the lead, recorded the fastest ever speed round the circuit – 123.207 mph, up from 122.958 – job done. First victory for the new Hawk Racing Team.

Heading to the TT, then, we had reason to be optimistic, if only mildly so. Winning the NW is nice but it's a run-out, no more. We knew that BMW would go hell for leather on developments and tweaks to try to catch us up, and they had the resources to do it. But as two people dumped by them, you'd have to say that what Steve and I had was worth something too. Money versus passion. In a few days' time we'd see what counted for more.

The conditions were perfect. I broke the practice lap record on the Friday on the Superbike. The first man to average over 131 mph. With the weather so good we kept going and going, learning the bike. We got in twenty, thirty laps, more than enough for anyone to know a machine. Mine had only been built that year by Stuart and Steve, but there could be no excuses after all those miles and I think the times we were getting showed the practice was paying off. By the end of the week it was me and Ian, with a gap behind us.

I'd have been happy with that if I were him. But the history between the teams makes it a bit spicy. We're both running BMWs except his is fully branded and mine's the mystery machine. We've painted it black; we don't want the association, to give them any publicity. But they know it's one of theirs and so do the fans. Which is why we start hearing all these whispers coming from the factory team. Loads of niggly stuff. Every microphone that gets shoved under Ian's nose, he's saying, 'Well, it's the first time I've ridden a BMW; other teams have an advantage.' Aye, the bullshit is starting to fly.

Come race day it's getting hot and heavy. John's away first. Then Bruce. James Hillier. Ian. Peter Hickman. Then me. I've got the hammer down immediately. I'm through Bray Hill flat out and by the end of the lap I've done 133.369 mph from a standing start. A new record.

That's not all. I broke seventeen minutes doing it.

With 16.59 I'm the fastest man in history around the track, but the second lap I do it again. Incredibly it's 16.58, and marginally quicker at 133.393 mph. Of course, I don't know this. As far as I'm concerned there have been places where I should have been pushing harder, being leaner.

In the pits is the first opportunity I have to get a fix on my position.

'You've got this. Don't take any risks.'

That's all I'm told. But it's enough.

At that stage I'm leading Ian, the next fastest man, by seven seconds. By the time we hit Glen Helen on lap three, that's more than doubled to fifteen seconds. Now he's actually within sight. John is the only other contender, and for a while we're all within each other's exhaust fumes. By Bungalow on the final lap I manage to get the lead on the road. With victory in the bag it's not the end of the world that Hutch nicks the chequered flag. I've got the win on the clock, that's all that matters.

In the press conference John is graciousness itself. Ian mutters about not having much time riding his bike and that it will prepare him for Friday. When it's my turn, I says, 'New bikes? Whatever. We were on a new bike we built.' For good measure I add, 'We were the underdogs here today.'

I'm sitting between a Honda man and BMW man. But the way Hutch is talking I half expect him to say we were the team with an advantage.

If it sounds like I'm having a dig, that's because I am. It winds me up that people think if they say the same crap often enough they'll be believed. If I'm shit I say I'm shit. If I'm beat, I hold my hands up. I don't blame this or that. That's pathetic, in my view.

Racing's changed even in my time. There's too much bullshit now, too much brown nosing. No one says what they mean. They bitch but they don't tell you straight. What pisses me off is that I get asked to comment and fall into it, and then I'm doing the same. Believe me, if I have a problem with you, I'm round your house. I'm not tweeting or giving interviews.

Afterwards, Steve was out of control. I was delighted for him. The way he'd been cast aside by BMW, he deserved this. I was happy for myself, too, of course. Putting a time in that's faster than anyone else has ever done can never be taken away. In a hundred years someone might go sixteen minutes. But I will always be the first guy to go under seventeen. That's just a fact. And, I have to say, it's one that gives me a smile even now. Grabbing a piece of history is up there with the best of my achievements. Of course, I always knew I'd bounce back. I'm arrogant like that. But doing it with Steve was the icing on the cake.

The ding-dong between me and Ian extended even when we weren't riding for our teams. In the Supersport I came a worthy second to him, but afterwards they found an illegal cam bucket on my bike. I think if it had happened to another team they'd still be arguing the toss now. Still denying it, at least. I have no time for that. Something's either right or it's wrong. And this, I knew, was wrong.

As soon as I saw it I ruled myself out. I could have argued and shouted and threatened all manner of things, and maybe made them keep me in first place. There was enough evidence to support that. Number one: the modification had zero impact on speed. Gary Thompson, clerk of the course, went on record to say that it was 'not a performance enhancing addition'. Number two: with or without it, I would still have made the podium. And three: we did it totally unwittingly. It came about because we lost an engine at the last minute, so Gary just acquired one and we stuck it in. We gave it a once-over to make sure it would last, but I didn't strip it. If I had done I'd have spotted the problem.

I believe I did the right thing. I like to think it's what my dad would have wanted me to do.

If you're a man you own up to your mistakes. Simple.

After the second Supersport, and another runner-up place behind Hutch, there was another controversy. Nothing to do with me this time, although certain players thought it was. I was accused of reporting Ian's bike to the scrutineers because it had overlong pistons, a clear infringement and, unlike mine, likely to give a performance boost. Here's the thing: I saw his bike and it was true. I don't care what anybody says – you can bring any lawyer to our house. I've been building Yamaha R6 engines since I was seventeen.

I'm not saying I'm the best engine builder in the world or the best engine tuner, but I know what an engine looks like – they were supposed to be standard pistons and these weren't standard pistons.

That's a fact. What anyone did with that information is nothing to do with me. I'm not a scrutineer or a clerk. I'm not ratting on anyone; it doesn't bother me. But sometimes talking the truth isn't a thing that helps you. Paranoia over at the Bavarian Motor Works was running high. Some people at Tyco were seeing conspiracies here, there and everywhere. Ian's all over social media slagging off officials, hinting at whisper campaigns, the usual bollocks.

Come Friday, the big one, and the main man from Tyco gets up in Gary's face. They have words. At the end the Tyco boy says, 'The best man is going to win.'

Gary says, 'I'll shake the winner's hand, whoever it is.'

I normally don't get involved in personal business but I did want to beat BMW. Not because Ian was riding it but because they'd done wrong by Steve and, to an extent, me, and they were running superior machinery. On paper, at least. Your biggest challenge in life is usually to beat someone with the same advantages as you. If everyone has an equal opportunity, then the winner is likely going to be the one boy with the most talent. The only thing more satisfying is whipping the backside of someone on superior equipment.

Ever since those stunning first practices involving me and Ian (when he seemed to know pretty well how to ride a BMW, by the way), the whole TT had been building up to the final Friday, and the Senior TT. It was the big climax, the great showdown, the final slug-out between the fortnight's two heavyweights.

Just as it had been two years earlier, all the big cheeses from Germany were over to watch their new boy's coronation. I'd met a few of them myself but there was a new face at the top, a new boss.

Eventually all the bullshit stops and on a beautiful sunny day, guaranteed to blind you on certain corners, we get going. I'm right on the limit from the word go. First lap, head down, I break my own record for the standing start. It's another sub-seventeen. Coming into the pits on the second lap I do a 133.962. If I'd known it was so close to 134 I'd have pushed harder.

I know from experience how quickly things can change around the Mountain Course. At the second pits I'm leading Hutch by nearly eleven seconds. That's nothing. A mistake with a tyre or fuel can destroy that kind of gap. But the boys do what they do best and when I get back out I've found another five seconds over the works BMW. Now I can see Ian and John on the track it's only a matter of time before I pass them. When I finish, it's with a lead of more than twenty seconds.

Ahead on the clock and ahead on the track. It doesn't get any better than this. Seeing one or two of the BMW boys looking a wee bit miffed that the billion-dollar boy hadn't done better with all that backing is a bonus. Nobody from Tyco offers to shake my hand, put it like that.

Bringing a non-factory Superbike home first in the Senior race at the TT is an achievement for anyone. But this win was personal for me, for Steve, and everyone. After the last two years of being undervalued by two factory giants and coming back to beat them both, it felt like a chapter closing. And what a chapter. As a team we're in the history books. As a rider I've made it clear I can ride anything and win. And do it in style.

As for the next chapter? Where do you go when you've won thirteen little ladies by the age of twenty-seven? What do you do when you hold the lap records for the biggest road race in the world? When you're already called the fastest rider of all time?

I'll tell you what you do: you go faster. You try harder. And you win again. You do it for yourself, you do it for your dad. You do it because you're a Dunlop.

You do it because you're a road racer. And it's in your blood.

ACKNOWLEDGEMENTS

I would like to express my gratitude to the many people who helped me with this book; to all those who provided support. Publishing the book would not have been possible without the backing of Clare Tillyer, Clara Nelson, George Maudsley and the team at Michael O'Mara Books. Not forgetting the perseverance and excellent assistance of David Riding, MBA Literary Agents Ltd.

A big shout out must go to all my sponsors, my team and the fans who have supported and encouraged me throughout the years, as without them, none of this would have been achievable.

Thank you to Jeff Hudson for helping me tell my story.

PICTURE CREDITS